Explaining Civil Society Development

Explaining Civil Society Development

A Social Origins Approach

LESTER M. SALAMON, S. WOJCIECH SOKOLOWSKI,
MEGAN A. HADDOCK, *and* ASSOCIATES

Johns Hopkins University Press

Baltimore

Johns Hopkins University Press
2715 North Charles Street
Baltimore, Maryland 21218-4363
www.press.jhu.edu

Library of Congress Cataloging-in-Publication Data

Names: Salamon, Lester M. | Sokolowski, S. Wojciech. | Haddock, Megan A.
Title: Explaining civil society development : a social origins approach /
    Lester M. Salamon, S. Wojciech Sokolowski, Megan A. Haddock, and associates.
Description: Baltimore, Maryland : Johns Hopkins University Press, [2017] |
    Includes bibliographical references and index.
Identifiers: LCCN 2016046940 | ISBN 9781421422985 (hardcover : alk. paper) |
    ISBN 9781421422992 (electronic) | ISBN 1421422980 (hardcover : alk. paper) |
    ISBN 1421422999 (electronic)
Subjects: LCSH: Nonprofit organizations. | Nonprofit organizations—Social aspects. |
    Civil society. | Welfare state.
Classification: LCC HD2769.15 .S64 2017 | DDC 338.7—dc23
LC record available at https://lccn.loc.gov/2016046940

A catalog record for this book is available from the British Library.

*Special discounts are available for bulk purchases of this book. For more information,
please contact Special Sales at 410-516-6936 or specialsales@press.jhu.edu.*

Johns Hopkins University Press uses environmentally friendly book materials,
including recycled text paper that is composed of at least 30 percent post-consumer waste,
whenever possible.

To the remarkable group of Local Associates who managed the work of this project in each of its target countries, without whom the data and related material reflected in this book would never have been assembled, and particularly to two of its members, Ledivina Cariño and Mark Lyons, who tragically passed away before this book saw the light of day.

A great painter does not content himself by affecting us with his masterpieces; ultimately he succeeds in changing the landscape of our minds.

ORHAN PAMUK, *MY NAME IS RED*, 195

CONTENTS

ACKNOWLEDGMENTS

This book represents the capstone of a 25-year saga undertaken to rescue a crucial component of the world's social and organizational infrastructure from the virtual obscurity to which it had been consigned in the world's academic institutions, policy discussions, media coverage, and statistical systems. The social and organizational infrastructure in question is the vast collection of private, but not-for-profit, schools, clinics, hospitals, social service agencies, symphonies, human rights groups, environmental organizations, think tanks, professional associations, disaster relief and development organizations, and dozens more groups that make up what is variously termed the nonprofit, voluntary, noncommercial, civil society, or nongovernmental sector and the charitable giving and volunteering that help to support it. Few sets of institutions have been more important to improvements in the quality of life around the world, yet few have been more invisible in basic data systems, neglected in scholarly and media attention, and consequently either largely ignored or enveloped in a variety of misleading myths.

This saga started when two intrepid academics, one a young, German-born sociologist and the other an American professor who had recently completed the first economic analysis of this sector in the United States, found themselves invited to an intimate gathering of major charitable foundation leaders from around the world in Bonn, Germany, in 1991. In attendance were 10 or 12 senior foundation executives from Germany, France, the United Kingdom, the United States, Japan, and the Netherlands.

Discussion at this session focused on the inability of those in the nonprofit sector to attract the attention of policymakers, the media, or the academic community, let alone to represent themselves effectively to their citizens and the world. Each of the foundation leaders had been asked to come prepared to describe the scope, scale, and situation of this nonprofit or civil society sector in his or her own country, but as the meeting proceeded it became clear that there was a serious problem. Everyone had a different idea of what this sector contained, most of them quite partial or confusing. Only the Americans had even the sketchiest idea about its contours, scale, or sources of support, and even that was relatively recent and far from fully understood.

Midway through this awkward discussion, the American professor sheepishly raised his hand and, after being given the floor, called attention to this embarrassing point. I suggested that there was a way to remedy the problem but cautioned that this would require a serious, systematic, comparative effort and a willingness to set aside a variety of myths and misperceptions. A deafening silence followed. Unmoved, the senior leaders continued their groping effort to portray the sector they were part of but had little solid basis to understand.

But my remarks apparently sank in with one of the participants. At a celebratory dinner in honor of his birthday that evening, the leader of a major US charity bellowed out: "Salamon, how much would it cost to finance the kind of project you were describing this afternoon?" I did some quick mental calculations and responded with a rough estimate. "Good, let's raise that right here," he announced, and he went around the table pressing each of the participants to pledge their support for such a project. After some hemming, hawing, and temporizing that included the signing of a written agreement with the chairman of the meeting's host organization stipulating the exchange rate between Deutschmarks and dollars at which the German contribution would be paid, all the parties agreed. Thus was launched the Johns Hopkins Comparative Nonprofit Sector Project, for which this book is the capstone product, though not everyone present realized they had made a binding commitment, so that it took more than a year to convert that night's pledges into actual support.

Once launched, the Johns Hopkins CNP set about assembling an exceptional team of dedicated research partners, the CNP Local Associates. This trailblazing group of scholars took on what seemed at the outset to be an impossible and unrewarding task of assembling empirical knowledge about a set of institutions and behaviors for which little solid information was available and that was off the beaten academic track. The project also began assembling local advisory committees in each of the countries in which it worked.

A central premise of the project was that in order to gain visibility in policy and media circles, it was necessary to add to the moving individual stories of this sector's accomplishments solid and reliable empirical figures describing the size and economic weight of the nonprofit sector. This meant that sector stakeholders could illustrate the importance of this sector in terms that policymakers and the media find most compelling and easy to comprehend. From the outset the project also had a number of other, even more ambitious, objectives: to test, and potentially challenge, some of the myths surrounding this sector and some of the early theories and beliefs purporting to explain why nonprofits arise and how they are financed; to legitimize the nonprofit sector as a field of study and foster a robust global community of scholars knowledgeable about this field and committed to work in it; and, most ambitious of all, to bring this sector into visibility in official statistics produced by national statistical agencies for the first time by changing the way the institutions and activities of this sector are treated in global statistical guidance systems.

Early on, the project had to confront the challenge of identifying a consensus definition of the sector it was proposing to measure. Such a definition needed to identify the same types of entities and activities in the enormously varied countries to which it would be applied, despite the enormous diversity of this sector and the vast differences in legal structures, economic circumstances, and cultural traditions that these different countries embodied. What is more, it had to do so in a way that could ultimately be incorporated into official international statistical systems. No wonder the whole enterprise met with considerable skepticism, and even some considerable derision, including within the sector itself.

But the project team persisted, thanks in important part to our Local Associates. Our commitment to a bottom-up process empowered them to start with the realities on the ground in our local sites and find the commonalities that would allow us to see the outlines of a true sector among the welter of individual organizations, behaviors, and national peculiarities. To our joy and amazement, as the first set of data began to hit the streets, other countries clamored to get into the project. As a consequence, the initial 8 countries with which we started this journey quickly grew to 13, and 13 to 23, and from there to 36, finally reaching well over 40 as of this writing, with good prospects of expanding further. As each group of countries joined the project, we repeated the same rigorous process of assembling reliable research partners, forming knowledgeable local advisory committees, testing our definition, assessing potential data sources, and making needed adjustments in the light of new information. Along the way, the project produced an entire book series published by Manchester University Press; 66 working papers; over 200 other articles, comparative reports, and book chapters; a series of project overview books; and two landmark additions to the official global statistical system—the *Handbook on Nonprofit Institutions in the System of National Accounts* (the UN *NPI Handbook* for short), published by the United Nations Statistics Division in 2003; and the *Manual on the Measurement of Volunteer Work,* published by the International Labour Office in 2011.

Inevitably, an undertaking of this scope and duration collects many debts to others without whose ingenuity, hard work, persistence, and support this project would never have achieved its promise. Altogether, 16 talented people worked at various times on the project's core staff during its 25-year life, somewhere between 150 and 200 international researchers worked on various aspects of the project in the CNP partner countries under the guidance of our remarkable group of Local Associates, another roughly 500 individuals served on the project's national and international advisory committees, and 94 separate organizations provided financial support. Partly out of this work as well has come a vibrant new international association dedicated to research on the global "third sector."

Space will not permit acknowledging each of these individuals and organizations by name here, so a separate section has been provided at the end of this volume to list the core staff, the advisory committee members, the funding organizations, and the Local Associates, if not all the local researchers. But I would be remiss if I did not identify at least some of those whose contributions have been especially important. First and foremost here would be Helmut Anheier, now the dean of the Hertie School in Berlin, who brilliantly and effectively served as my right hand in guiding the project as its associate director during its formative first decade. Equally pivotal has been S. Wojciech Sokolowski, who has been the genius keeper of the project's critical database and protector of its scientific integrity, working closely with Local Associates on all aspects of the project's conceptualization, data assembly, data analysis, and integration into the international statistical system. The project has also been well served by two very able and dedicated managers, initially Regina Rippetoe List and more recently Megan A. Haddock. We could also not have survived without the production and communication skills of Mimi Bilzor and Chelsea Newhouse or the administrative support of Jackie Perry.

Special thanks are also due to John Richardson, the first executive director of the European Foundation Center (EFC), who made the EFC Annual Meeting available as a launching pad for our initial set of project findings and ultimately for the project's expansion to other countries; to Herman Habermann, the director of the United Nations Statistical Division in the mid-1990s, who first gave us entry into the official System of National Accounts in order to institutionalize the capacity to produce official data on the nonprofit sector globally; to Ivo Havinga and Herman Smith, who have worked closely with us on the preparation of the initial UN *NPI Handbook* and more recently on a major revision and broadening of its coverage; to Sylvester Young and Rafael Diez de Medina, successive directors of the ILO's Statistical Department who opened the door to integrating the measurement of volunteering into official international statistics through issuance of the ILO *Manual on the Measurement of Volunteer Work,* and to the United Nations Volunteers Program for providing the bulk of the funding needed to bring it into being; to Luc Tayart de Borms of the King Baudouin Foundation, who chaired the project's International Advisory Committee for a number of years and was especially creative in seeing the value of the data the project generated; to Ksenija Fonovic and Renzo Razzano of Italy's Associazione Promozione e Solidarietà Society (SPES), who have been especially effective in promoting the implementation of the UN *NPI Handbook* and ILO *Manual* not only in Italy but in Europe more broadly; and to several funding organizations that were especially generous in their core financial support to the project over extended periods, among them Atlantic Philanthropies, the Ford Foundation, and the Charles Stewart Mott Foundation.

To all of these individuals and organizations, both those cited here and those identified as members of the Johns Hopkins Comparative Nonprofit Sector Team in the special listing at the back of this book, I am deeply grateful. This project has always been a group effort, and whatever credit is due to it is appropriately shared with all of them. It is for this reason that I dedicate this book to our CNP Local Associates, without whom this project could not have proceeded. While whatever credit this project deserves is widely shared, whatever shortcomings the project may have had, including any reflected in this book, are my responsibility alone as the project's director, and I accept it fully.

Lester M. Salamon
Annapolis, Maryland

Explaining Civil Society Development

CHAPTER ONE

Introduction

The Puzzle of Civil Society Development

LESTER M. SALAMON

> No one ever obliges us to know, Adso. We must, that is all,
> even if we comprehend imperfectly.
>
> —UMBERTO ECO, *THE NAME OF THE ROSE*, 547

THIS BOOK SEEKS to unravel a puzzle that has emerged from work that the present authors have undertaken over the past two decades to document the scope and structure of the nonprofit, or civil society, sector in countries throughout the world. That puzzle simply stated is this: How can we explain the enormous variations in civil society/nonprofit sector size, structure, financing, and role revealed by the powerful body of comparative data that this work has generated in more than 40 countries scattered widely across the world?[1] Why is it, for example, that the nonprofit workforce varies from a low of barely 1 percent of the working-age population in Pakistan to over 15 percent in the Netherlands? The level of development likely plays a role here, but why, then, does the paid workforce of the civil society sector stand at nearly 10 percent of the country's working-age population in Belgium but only 2.5 percent in Sweden—even though these two countries are at comparable levels of development? Why does government account for 65 percent of nonprofit revenue in Germany and only 36 percent in nearby Italy? And how is it that the overall size and structure of the Mexican nonprofit sector is virtually identical with that in Russia, a country seemingly worlds away?

Answers to these questions are crucial to a proper understanding of the nonprofit sector and its evolution and role. But their importance goes well beyond this. With government resources barely growing or in decline while the problems of poverty, distress, and environmental degradation are deepening daily, private, nonprofit, or civil society organizations have come to be viewed as crucial allies in the struggle to improve the quality of life on a

I

global scale. Because of their unique combination of private structure and public purpose, their generally smaller size, their connections to citizens, their flexibility, and their capacity to tap private initiative in support of public purposes, these organizations are increasingly being called upon to perform a number of critical functions: to help deliver vital human services; to empower the disadvantaged; to bring unaddressed problems to public attention; to give expression to artistic, religious, cultural, ethnic, social, and recreational values and impulses; to build community and foster those bonds of trust and reciprocity that are necessary for political stability and economic prosperity; and generally to mobilize individual initiative in pursuit of the common good.

Reflecting this, the accomplishment of the vast majority of the seventeen "Sustainable Development Goals" recently identified by the United Nations as the priority objectives of the international community's "post-2015 development agenda" seem likely to depend critically on the contributions of private, civil society organizations.[2] Understanding the factors that give rise to such organizations and shape their contours and roles may therefore hold the key to the success of this post-2015 agenda.

More fundamentally, unraveling this puzzle promises to provide the missing link in recent efforts to explain why nations fail. In a recent book with this title, Daron Acemoglu and James A. Robinson argue that "[w]hile economic institutions are critical in determining whether a country is poor or prosperous, it is politics and political institutions that determine what economic institutions a country has."[3] But what is it that determines the kind of politics and political institutions a country has? According to one promising line of research, a major part of the answer to this question lies in the presence of civic traditions emphasizing norms of trust and reciprocity—traditions that turn out to be associated with the presence of robust networks of associations, what we have termed nonprofit or civil society organizations.[4] But what is it that gives rise to robust networks of civil society organizations? It is this question that this book seeks to answer.

Our answer departs, however, from the prevailing theories that have long dominated the academic literature on the nonprofit sector, and it challenges as well a number of popular beliefs that these theories, at least implicitly, have helped to sustain. These theories would have us believe that what gives rise to nonprofit organizations are the market-based *preferences* of individual consumer/voters and producers of goods and services and/or the *sentiments* bequeathed by cultural traditions of altruism and caring.

More specifically, the *preference theories* argue that nonprofit organizations emerge to fulfill unsatisfied demands for collective goods on the part of consumers/voters caused by inherent limitations of the market system and democratic political institutions, particularly in heterogeneous societies. Also at work, they argue, are the preferences of various social entrepreneurs or religious zealots who come forward to provide the supply of organizations to meet this demand because they see in the creation of nonprofit organizations a way to attract adherents to their religion or cause. The *sentiment theories* emphasize instead certain cultural values, frequently arising from religious beliefs, that incline individuals toward altruistic behaviors that require nonprofit institutions for their fulfillment.

Both of these sets of theories have a certain surface logic to them. Beyond that, they have conveniently supported a variety of firmly held popular beliefs about the nature and character of nonprofit institutions—such as the belief that nonprofit institutions are fundamentally supported by private charity and that they are a peculiarly American phenomenon and are far less prominent in countries that have established highly developed "welfare states" instead.

In the absence of solid comparative data on the scope and structure of the civil society sector around the world, it has been impossible to subject these theories to serious, cross-national, empirical testing. It has therefore been possible to believe them on faith or on the basis of their logical consistency with classical economic reasoning. But thanks to the work of the Johns Hopkins Comparative Nonprofit Sector Project in which I and an international team of collaborators have been involved for the past two decades, a robust body of solid, comparative data has been assembled on the civil society sectors in over 40 countries scattered broadly around the world using a common definition and common data-gathering protocols (table 1.1 lists these project countries).[5] As a consequence, we now have systematic data on the size of the workforce, both paid and volunteer, of the civil society sector; the fields in which these organizations work and the scale of activity in each; the revenues of these organizations, both overall and by major source; and the economic impact these organizations generate.

As these data have come online, they have rescued the global nonprofit sector from its long-standing position as the invisible subcontinent on the landscape of modern society. In the process, we have come to recognize how far the realities of nonprofit operations globally diverge from some of the

TABLE 1.1   Country coverage of the Johns Hopkins Comparative Nonprofit Sector Project as of 2014

Region (number of countries)	Countries	
Western Europe (15)	Austria	Netherlands
	Belgium	Norway
	Denmark	Portugal
	Finland	Spain
	France	Sweden
	Germany	Switzerland
	Ireland	United Kingdom
	Italy	
Central and Eastern Europe (6)	Czech Republic	Romania
	Hungary	Russia
	Poland	Slovakia
North America (3)	Canada	United States
	Mexico	
South America (5)	Argentina	Colombia
	Brazil	Peru
	Chile	
Africa/Middle East (5)*	Israel	Tanzania
	Kenya	Uganda
	South Africa	
Asia (7)	Australia	New Zealand
	India	Pakistan
	Japan	Philippines
	Korea, Republic of	
Total (41)*		

*Two additional countries, Egypt and Morocco, were covered in the project but were not included in the analysis here due to the unavailability of data on all variables.

most fervently held popular beliefs that existed about this sector when we began this work. Included here were beliefs such as the following:

- *That no such thing as a distinctive nonprofit "sector" truly exists, but rather a confusing congeries of institutions and behaviors that blur too completely with other social institutions—market producers, governments, and households—to be capable of conceptual differentiation, let alone empirical study.*[6] To the contrary, the work we carried out through the Johns Hopkins Comparative Nonprofit Sector Project has validated the existence of a set of institutions exhibiting a common set of objective definitional features in well over 40 countries that are scattered broadly throughout the world and that represent widely divergent levels of economic and social development as well as patterns of religious belief.

- *That the civil society sector, whatever its social importance, is not a significant economic presence.* In fact, this sector is a major economic force, with a workforce that ranks among the top two or three industries in a wide range of countries.

- *That to the extent a nonprofit sector exists, it is largely an American phenomenon, reflecting the extraordinary generosity of the American public and the unusual American emphasis on individualism.* In fact, the United States turns out to be not only not the sole country with a sizable nonprofit sector but not even the country with the largest such sector measured in terms of the relative size of its nonprofit workforce.[7]

- *That unlike the United States, which developed a robust nonprofit sector to handle social-welfare provision, the countries of Europe have created "welfare states" dominated by governmental provision of such services.* In fact, what many of the countries of Europe have developed are "welfare partnerships" featuring extensive reliance on private nonprofit groups to deliver state-financed welfare services. In the process, the resulting nonprofit sectors have grown much larger in relative terms than their US counterpart.

- *That private charitable contributions—from individuals, foundations, and corporations—are the key to sustaining a vibrant set of nonprofit institutions.* In fact, however, charitable contributions now account for a relatively small fraction of nonprofit revenues. Even in the United States, where many organizations do still rely heavily on charitable support, at least during their start-up periods, the sector as a whole, as defined in this project, receives less than 13 or 14 percent of its revenue from all sources of charitable giving combined. Far more important is the nearly 40 percent of all support coming from government and the 50 percent coming in the form of fees and charges. And the situation elsewhere is even more dramatic, with government accounting for 60 or 70 percent of the income of nonprofits in the countries with the largest and most fully developed nonprofit sectors.

More importantly for our purposes here, we discovered enormous variations in almost every dimension of the civil society sector on which we were able to generate reliable data—variations that do not seem consistent with either the preference or sentiment theories dominant in the literature. For example, as will be detailed more fully in chapter 3, the presence or absence of robust nonprofit institutions does not seem to correspond with the level of diversity of national populations, as predicted by the preference theories. What is more, we could find no religious tradition that failed to emphasize personal altruism, making it unlikely that variations in popular sentiments of caring or altruism could explain the wide variations in the size or shape of the civil society sector among countries that our data revealed. Indeed, some of the countries with the strongest religiously inspired traditions of charity and giving have some of the least fully developed civil society sectors.

As this evidence mounted, it forced us to rethink prevailing theories of the growth and development of civil society institutions. More generally, we came to the conclusion that the narrow focus on the rational choices of individual actors maximizing their preferences for goods or services or responding to abstract cultural values emphasized in the preference and sentiment theories, whatever its value in selected circumstances, was inadequate to explain the varied dimensions of civil society development revealed by our data. In particular, these existing explanations suffered from a more general shortcoming common to classical and neoclassical economics—a shortcoming that theorist Mark Granovetter has termed "an atomized, undersocialized conception of human action."[8] As Granovetter puts it: "Actors do not behave or decide as atoms outside a social context, nor do they adhere slavishly to a script written for them by the particular intersection of social categories that they happen to occupy. Their attempts at purposive action are instead embedded in concrete, ongoing systems of social relations."[9]

Fundamentally, we will argue that this concept of "embeddedness" applies forcefully to the development of nonprofit institutions. Choices about whether to rely on the market, the civil society sector, the state, or kinship networks in the provision of key human services are not simply made freely by individual consumers or service providers in an open market, as the preference theories seem to imply. Nor are they determined solely by free-standing cultural or religious traditions. Rather, these choices, and these cultural traditions, are heavily constrained by existing social and political relationships that are inherited from the past and shaped by complex interrelationships among the varying social strata and social institutions that make up any society. These outcomes are therefore heavily affected not simply by sentiments and preferences but also by the exercise of political, so-cial, and economic *power* among key social groupings and institutions at critical turning points in societal development.

This is not, of course, an entirely new observation. As Seibel has reminded us, nonprofit organizations "are not only providers of goods and services but important factors of social and political coordination."[10] As a consequence, they do not float freely in social space responding merely to sentiments and preferences, as the prior theories seem to suggest. Rather, they are firmly embedded in prevailing social, political, and economic structures, often serving, in Seibel's words, as "the knots within networks of elites with repu-tation, finance, and power." Civil society theorists such as John Hall have acknowledged this point as well, despite not working out its full implications. Hall thus ascribes the emergence of civil society in Europe to "the peculiar balance of forces among kings, nobility, and urban middle class elements."[11] Similarly, Gramsci points to civil society organizations as crucial compo-nents of "the 'trenches' and the permanent fortifications of the front in the war of position . . . between the forces of revolution and the forces of resto-ration."[12] More recently, Howell and Pearce similarly emphasize civil soci-ety's character as an arena where "power relationships" are "reproduced" as well as "challenged."[13]

Yet embeddedness in power relations has been conspicuously absent from the dominant academic theories purporting to explain the scope and char-acter of the nonprofit sector. To be sure, some observers have commented on the role of civil society as a potential *source* of power. But whether because of the heavy emphasis that sentiment theories put on civil society as an ex-pression of cherished values of altruism or solidarity, or some other factor, the possibility that the civil society sector could also be a product of power rela-tions has largely been downplayed or ignored.

It is the argument here that this inattention needs to be corrected if we are to comprehend the puzzling variations in the size, form, structure, and financing of civil society organizations globally. But which power relation-ships are most relevant?

Fortunately, we are not completely at sea in searching for possible an-swers to this question. One important clue is offered by political scientist Robert Putnam, who found himself drawn "deep into the contrasting pasts of Italy's regions" in order to explain the striking variations in civic traditions and civil society development that he argues lay behind the considerable vari-ations in the performance of Italian regional governments in the 1970s and

1980s.[14] This comparative historical approach and its emphasis on "path dependence"—the durability of historically rooted social relationships—is even more fully reflected in the pioneering work of Barrington Moore, Jr., and Dietrich Rueschemeyer and his colleagues on the "social origins" of fascism and democracy[15] as well as in the work of Gøsta Esping-Andersen and Theda Skocpol on the origins of the modern welfare state.[16]

Using this mode of analysis, Moore discerned in the historical records of England, France, Germany, and China three distinct "routes to the modern world"—democratic, fascist, and communist—each of which could be attributed to a particular constellation of relationships among landed elites, the rural peasantry, urban working and middle classes, and the state.[17] Focusing on Latin America, Rueschemeyer and his colleagues extended the range of relevant power relationships beyond indigenous social classes to embrace international actors such as colonial powers and a variety of essentially political structures—such as governmental institutions and political parties—that can magnify or lessen the power and influence that different social groupings can wield.[18] This latter perspective emphasizing the role of such political filters can also be found in the works of Esping-Andersen and Skocpol in explaining various patterns of "welfare regimes" in Europe and the United States.[19]

While neither Moore nor Esping-Andersen applies his analysis to the variations in the development of the civil society sector, and Rueschemeyer et al. and Skocpol do so only in part, there are strong reasons to believe that the mode of analysis they utilize should have considerable relevance to this question. This suggests the need for a more complex, historically rooted "social origins" analysis to account for the varied size, composition, and structure of the civil society sector in different societies.

Drawing on these insights, we formulate and test such a "social origins" explanation of global civil society development here. As is spelled out more fully in chapter 4, this explanation posits two fundamental propositions: first, that underlying the apparently random cross-national variations in key dimensions of the civil society sector lie some identifiable patterns that invite an attempt at explanation; and second, that these patterns are strongly associated with distinctive constellations of power relationships among a variety of socioeconomic groups and institutions, including landed elites, middle-class commercial and industrial interests, peasants, workers, and the institutions through which these groupings come together and express their interests and perspectives at critical moments in the histories of their societies. These critical moments often set a path, or establish propensities, that affect the evolution of important societal institutions and behaviors—including particularly civil society organizations and behaviors—for decades afterward.

Structure of Presentation

To explore these hypotheses, the discussion in the balance of this volume falls into two parts. Part I, which follows this introduction, consists of five chapters that carry the main thrust of the book's message. Taken together, these chapters first outline in more detail the set of facts about the development of the civil society sector that this book seeks to explain and then test the ability of both the prevailing theories and the hypothesized social origins theory to explain these facts.

Thus, chapter 2 details the basic contours of the global civil society sector in the more than 40 countries on which systematic data have been assembled through the Johns Hopkins Comparative Nonprofit Sector Project (CNP Project). Two central conclusions emerge from this chapter: first, that the global civil society sector is far larger and more significant in more places than previous portrayals and popular assumptions suggest; and second, that some striking variations exist in many different facets of this sector, raising the intriguing possibility that these variations may hold important clues about the causes of civil society growth and development. Readers who have followed previous publications on these findings will be interested to find that the account here provides data on 10 additional countries either newly added to the project's database or on which updated data have become available.

Against this background, chapter 3 outlines the various strands of the prevailing sentiment and preference theories and offers a first empirical test of the ability of these two sets of theories to account for the striking variations in civil society sector size and contours that chapter 2 documented. The central conclusion that emerges from these tests is that, at best, these dominant theories of civil society development account for a highly limited range of the observed variations, and at worst they support expectations that are the reverse of what the observed facts show.

Chapter 4 then lays out the proposed alternative social origins theory and the hypothesized patterns of civil society structure and functions that grow out of it. As suggested above, the heart of this theory is a model that sees the scope and structure of the civil society sector as the outcome of particular constellations of relationships among key social actors whose power is magnified or moderated by a number of important intervening factors during critical periods of development in different countries. Viewed through the lens of this theory it is possible to hypothesize the existence of at least five different patterns of civil society development and to identify the social origins likely to be associated with each.

Chapter 5 then tests this theory against the empirical data we have assembled on the size, composition, funding, and workforce structure of the civil society sector in our 41 CNP countries. It does so first by testing the extent to which the five patterns of civil society development hypothesized by the theory actually appear in the empirical record of these countries, then by determining the extent to which the factors that the theory hypothesizes to be responsible for the emergence of these patterns are actually evident in the historical record of these countries, and finally by assessing the ability of the theory to explain why some countries do not seem to fit any one of the five patterns and what development trajectory they may be on. In doing so, the chapter tests the ability of this theory not only to account for past developments but also to account for ongoing changes.

A concluding chapter to this central part of the volume—chapter 6—then summarizes the book's major conclusion, fundamentally validating the social origins theory's explanation of the causes of the different observed patterns of civil society sector development observed in the data, acknowledges the limitations that this major conclusion nevertheless also confronts, and suggests how this theory can be deployed not only to explain the past but also to predict likely future developments.

Part II of the volume then turns from the analytical task of explaining the widespread variations in patterns of civil society development to a detailed look at the scale and shape of the civil society sector in the 10 individual countries newly added to the CNP Project's research base or for which we now have updated data. This follows a practice of profiling newly added countries set in previous volumes in the series of books generated by this project. Given the analytical thrust of the present volume, however, we have extended the discussion in these 10 chapters to comment at least briefly on how well the social origins theory developed in the body of the book seems to account for the patterns that are evident in these additional countries. Since some of these are countries on which we now have data illustrating changes over time, we also assess the ability of our social origins theory not only to explain civil society sector realities at a point in time but also to understand what might be causing observed changes.

Caveats

As with any empirical study, important decisions have had to be made about the scope of this inquiry, the variables about which it has been possible to generate solid data, and the tests that could consequently be run. In particular, our focus is on what we consider to be the organizational heart of the civil society sector—the set of institutions and associated individual behaviors that lie in some sense outside the boundaries of the market, the state, and the household and that meet a set of defining features worked out through a collaborative process involving an international team of scholars at the outset of this project and then subsequently tested in each of the over 40 countries on which we conducted empirical research.[20] As outlined more fully in appendix A, this definition focused our attention on entities that are (i) organizations, whether formally or informally constituted and whether legally registered or not; (ii) institutionally separate from government; (iii) prohibited from distributing any profits they may generate to their investors, managers, or directors; (iv) self-governing and able to put themselves out of existence on their own authority; and (v) noncompulsory, that is, engaging participants without compulsion.

We are well aware of the fact that alternative types of organizations and individual behaviors are sometimes considered parts of the civil society sector and that many other terms are often used to depict these entities and activities. When the work described here was initiated, however, the idea that any distinguishable sector of society could be identified outside the boundaries of the state and the market—let alone that it might be possible to gather systematically comparable data on it across a broad range of countries—was widely doubted and, at least in some quarters, vehemently resisted. Under the circumstances, it seemed prudent, and also highly useful, to focus on what we ultimately found through a bottom-up research process to constitute the institutional heart of this sector in the widest set of countries, recognizing that others could build on this foundation as they felt appropriate to encompass other types of institutions (e.g., cooperatives and mutuals that do not adhere to the nondistribution constraint incorporated in our definition) or other types of behaviors (e.g., unstructured forms of citizen engagement). Also weighing on our decisions was the hope that our work could influence existing official statistical systems, which had fundamentally buried the civil society sector in national economic statistics until the work of this project was able to demonstrate its true scope and size. It was therefore important to utilize a definition that could potentially be incorporated into the System of National Accounts, which guides official economic statistics around the world—a decision that paid off handsomely in the adoption by the United Nations Statistics Division in 2003 of a *Handbook on Nonprofit Institutions in the System of National Accounts* that incorporated our project's definition and approach, in the issuance in 2011 by the International Labour Organization of a *Manual on the Measurement of Volunteer Work,* and in a new edition of the UN *NPI Handbook* in 2017 that extends the reach of the initial UN *NPI Handbook* to a broader range of so-called social economy institutions and direct volunteer activity.[21]

Given the breadth and exploratory nature of this inquiry, moreover, it was necessary to impose some limits on the range of variables on which to focus. We selected variables that most clearly reflected the forms and levels of activity of our defined civil society organizations. We thus did not spend much time gathering data on the number of such organizations, since such data are notoriously misleading and inaccurate. Rather, we focused on employment, both paid and volunteer, expressed in full-time equivalent terms as a share of the economically active population in order to make them cross-nationally comparable;[22] on the shares of revenue from various sources (philanthropy, government, and service fees); and on the fields in which organizations operate, classified using a special International Classification of Nonprofit Organizations (ICNPO) that built upon, but elaborated on, the International Standard Industrial Classification system used in most international economic statistics. Most of the data reported here were generated over an 18-year period stretching from 1995 through 2012. In a number of countries, time series data are available covering significant portions of the period, while in others work was undertaken more recently and earlier data are not available.

Despite these limitations, we are convinced that the data assembled and analyzed here represent the most detailed and reliable cross-national empirical picture of the global civil society sector available in the world. The data were generated using exacting standards of comparability by teams of researchers guided by a common set of research protocols and an agreed-upon common definition and were carefully monitored by a skilled staff. What is more, the data gain further credence from the fact that the project's procedures and definition were subsequently incorporated into the official *Handbook on Nonprofit Institutions in the System of National Accounts*, issued as a publication of the United Nations Statistics Division in 2003, and adopted to date by 20 countries ranging from Canada to Kyrgyzstan and from New Zealand to Norway. We therefore believe that this body of data, while far from perfect, is sufficiently robust, reliable, and comparable to sustain the analysis presented here and that it offers important insights into the patterns of development of civil society institutions in an exceedingly wide range of countries embodying widely disparate levels of economic development, extensive regional diversity, and virtually every major religious tradition.

Finally, although we believe this book makes a significant contribution to our understanding of the dynamics of civil society sector development by calling attention to a set of factors that has been overlooked or downplayed in previous accounts, we are well aware of the enormous complexity of the social processes our book attempts to unravel and are not suggesting any single causal explanation. Indeed, the social origins theory elaborated here itself embraces a diverse mixture of factors that interact in complex and dynamic ways. Nor do we expect that the tests we have been able to generate on this theory constitute a definitive proof for all countries for all time. As we note again in the conclusion, data on countries not covered by this study may yield new evidence that will require modifications or even substantial revisions of this approach. Our contention, rather, is that the factors associated with this theory seem to help significantly in accounting for the known facts and should therefore no longer be ignored.

With these caveats in mind, we turn now to what these data tell us about the scope, structure, financing, and role of the global civil-society sector and about the country-by-country variations in these dimensions that are also powerfully apparent.

Notes

1. The terms "civil society sector" and "nonprofit sector" are used interchangeably in this book, although they carry slightly different connotations. We consider nonprofit organizations to be a central component of the civil society concept, though we recognize that it does not exhaust the concept. On the variety of understandings of the concept of civil society, see Seligman 1992, Edwards 2004, Edwards 2011, and Hall 1995b. In this account, we differentiate the term "civil society" from its more

narrow cognates—"civil society organization" and "civil society sector"—and generally utilize the latter terms to signal our focus on the organizational core of the broader and more abstract civil society concept. For prior reports on the results of the Johns Hopkins Comparative Nonprofit Sector Project that generated the data referred to here, see Salamon, Anheier, List, et al. 1999; Salamon and Anheier 1997b; and Salamon, Sokolowski, and Associates 2004.

2. Salamon and Haddock 2015.

3. Acemoglu and Robinson 2012.

4. Putnam 1993; Fukuyama 1995; Coleman 1990.

5. A total of 41 countries are included in the analysis here. Two additional countries—Egypt and Morocco—were covered in the project but are not included in this analysis due to limited data availability.

6. This view is most clearly evident in the official guidance system for international economic data, the so-called System of National Accounts (SNA), which until 1993 made no provision for a distinctive "nonprofit institution" (NPI) sector—and even after that restricted this sector to what it termed *nonprofit institutions serving households*, which operationally includes only institutions supported wholly or overwhelmingly by charitable contributions. Other nonprofit institutions are assigned to the corporations, government, or household sectors. Not until 2003, largely as a result of work reported in this volume, did the SNA officially acknowledge the existence of an NPI sector, which remains restricted to presentation in "satellite accounts" and not in the SNA proper. A 2008 revision of the SNA did add a dedicated chapter devoted to NPIs and called on countries to identify NPIs separately in the other institutional accounts to which they are allocated in their core SNA reporting; this step makes it far easier for statistical agencies or outside experts to produce the NPI satellite accounts. In 2017, a revision of the 2003 UN *NPI Handbook* was released that broadened the coverage beyond NPIs to include direct volunteering as well as those cooperatives, mutual associations, and social enterprises that operate under a significant limitation on their distribution of profits.

7. For empirical verification of this and subsequent global nonprofit dimensions, see Salamon, Sokolowski, and Associates 2004 and chapter 2 of this volume.

8. Granovetter 1985, 483.

9. Ibid., 487.

10. Seibel 1990, 46.

11. Hall 1995b, 5.

12. Gramsci 1999.

13. Howell and Pearce 2001, 3.

14. Putnam 1993, 121. In his superb analysis of the 11th- and 12th-century origins of Italy's divergent civic cultures, Putnam effectively utilizes what we will here term a "social origins approach" emphasizing the power that landed elites, later joined by colonial powers, exercised over a submerged peasantry to explain the absence of associational life in southern Italy. His discussion of the rise of "associationalism" in Northern Italy, by contrast, relies more heavily on the somewhat shakier

grounds of a sentiments argument emphasizing the role of ideas, particularly the idea of civic virtue, in creating Northern Italy's strong associational tradition.

15. Moore 1966; Rueschemeyer, Stephens, and Stephens 1992. For a theoretical exposition of this "path dependence" theory, see Arthur 1994; for its application to organizational ecology, see Krugman 1991.

16. Esping-Andersen 1990; Skocpol 1995.

17. Moore 1966. Brenner (1982) brought a similar line of argument to bear to explain differences in the institutional development of continental Europe and England, arguing that these differences can be traced to different power relations between the landed gentry and peasantry in the Middle Ages, which made it necessary for landed elements to rely heavily on the state to control the peasantry in Europe whereas English landlords utilized market-type relationships instead.

18. Rueschemeyer, Stephens, and Stephens 1992, 5.

19. Esping-Andersen 1990; Skocpol 1995. This emphasis on political factors has been further validated in Timberger 1978 and Evans, Rueschemeyer, and Skocpol 1985.

20. For a discussion of the process that led to the formulation of the project's definition of the civil society, or nonprofit, sector and the applicability of this definition to a wide range of countries, see chapter 2 in this volume and Salamon and Anheier 1997b, as well as the individual country chapters in this book.

21. United Nations 2003; International Labour Organization 2011; United Nations 2017 (forthcoming).

22. The measure of employment used was the number of hours worked in civil society institutions by paid employees and volunteers during a year divided by the typical hours considered to represent full-time employment in a country to yield the number of "full-time equivalent" (FTE) workers. This measure avoids the danger of double counting that may result from simply adding together the number of persons working for these organizations in either capacity without adjusting for the limited time that volunteers typically serve. To standardize this measure across countries of different sizes, this figure was then divided by the overall size of each country's respective economically active population (EAP). EAP was used instead of "labor force" because of the variations in the definition of the labor force in different countries and the fact that in many countries, particularly in the global South, large numbers of workers are in the informal economy and therefore not included in counts of the "labor force."

PART ONE

Social Origins of Civil Society

LESTER M. SALAMON, S. WOJCIECH SOKOLOWSKI,
and MEGAN A. HADDOCK

CHAPTER TWO

What Is to Be Explained?

Variations in Civil Society Development

> I have never doubted the truth of signs, Adso; they are
> the only things man has with which to orient himself
> in the world. What I did not understand was the relation
> among signs.
>
> —UMBERTO ECO, *THE NAME OF THE ROSE,* 599

BEFORE TESTING ANY BODY of theory it is essential to be clear about what the theory is being called on to explain. While this would be a trivial undertaking under normal circumstances, it turns out to be a daunting obstacle when it comes to the nonprofit or civil society sector. This is so for several reasons. Most fundamentally, the enormous diversity of the set of entities and activities that could potentially be embraced within this sector has raised serious doubts in the minds of many about whether any such sector exists and, if so, about what it contains. Even among those willing to concede that it is possible to identify some distinguishable sector of social or economic life outside of the market, the state, and the household there are significant differences regarding what criteria to use for fixing the boundaries—with some observers limiting the sector to concrete organizations and behaviors and others stretching it to embrace attitudes and values that exist apart from tangible institutional or behavioral expressions. Even among those who focus on more tangible institutional and behavioral manifestations of this sector, significant differences exist over whether the defining features should be the source of organizational income, the treatment of any operating surplus, who the organizations serve, how they are treated in tax laws, what their legal status is, how extensively they rely on volunteers, how they are governed, what their objectives are, or any of a number of other features.[1] Not surprisingly, these different defining features yield, in turn, a corresponding terminological tangle, with a welter of different names advanced to brand this sector: civil society sector, nonprofit sector, nongovernmental sector, social economy sector, voluntary sector, charitable sector, independent sector, noncommercial sector, third sector, social sector, and many more.

Quite apart from this conceptual and definitional challenge, moreover, important questions arise about what facets of this sector's existence it is important to know about. For some, this sector should be treated like any other, with measures developed on its overall size, its economic footprint, the number of people it engages, and its overall impact on social and economic life. Others, however, consider any effort to reduce the importance of this sector to crude economic measures to be a distortion of the ethical and normative dimensions that really express this sector's true contributions.

In this chapter, we take up these conceptual and empirical questions and identify what it is that our explanatory theory of this sector is intended to explain. To do so, the discussion draws heavily on the results of the Johns Hopkins Comparative Nonprofit Sector Project (CNP Project) in which the principal authors have long been involved. This body of work remains the major source of solid empirical knowledge about the organizational and behavioral manifestations of the nonprofit, or civil society, sector at the international level and the principal source of empirical data on which this book relies. Although the System of National Accounts (SNA), the guidance system for official economic statistics generated by national statistical offices, has, since 1993, contained data on a separately identified economic "sector" called Nonprofit Institutions Serving Households (NPISH), we discovered early in our work that the entities covered in this sector actually account for relatively little of the economic activity carried on by nonprofit institutions.[2] The data on which this chapter, and this book, are based were generated in order to overcome this gap in existing information sources.

The purpose of this chapter is to outline some of the major features of this sector as they emerge from this body of work. More specifically, the discussion here falls into three sections. In the first we identify the defining features of the entities and behaviors that are the focus of our attention and explain the rationale for the choices we have made. The second section then documents some of the key attributes of this sector, drawing on the data we have assembled in over 40 countries.[3] A central conclusion that emerges from these data is that the global civil society sector is quite a bit larger than widely assumed, engages in a wide variety of activities, and supports itself from a surprisingly diverse set of sources. The third section then zeroes in on what turn out to be enormous variations in the scope, structure, financing, and role of this sector from country to country.

Defining the Civil Society Sector

The concept of the "nonprofit" or "civil society" sector adopted in this book was first introduced in the early 1990s as part of the Johns Hopkins Comparative Nonprofit Sector Project's effort to forge a common understanding and body of reliable empirical data on what was variously termed the charitable, nonprofit, or civil society sector at the global level.[4] As noted previously, no agreed, cross-national definition of this sector, and certainly no systematic comparative data on the sector so defined, existed at the time. To generate a consensus definition of this sector, work on this project proceeded in four steps as follows.

In the first place, we identified a set of criteria that could guide our search for a valid definition of the nonprofit or civil society sector. Because our goal embraced the development of a rigorous body of comparative empirical data on the sector so defined, and a body of data that could be replicated over time by official statistical offices, this step had to proceed with special care and with the requirements of statistical data gathering very much in mind. In practice, this meant a definition capable of meeting five key criteria:

1. Sufficient *breadth* and *sensitivity* to encompass the great diversity of this sector in its various geographic manifestations;
2. The *clarity* to differentiate civil society organizations from the other major types of social units with which they are sometimes confused—government agencies, private businesses, and families;
3. *Comparability*, to highlight similarities and differences among countries and regions;
4. *Operationalizability*, to permit the development of concrete empirical measures of various facets of the entities covered; and
5. *Institutionalizability*, to permit its potential integration into official national statistical systems so that regular data on this set of institutions and behaviors could be generated by statistical agencies on an ongoing basis.

Consistent with these criteria, we resolved to focus this initial effort on the institutional core of the civil society sector and on the individual behaviors related to it. This focus on the tangible, organizational dimensions of the civil society sector made both operational and conceptual sense. Operationally, it allow us to ground our empirical work on tangible manifestations of the civil society concept rather than more intangible and abstract ones and thus to ensure a degree of rigor that few other options permitted. Conceptually, many scholars have emphasized the centrality of organization to the civil society sector's role and impact. In his pivotal work *The Politics of Mass Society,* for example, political scientist William Kornhauser identified the presence of mediating institutions between the individual and the state as the key to avoiding the emergence of totalitarianism.[5] Gamson examined social movements in the United States in historical perspective and found that having an organizational structure is a key factor that determines whether a movement succeeds in achieving its goals.[6] Conservative theorists such as Robert Nisbet, Peter Berger, and John Neuhaus have similarly identified the institutional dimension of civil society as being particularly crucial.[7] As Nisbet put it: "The real conflict in modern political history has not been, as is so often stated, between state and individual, but between state and social group."[8]

This emphasis on the organizational dimension of civil society is also a common theme among activists. Africa's popular independence leader Kwame Nkrumah understood this point well when he observed in a celebrated 1949 article: "In order to restore self-government, we must unite, and in order to unite, we must organize. We must organize as never before, for organization decides everything."[9] The experiences of 2013–14's Arab Spring has only reinforced this point, demonstrating that spontaneous social movements not backed by organization often produce only ephemeral gains.

This is not to say that our emphasis on organizations and the behaviors associated with them ignores the more informal, or subjective and normative, dimensions of civil society or the more abstract notions of civil society as a "public space," as advanced by theorists such as Jürgen Habermas.[10] Rather, we chose to capture these dimensions as they become manifest in concrete behaviors and organizations and to capture the "public space" as citizens choose to enter it. As will become clear, one way this was done was to capture informal volunteer behavior in addition to more formal work.

But what does the civil society sector so conceived embrace? To answer this question, we launched a bottom-up mapping exercise seeking to identify the concepts, entities, and behaviors commonly thought to be embraced within a civil society or nonprofit sector concept in an initial set of 13 countries scattered widely across the globe. For this purpose, we recruited a network of Local Associates and organized a set of practitioner "advisory panels" to root the inquiry in local circumstances and understandings. These national experiences were then compared to see where they overlapped and to identify the basic characteristics of the entities that fell into the resulting overlapping area. Finally, we made note of the "gray areas" that existed on the fringes of this core concept and created a process for Local Associates to consult with us to determine how to treat entities that occupied these gray areas.

What emerged from this process after much discussion was a consensus structural-operational definition of the civil society sector that identified five features that any entity had to possess to be considered in-scope of the civil society sector. In particular, under this definition, the civil society sector is composed of entities that are:

- *Organizations*, that is, they have some structure and regularity to their operations, whether or not they are formally constituted or legally registered. This means that our definition embraced informal, nonregistered groups as well as formally registered ones. The defining question is not whether the group is legally or formally recognized but whether it has some organizational permanence and regularity as reflected in regular meetings, a membership, and a set of procedures for making decisions that participants recognize as legitimate, whether written or embedded in spoken tradition.

- *Private*, that is, they are institutionally separate from the state, even though they may receive support from governmental sources. This criterion differentiates civil society organizations from government agencies without excluding organizations that receive a significant share of their income from government, as many civil society organizations do.

- *Not profit-distributing*, that is, they are not primarily commercial in purpose and do not distribute any profits they may generate to their owners, members, or stockholders. Nonprofit institutions can generate surpluses in the course of their operations, but any such surpluses must be reinvested in the objectives of the organizations rather than distributed to those who hold financial stakes in the organizations. This criterion differentiates nonprofit institutions from for-profit businesses and thus meets both the *clarity* and *operationalizability* criteria we set, since the vast majority of countries embrace such a nondistribution constraint in their legal structures. It also aligned our definition with existing statistical usage, since this feature is a crucial differentiating factor in national accounts definitions of a "nonprofit institution," enhancing the prospect that we could engage the international statistical system to carry on the data-gathering work that we were undertaking, as has in fact taken place.

- *Self-governing*, that is, they have their own mechanisms for internal governance, are able to cease operations on their own authority, and are fundamentally in control of their own missions and purposes. This criterion differentiates nonprofit institutions from subsidiaries or agencies of other legal entities, including units of government.

- *Noncompulsory*, that is, membership or participation in them is contingent on an individual's choice or consent, rather than being legally required or otherwise compulsory. This criterion is useful in differentiating civil society organizations from kin-based groups (e.g., extended households or castes) whose membership is determined by birth rather than individual consent.

This process was then repeated as subsequent countries were added to the project and refinements made in the terminology used to convey the central defining features. As a result, the project's working definition of the civil society sector has been tested and validated in over 40 countries representing virtually every continent, every known religious tradition, and every level of social and economic development. Ultimately, it was given official international sanction by being incorporated into the 2003 United Nations *Handbook on Nonprofit Institutions in the System of National Accounts.*

Out of this process has come a quite broad conceptualization of the civil society sector, encompassing *informal* organizations (organizations that are not registered, not observed, or staffed entirely by volunteers) as well as *formal* organizations (those that are registered or otherwise visible to statistical authorities); *religious* as well as *secular* organizations;[11] primarily *member-serving* organizations such as professional associations, labor unions, and business associations in addition to primarily *public-serving* organizations, such as hospitals, clinics, social service organizations, food kitchens, and cultural institutions; organizations with paid staff and those staffed entirely by volunteers; and organizations performing essentially *expressive* functions—such as advocacy, cultural expression, community organizing, environmental protection, human rights, religion, representation of interests, and political expression—as well as those performing essentially *service* functions—such as the provision of health care, education, or welfare services—or performing both.

While the structural-operational definition of the civil society sector does not embrace direct individual forms of citizen action—such as helping neighbors, voting, and writing to legislators directly—it nevertheless embraces all such forms that are in some sense mediated by organizations, whether formal or informal, including social movement organizations. What is more, because the CNP Project treats volunteers as part of the civil society organization workforce and its methodology for measuring volunteering takes the form of household interviews, it actually picks up a reasonable portion of the individual advocacy and social movement activity.

Far more difficult to embrace within this definition of the civil society sector have been two other clusters of organizations widely considered to be at least next-of-kin to the civil society sector as we have defined it: first, cooperatives and mutuals, sometimes referred to as "social economy" organizations, and second, "social enterprises." To be sure, many cooperatives, mutuals, and social enterprises are organized as nonprofit organizations subject to the non-distribution-of-profit restriction that is a central component of our structural-operational definition. As such, they are in-scope of the civil society sector as we have defined it. But other cooperatives and mutuals, as well as many social enterprises, do distribute profits to members, owners, or investors. Indeed, in many countries some quite large cooperatives and mutuals are indistinguishable from regular for-profit enterprises. Much of the huge French banking and insurance industries, for example, are organized on a mutual basis. Including cooperatives, mutuals, and social enterprises not subject to a nondistribution of profit restriction would thus violate a key defining feature of entities in-scope of the defining features established for our inquiry, though subsequent work by two of the present authors have identified a consensus approach to addressing this issue in future research.[12]

Perhaps most importantly, the structural-operational definition used here has proved its applicability in over 40 countries scattered widely throughout the world and representing virtually every major region and religious and cultural tradition. The definition embraces elements that go beyond the usage in any particular country or region while still being workable in almost all of them. Thus, it includes, but also extends beyond, the narrow concept of "nongovernmental organizations," or NGOs, common in many developing areas. It also differs significantly from usage in the United States, where member-serving organizations such as trade associations, professional associations, and labor unions are not typically embraced within the academic and common public conception of the nonprofit sector, which typically focus more narrowly on so-called 501(c)(3) "charitable" organizations.[13] Reflecting this, the definition was given formal international sanction by being embraced by the United Nations Statistical Commission in the UN's 2003 *Handbook on Nonprofit Institutions in the System of National Accounts.*

To distinguish this conceptualization of civil society from related concepts used in political science, social movement, or normative social-theory literature, we will refer to the entities that meet our definition as "civil society organizations" (CSOs) and the collection of such entities and behaviors that meet this definition as the "civil society sector" (CSS). The scope of this concept is for the most part similar to that of "nonprofit institutions" (NPIs) or "the nonprofit sector" used in the United Nations' System of National Accounts, but we choose not to rely on these terms because they focus too narrowly on the non-profit-distribution feature of these organizations to the exclusion of other features and because they often confuse readers into believing that our definition is restricted to entities referred to in the United States by these terms when in fact it extends well beyond them.

The Size and Contours of the Civil Society Sector: The Aggregate View

Armed with this definition of the civil society sector and with a common set of research protocols, researchers in over 40 countries operating under the auspices of the CNP Project have taken a huge step toward putting this sector on the statistical map of the world.[14] The result is the most extensive, systematic, comparative body of data ever assembled on the world's civil society sector covering the sector's size (measured in terms of its full-time equivalent workforce, both paid and volunteer), its contribution to the gross domestic product (GDP), its activities, the composition of its revenues, and its recent rate of growth. (See appendix B for complete data.)

As already noted, these data challenge a number of myths that have long stood in the way of full understanding of the civil society sector and the contribution it makes. More specifically, two overarching findings emerge from this body of work:

1. The civil society sector turns out to be a much larger and more ubiquitous presence around the world than previously recognized; but
2. Enormous variations exist in virtually all dimensions of this sector from place to place—variations that seem to defy conventional explanations.

In this section we take up the first of these findings to set the context for the consideration of the variations in civil society scale, composition, functions, and financing that we then take up in the balance of this chapter. These latter findings, in turn, pose the puzzle that the subsequent chapters in this book will seek to unravel.

A MAJOR ECONOMIC PRESENCE

Perhaps the major aggregate finding that has emerged from the work reported here relates to the sheer scale of the civil society sector around the world. In particular, contrary to previous assumptions, the civil society sector that comes into view through our data turns out to be an enormous economic force, outdistancing major industries in the scale of its workforce and in its contribution to social and economic life.[15] Taken together, CSOs as defined above engaged an estimated 54 million full-time equivalent (FTE) workers in the 41 countries on which a full set of workforce and financial data are available.[16] This means that, in the aggregate, nearly one-third more people work in the civil society sector in these countries than are employed by government at all levels, and civil society organizations employ eight times more workers than the utilities industry and 17 percent more than all of transportation and communications (figure 2.1).

Put somewhat differently, the civil society sector engages, on average, 5.7 percent of the economically active population in these 41 countries.[17] This is significant because any industry that accounts for 5 percent of the employment of a country is considered to be a major industry. What is more, in the fields in which they operate, CSOs turn out to play an even more dominant role. Data generated by the National Bank of Belgium using a definition of the civil society sector equivalent to that outlined here indicated that civil society organizations accounted for 66 percent of the value of all social service activities in that country and 40 percent of all the value produced in the health field. And this was in a country considered to be an example of a typical European "welfare state."

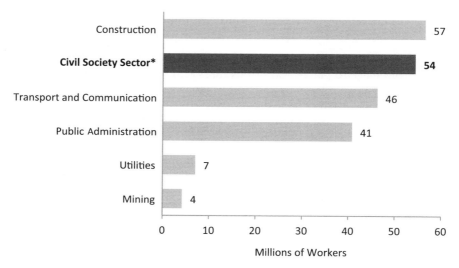

FIGURE 2.1. Civil Society workforce vs. workforce in major industries, 2005 estimates, 41 countries. *Source:* Johns Hopkins Center for Civil Society Studies Global Nonprofit Data Files. See appendix A for further detail. *Including full-time equivalent number of volunteer workers.

A MOBILIZER OF VOLUNTEERS

A second characteristic feature of the civil society sector around the world is its engagement of volunteers. The CSS workforce is distinctive in this respect since it includes both paid employees and volunteers. In fact, of the nearly 54 million full-time equivalent workers in the civil society sector in the 41 countries on which we have data, 37 percent are volunteers.[18] Using our 41 countries as a base, we project that this translates into a global volunteer workforce of 35 million full-time equivalent workers. The actual number of volunteers is substantially higher than this, of course, since most volunteers work only part-time. Focusing just on the volunteers that work in or through nonprofit organizations, we estimate that the total number of such persons volunteering globally is over 350 million. Put somewhat differently, if all the civil society sector volunteers around the world lived in a single country, this "Volunteerland" would be the third most populous country in the world, behind only China and India (figure 2.2).[19] Clearly, this ability to mobilize a veritable army of volunteers is another potent measure of the reach and power of the civil society sector.

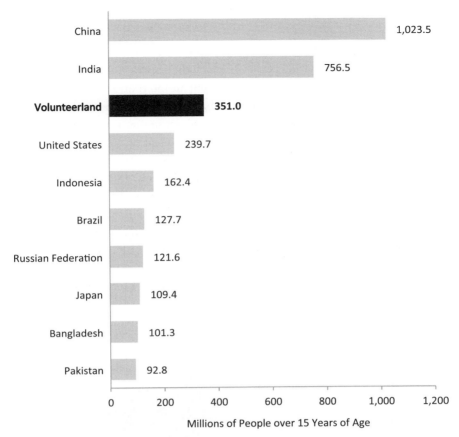

FIGURE 2.2. "Volunteerland" population vs. adult population of selected countries, ca. 2005. *Source:* Salamon, Sokolowski, and Haddock 2011. *Note:* Includes only volunteering through civil society organizations.

A WIDE RANGE OF FUNCTIONS

Civil society organizations are important not only in economic terms but also socially, politically, and culturally. Indeed, CSOs perform a multitude of social functions. For one thing, they are service providers, delivering significant shares of such services as health care, education, environmental protection, disaster relief, and economic development promotion. Beyond this, however, they function as policy advocates, as promoters of a sense of community, as guardians of a crucial value emphasizing the importance of individual initiative for the common good, and as vehicles for giving expression to a host of interests and values—whether religious, ethnic, social, cultural, racial, professional, or gender-related.[20]

To gain some insight into the relative level of activity civil society organizations generate in the various fields in which they operate, we have classified CSOs in terms of their principal activity using an International Classification of Nonprofit Organizations built on the base of the International Standard Industrial Classification used in most official economic statistics. We then calculated the share of the total CSO workforce each of these activity fields accounts for. To be sure, this is not a fully complete picture of the work of CSOs, since many organizations perform more than one function, but it provides at least a first approximation of the activities that these organizations perform.

Using this approach, figure 2.3 shows that the *service* functions of the civil society sector—education and research, social services, health care, and housing and development—engage 59 percent of the CSO full-time equivalent paid and volunteer staff effort in the 41 countries on which data are

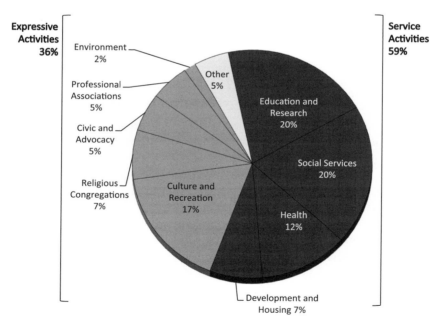

FIGURE 2.3. Distribution of CSO workforce by field. *Source:* Johns Hopkins Center for Civil Society Studies Global Nonprofit Data Files. See appendix B for further detail.

available. Education and social services each absorb approximately 20 percent of that effort. Health comes next with approximately 12 percent of CSO workforce effort. By comparison, the *expressive* functions—culture and recreation, religion, civic and environmental protection, business and professional representation—occupy about 36 percent of this activity. The remaining fields, philanthropy, international activities, and activities not elsewhere classified, account for about 5 percent.

The distribution of paid and volunteer staff among these different functions differs, however. Thus, as shown in figure 2.4, the bulk (69 percent) of the paid staff effort of CSOs in these 41 countries is devoted to service functions. By contrast, the majority (51 percent) of the volunteer staff time is spent in expressive activities, principally culture and recreation (25 percent) and religion (11 percent). Considerable proportions (43 percent) of the volunteer staff effort is also devoted to service activities, however, particularly social services (22 percent), education (8 percent), and development and housing (7 percent).

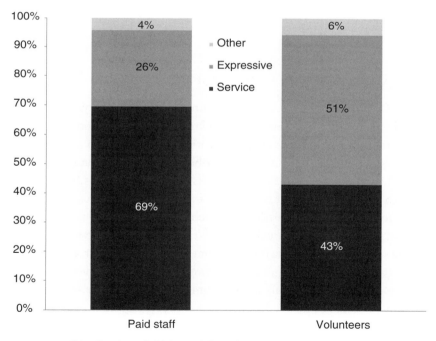

FIGURE 2.4. Distribution of CSO workforce by service vs. expressive activity, paid staff vs. volunteers. *Source:* Johns Hopkins Center for Civil Society Studies Global Nonprofit Data Files. See appendix B for further detail.

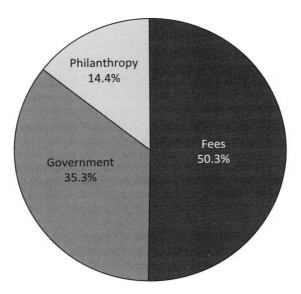

FIGURE 2.5. Sources of revenue of civil society organizations, 41-country average.
Source: Johns Hopkins Center for Civil Society Studies Global Nonprofit Data
Files. See appendix B for further detail. *Note:* Unweighted average.

AN UNEXPECTED REVENUE STRUCTURE

As noted in chapter 1, the revenue structure of the civil society sector differs
markedly from what most observers tend to believe. While charitable giving
attracts the most public and media attention, it turns out to account for a
relatively small share of CSO revenue globally. Thus, as shown in figure 2.5,
taken all together, *charitable contributions*—from individuals, foundations,
and corporations—account on average for just over 14 percent of overall
CSO revenue in the 41 countries on which revenue data are available.[21] By
contrast, *fee income,* which includes private payments for services, membership dues, and investment income, accounts for a much larger 50 percent of
income on average. Finally, *government support,* which includes grants, contracts, and voucher payments by governments for particular services, such
as health care, makes up the balance of just over 35 percent of civil society
organization revenue.

This overall pattern of fee income dominance does not vary much among
different fields. Fee income dominates the revenue picture of civil society
organizations in 8 of the 12 fields of CSO activity identified in the Interna-

tional Classification of Nonprofit Institutions. In five of these fields, including professional organizations, culture, development and housing, and foundations, fee income accounts for half or more of total revenue; in three others (education, civic associations, and environment), fees constitute the largest single source of income even though they account for something less than half of the total.

DYNAMISM

One final notable dimension of CSO activity has been its recent dynamism. As it turns out, the civil society sector has recently been in the midst of significant growth in a number of countries—growing at a rate that exceeds the growth of overall employment, of the economically active population, and even of the overall economy.[22] Thus, between the mid-1990s and the early years of the new century, paid employment in the civil society sector grew at an annual average rate of 4.6 percent in the 14 countries on which comparative time-series data are available. By comparison, as shown in figure 2.6, overall employment in the service sector in these same countries grew at an average annual rate that was less than half as great (2.2 percent), and total employment grew at a rate that was barely one-fifth as great (1.1 percent).

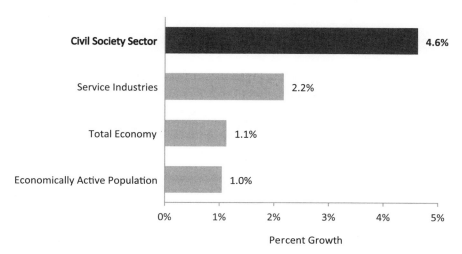

FIGURE 2.6. Average annual employment growth rates, civil society sector vs. service industries and rest of the economy, 14-country averages. *Source:* Johns Hopkins Center for Civil Society Studies Global Nonprofit Data Files. See appendix B for further detail.

This picture of dynamism has also been evident in the finances of the civil society sector between the late 1990s and the early years of the new century. Thus, for example, in the 14 countries on which we have been able to assemble comparable revenue data, the average annual rate of growth of civil society sector revenue was 6.7 percent after adjusting for inflation from the late 1990s into the early years of the new century. By comparison, the GDP of these countries grew at a rate that was less than half as great (3 percent) during this same period, and this general pattern was evident in 11 of the 14 countries for which data are available.[23] This growth of CSS revenue came mainly from two sources: government and philanthropy. The government share of CSO revenue increased in 10 of the countries, and the philanthropy share increased in 9 out of 14 countries on which data are available. In seven of these countries where government shares increased, the shares of philanthropy also increased, while fee shares decreased. By contrast, in the five countries in which the government share of CSO revenue decreased, the philanthropy share decreased as well in three of them, while the fee share increased. These changes debunk another popular myth that government funding displaces private philanthropy and an increase in government support will lead to a decline in private philanthropy. In fact, the opposite seems to be true, and a loss of government support is likely to result in an increase in fee income rather than an increase in philanthropic support.

Cross-National Variations

Important though these aggregate features of the global civil society sector in our 41-country database are, they can be misleading, for behind the aggregate picture lie some enormous variations. What is more, these variations apply to each of the dimensions of the civil society sector that we have been able to examine and often in apparently confusing ways. Is it possible that these variations hold the key to explaining what causes the differences in the size, shape, functions, and financing of the civil society sector among countries across the world? In order to answer this question, we must first examine what these variations are.

OVERALL SCALE

A useful starting point for this discussion of cross-national variations in the contours of the civil society sector is with the sector's basic scale; for the general story of substantial civil society social and economic scale obscures a significant subtext of enormous variation. As figure 2.7 and appendix B show, measured as a share of the economically active population of each country in order to offset the fact that countries differ in aggregate size, the CSO workforce, including both paid and volunteer workers, ranges from a high of 15.9 percent of the economically active population in the Netherlands to a low of 0.7 percent in Romania, a spread of 23:1, with substantial variations up and down the distribution.

As figure 2.7 suggests, there appears to be a relationship between the relative size of the civil society sector and the level of economic and social development of a country. Thus, the countries with higher proportions of civil society workers as a share of their economically active populations tend to be more developed. At the same time, however, this relationship is far from perfect. Thus, for example, although Finland and the Netherlands are both highly developed, the relative scale of the Dutch CSS is still three times greater than that in Finland. Clearly other factors are at work in explaining the relative scale of the civil society sector in different countries.

VOLUNTEER SHARE OF CIVIL SOCIETY WORKFORCE

Not only does the overall size of the civil society workforce vary among countries, but so does the share of that workforce made up of volunteers. As noted earlier, this is a particularly distinctive facet of the CSS workforce. But it is not equally in evidence everywhere, and its presence does not seem to depend on the income level of the country. Thus, as shown in figure 2.8, among the countries with the highest share of volunteer workers in the civil society sector workforce are high-income countries such as Sweden, New Zealand, and Norway but also relatively low-income countries such as South Africa, Tanzania, and Uganda. This suggests that a more complex array of factors may be at work in shaping the extent of volunteer activity in different countries.

CIVIL SOCIETY SECTOR FUNCTIONS

As with other aspects of the civil society sector, enormous variations also exist from place to place in the distribution of the CSS workforce between service and expressive functions. Thus, as shown in figure 2.9, the share of the CSO workforce engaged in service functions varies from a high of

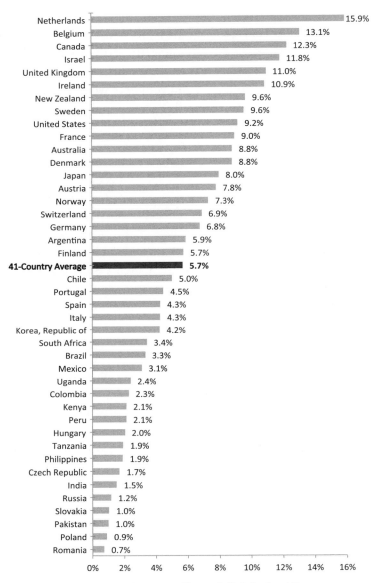

Netherlands 15.9%
Belgium 13.1%
Canada 12.3%
Israel 11.8%
United Kingdom 11.0%
Ireland 10.9%
New Zealand 9.6%
Sweden 9.6%
United States 9.2%
France 9.0%
Australia 8.8%
Denmark 8.8%
Japan 8.0%
Austria 7.8%
Norway 7.3%
Switzerland 6.9%
Germany 6.8%
Argentina 5.9%
Finland 5.7%
41-Country Average **5.7%**
Chile 5.0%
Portugal 4.5%
Spain 4.3%
Italy 4.3%
Korea, Republic of 4.2%
South Africa 3.4%
Brazil 3.3%
Mexico 3.1%
Uganda 2.4%
Colombia 2.3%
Kenya 2.1%
Peru 2.1%
Hungary 2.0%
Tanzania 1.9%
Philippines 1.9%
Czech Republic 1.7%
India 1.5%
Russia 1.2%
Slovakia 1.0%
Pakistan 1.0%
Poland 0.9%
Romania 0.7%

0% 2% 4% 6% 8% 10% 12% 14% 16%

Percentage of Economically Active Population

FIGURE 2.7. Size of the civil society sector workforce as share of economically active population, by country. *Source:* Johns Hopkins Center for Civil Society Studies Global Nonprofit Data Files. See appendix B for further detail.

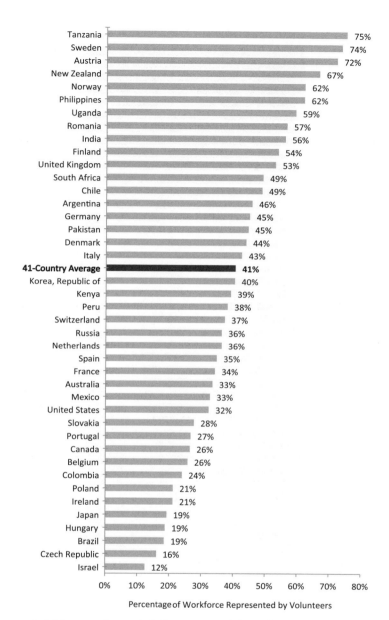

Country	Percentage
Tanzania	75%
Sweden	74%
Austria	72%
New Zealand	67%
Norway	62%
Philippines	62%
Uganda	59%
Romania	57%
India	56%
Finland	54%
United Kingdom	53%
South Africa	49%
Chile	49%
Argentina	46%
Germany	45%
Pakistan	45%
Denmark	44%
Italy	43%
41-Country Average	**41%**
Korea, Republic of	40%
Kenya	39%
Peru	38%
Switzerland	37%
Russia	36%
Netherlands	36%
Spain	35%
France	34%
Australia	33%
Mexico	33%
United States	32%
Slovakia	28%
Portugal	27%
Canada	26%
Belgium	26%
Colombia	24%
Poland	21%
Ireland	21%
Japan	19%
Hungary	19%
Brazil	19%
Czech Republic	16%
Israel	12%

Percentage of Workforce Represented by Volunteers

FIGURE 2.8. Volunteer share of civil society workforce, by country. *Source:* Johns Hopkins Center for Civil Society Studies Global Nonprofit Data Files. See appendix B for further detail.

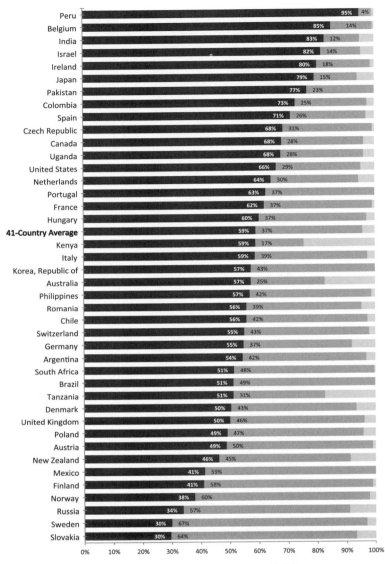

FIGURE 2.9. Share of civil society paid vs. volunteer workforce by service vs. expressive activity, by country. *Source:* Johns Hopkins Center for Civil Society Studies Global Nonprofit Data Files. See appendix B for further detail.

95 percent in Peru to a low of 30 percent in Slovakia. Conversely, the expressive share varies from a high of 67 percent in Sweden to a low of 4 percent in Peru. Although the service functions dominate the activities of the civil society workforce in most countries, six countries deviate from this pattern, and three of these six are Nordic countries—Finland, Norway, and Sweden—suggesting a distinctive pattern of civil society development in these countries, a point to which we will return in chapter 4.

REVENUE STRUCTURE

Similar disparities exist in the structure of CSO finances in the various countries. To be sure, one commonality is the secondary role played by philanthropy: in no country is philanthropy the major source of CSO revenue (see figure 2.10). Rather, the revenue source that is dominant in the largest number of these countries (27) is fees and charges. In six of these countries (Brazil, Philippines, Kenya, Mexico, Colombia, and Peru), fee income accounts for an especially sizable 70 percent or more of CSO revenue. This is somewhat paradoxical since these are among the poorest countries examined.

In the remaining 14 countries, the dominant revenue source is government, and in most of these government accounts for over half of total CSO income. Indeed, in seven of these countries (Belgium, Ireland, Israel, Germany, the Czech Republic, France, and the Netherlands), government accounts for over 60 percent of CSO income. This result is also somewhat paradoxical and, as we will see below, runs counter to one of the major theories long thought to explain nonprofit development.

Although private philanthropy is not the major source of revenue in any country, it does play a fairly significant role in a number of them. Thus, philanthropy accounts for over 40 percent of nonprofit revenue in Pakistan, for 38 percent in Uganda, and for about 25 percent in Romania and South Africa. Here, again, the empirical results run counter to received wisdom, which would predict higher levels of charitable giving in countries with greater private wealth.

Conclusions

Three conclusions thus emerge from this initial overview of the global civil society sector as viewed through the empirical data generated on over 40 countries around the world.

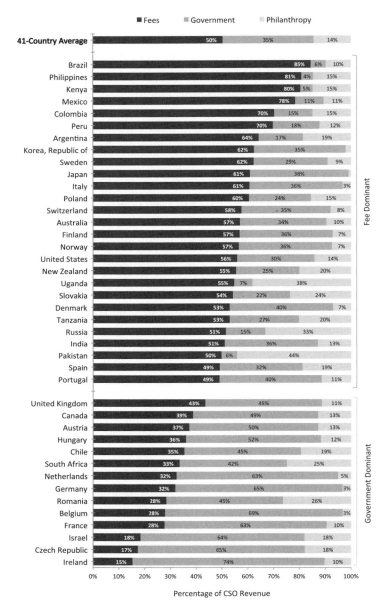

FIGURE 2.10. Share of civil society organization revenue, by major source, by country. *Source:* Johns Hopkins Center for Civil Society Studies Global Nonprofit Data Files. See appendix B for further detail.

SOCIAL ORIGINS OF CIVIL SOCIETY

- In the first place, it is possible to formulate a coherent, systematic, and operational cross-national definition of this sector that can be utilized to generate comparable and reliable data on this sector in a wide assortment of countries.

- Second, an initial effort to generate such data reveals a global civil society sector that is far more widely dispersed and far larger than previously recognized, ranking as one of the largest employers and contributors to economic life of all major industries and providing vehicles for the expression of a host of values and interests that add enormously to the quality of national life.

- Finally, although this sector is quite extensive in the aggregate, it also exhibits enormous variations from country to country. These variations go well beyond the simple dimensions of size and economic impact to encompass how different civil society sectors go about their work, what functions they perform, how they support themselves, and what trajectories they are on. And all of these facets are crucial to the role and impact these organizations can have.

How can we explain these variations, and what implications do they have for the future evolution of this set of institutions and for efforts to assist their development? Armed with this rich body of data, it is possible to begin searching for answers to these questions. We begin in the following chapter by bringing to this rich body of data the dominant preference and sentiment theories introduced in our initial chapter to see how far they can take us in explaining the variations that are now apparent.

Notes

1. Evers and Laville 2004; Salamon and Anheier 1997b; Salamon 2010.
2. The SNA does cover all of what it terms nonprofit institutions (NPIs), but the economically most active of these get allocated to other sectors, principally the corporations and government sectors, where they lose their identity as NPIs. This is so because the so-called allocation rules used in the SNA to assign economic entities to different sectors focus most heavily on how organizations are financed rather than their legal form or other features. Since government contracts and "voucher" payments are treated as "market sales," and since nonprofits receive significant support from these sources as well as from private purchases, most of the economically significant nonprofit institutions get allocated to either the financial or the nonfinancial *corporations sector*, while other nonprofits heavily financed by government grants

are assigned to the general government sector. In either case, NPIs are invisible in the data on corporations and units of government. To remedy this, we have worked with the United Nations Statistics Division to fashion a *Handbook on Nonprofit Institutions in the System of National Accounts* to guide countries in producing "satellite accounts" portraying the full nonprofit sector. Over 20 countries have implemented this *Handbook* as of this writing, and an updated version has now been issued extending its reach to a broader set of institutions and individual volunteer activities, as indicated in chapter 1.

3. As noted in table 1.1, 2 of the 43 countries on which we launched empirical work were ultimately unable to generate the full data set required for our analysis. Hence, the discussion here covers 41 countries.

4. For a discussion of our usage of these terms, see chapter 1, note 1, of this volume.

5. Kornhauser 1959.

6. Gamson 1990.

7. Nisbet 1962; Berger and Neuhaus 1977.

8. Nisbet 1962, 109.

9. Nkrumah 1973.

10. Heinrich 2005; Edwards 2004; Habermas 1989.

11. Religious organizations can take at least two different forms: (1) places of religious worship, and (2) service organizations, such as schools and hospitals with a religious affiliation. Both of these are included within the project's definition of a civil society organization, though, as noted below, where it was possible to differentiate the two, the religiously affiliated service organizations were grouped together with other service organizations in their respective fields and the religious worship organizations identified separately. Data on religious worship organizations were not available on all countries, however, and in countries where state churches operated, the religious organizations did not properly belong to the nonprofit or civil society sector.

12. For a critique of the approach adopted here on these grounds, see Evers and Laville 2004, 11–44. Two of the present authors have recently spearheaded an effort launched with European Commission support to formulate a broader conceptualization of a "third sector" that encompasses at least those cooperatives, mutuals, and social enterprises that operate under some clear limitation, if not complete prohibition, on the distribution of profit. For a fuller discussion of this effort, see Salamon and Sokolowski 2014. This broader conceptualization has now been incorporated into the 2017 revised edition of the UN *Handbook,* as mentioned in note 2.

13. Salamon 2012a, 2012b; Powell and Steinberg 2006.

14. More recently, this work has been fundamentally validated by the work of official statistical agencies in over 20 countries that, as of this date, have implemented the United Nations *Handbook on Nonprofit Institutions in the System of National Accounts,* itself a byproduct of this same CNP Project. A number of additional countries have such work under way as of this writing.

15. We use employment, both paid and volunteer, as our measure of the scale of the civil society sector because it is the best indicator of the actual level of activity in this sector. Financial measures can be seriously understated or otherwise distorted by the presence of volunteer labor and free provision of goods and services by nonprofits.

16. The base year utilized in the collection of data for this project differed from country to country. To normalize the estimates to a common base year for the absolute estimates reported in figure 2.1, we calculated the ratio of CSO workforce to the economically active population (EAP) in the year the data were collected and then applied this ratio to the 2005 EAP of the country. We believe this estimate is conservative since there is evidence that the CSO share of the EAP is rising in most countries for which data are available, as will be detailed below.

For all other analyses focusing on the CSO workforce, the variable used is the ratio of the CSO workforce size to the EAP in the country in the year in which our data were generated. We used the economically active population as the base against which to measure the civil society sector workforce because it is the most universal measure available. As noted previously, alternative measures such as "labor force" vary widely in concept among countries and are also sensitive to variations in how economic activity is carried out. In India, for example, much of the economic activity takes place in the informal economy, whose workers are not counted in the official labor force. By contrast, the EAP includes all people between the ages of 16 and 65 who are not institutionalized or otherwise unavailable for work. Because volunteers and some paid workers work part-time or episodically, we converted all employment data into full-time equivalent (FTE) workers. This was done by dividing the total hours of paid or volunteer work by the number of hours considered to represent full-time work in each country. This approach allowed us to normalize this key variable by controlling for the vast differences in the size of national economies while adjusting the count of volunteers by the time they are actually involved in this activity.

17. This figure is the unweighted average, which takes each country as an observation, regardless of its size. The weighted average, which takes account of the size of the economies in question, is 4.2 percent. This is because several of the countries with the lowest shares of CSO employment are relatively large countries.

18. This is the weighted share of volunteers in the civil society workforce in these 41 countries. The unweighted average of the 41 countries is 42 percent. The unweighted average is higher than the weighted average since the unweighted average treats all countries equally in computing the average and many of the smaller countries have higher volunteer shares of their civil society workforce than do the larger countries.

19. Including direct volunteering, and not just volunteering through organizations, the total number of volunteers globally likely exceeds 900 million people, just shy of the number of people living in China. For the derivation of these estimates, see Salamon, Sokolowski, and Haddock 2011.

20. Salamon 2012a.

21. The figures reported here are unweighted averages that treat all countries equally, regardless of the size of their civil society sectors.

22. The exact dimensions of this growth are difficult to ascertain precisely for a number of reasons. In the first place, we have been able to secure time series data on only 16 of our 41 countries, and these data cover somewhat different time periods. Second, due to improvements in the basic data sources and data assembly techniques between the initial CNP Project analyses in the mid-1990s and both the CNP update and Nonprofit Institution Satellite Account (NPISA) work carried out a decade later, some of the apparent growth in the CSO sector may be due to differences in the measurement methodologies rather than a change in the CSO universe. Finally, while an effort was made to integrate the key concepts of the CNP Project into the United Nations *NPI Handbook* and thus into the nonprofit institution satellite accounts resulting from it, countries implementing the *Handbook* did not always adhere to these concepts fully in their NPI satellite account work. One of the major areas where such deviations occurred was in the measurement of the sources of CSO revenues.

23. Further confirmation of this finding is evident in data reported in NPI satellite accounts assembled by national statistical offices in eight countries. According to these data, the value added to GDP by the civil society sector in these countries grew at an average annual rate of 5.8 percent before adjusting for inflation, which is 0.5 percentage points higher than the growth rate of overall gross domestic product. What is more, the rate of growth of CSO value added exceeded the rate of growth of the overall GDP in seven of these countries, testifying further to the strength of this finding.

CHAPTER THREE

Explaining Civil Society Development I

Preference and Sentiment Theories

LESTER M. SALAMON *and* S. WOJCIECH SOKOLOWSKI

> Solving a mystery is not the same as deducing from first
> principles . . . It means, rather, facing one or two or three
> particular data apparently with nothing in common, and
> trying to imagine whether they could represent so many
> instances of a general law you don't know, and which
> perhaps has never before been pronounced.
>
> —UMBERTO ECO, *THE NAME OF THE ROSE,* 365

THE PRECEDING CHAPTER demonstrated that wide variations exist in virtually every dimension of the civil society sector we have been able to examine across the 41 countries covered by the Johns Hopkins Comparative Nonprofit Sector Project (CNP Project). In this chapter we turn from description to analysis in a search for explanations of these variations. More specifically, we focus here on three sets of possible explanations—one common to more general explanations of democracy, education, and other facets of modern society and the other two related more closely to the nonprofit and civil society field. As will become clear, our general conclusion is that these theories do provide some insight into the dynamics at work with regard to some dimensions of the civil society sector in some places, but none of them can withstand much exposure to close empirical scrutiny across the range of dimensions of the civil society sector of interest to us here. We begin with the well-known explanations linking democracy (and by implication the rise of the civil society sector) to economic development and then turn to the theories linking the size and shape of the civil society sector to two other sets of factors, which we have termed *sentiments* and *preferences.*

Economic Development Theories

Few findings in the annals of social science research have successfully withstood more assaults or established themselves with more powerful support than the one first articulated by Seymour Martin Lipset in a 1959 paper attributing the emergence of democracy to economic development. Using cross-sectional data on a wide range of countries, Lipset showed that "the more well-to-do a nation, the greater the chances that it will sustain democracy."[1] A long array of supporters and detractors, using a variety of alternative statistical techniques and different measures of both economic development and democratic governance, have tested this association and ended up confirming its basic statistical validity.[2]

Because the emergence of civil society institutions is itself often seen as related to democratization, and because the data examined in chapter 2 above themselves suggested some relationship between at least the size of a country's civil society sector workforce and its level of economic development, it is incumbent on us to see how far this line of thinking can carry us toward an explanation of the variations in civil society development before venturing into more complex explanations. To what extent, therefore, does this relationship help us get to the bottom of the causes of the variations we have identified?

The answer, it seems, is not very. Table 3.1 reports the results of a series of cross-sectional correlations between the level of economic development in our project countries and various dimensions of the civil society sector in these countries.[3] There does seem to be a fairly robust positive relationship between the level of economic development in a country and the size of the CSO workforce measured as a share of the country's economically active population, at least for the full range of countries. This relationship explains an impressive 61 percent of the variance in the size of the civil society sector among our 41 countries. Interestingly, however, when we narrow the focus to the economically better-off countries, much of this impact disappears, leaving only 16 percent of the variation explained for these countries. This suggests that there is a nonlinear relationship between economic development and the size of the CSO sector and that past a certain threshold, further gains in per capita income do not translate into further growth of the CSO sector.

Beyond this one overall relationship, however, level of economic development does not seem to be related very strongly to other characteristics of the

TABLE 3.1 Relationship between per-capita GDP and dimensions of the CSO sector, 41 countries

	Relationship between GDP per capita and	Predicted relationship	Pearson's r	Variance explained (%)
1	CSO workforce as % of EAP,* all countries	+	+.78	61
2	CSO workforce as % of EAP, rich countries	+	+.39	16
3	Volunteer share of CSO workforce	–	.03	0
4	Service activities as % of CSO workforce effort	+	–.04	0
5	Government share of CSO income, all countries	+	+.50	25
6	Government share of CSO income, rich countries	+	–.15	2
7	Philanthropy share of CSO income, all countries	+	–.60	35
8	Philanthropy share of CSO income, rich countries	+	–.36	13

Data sources: Per capita Gross Domestic Product (GDP): United Nations Statistics Division, http://unstats.un.org/unsd/snaama/dnllist.asp. CSO data: Johns Hopkins Center for Civil Society Studies Global Nonprofit Data files.
*EAP = Economically active population.

civil society sector. No meaningful relationship thus exists between gross domestic product (GDP) per capita and the volunteer share of the CSO workforce or the share of the CSO workforce that engages in service activities. Increased economic development does seem related positively to the government share of CSO income for all countries, but this relationship largely disappears among the economically better-off countries—again suggesting a nonlinear relationship and a ceiling on the impact that increased per capita income has on the government share of CSO income. Finally, there seems to be a relationship between the level of economic development and the philanthropy share of CSO income, but this relationship turns out to be negative. This runs counter to what might be expected, namely, that giving would expand as income level expands. But it turns out that charitable giving is inelastic: as a share of GDP it rarely rises above 1 percent of national income, regardless of the level of per capita income in a country, as shown in figure 3.1.

Even if the relationships between the level of economic development and these various dimensions of the CSO sector were more robust than they

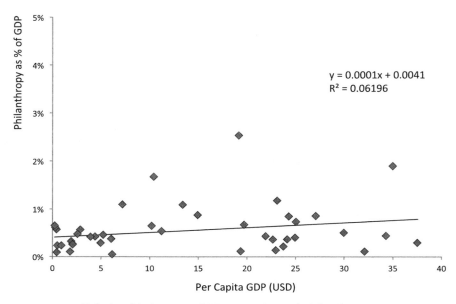

FIGURE 3.1. Relationship between GDP per capita and philanthropy, 41 countries. *Sources:* Per capita GDP, World Bank (http://data.worldbank.org/indicator/NY.GDP .PCAP.CD); Philanthropy, Johns Hopkins Center for Civil Society Studies Global Nonprofit Data Files.

seem to be, however, there would still be questions about the explanatory power of this set of explanations. It is well known that statistical correlations can at best establish relationships; they cannot prove which of two related phenomena is the cause and which the effect. As Rueschemeyer et al. observe: "Any correlation—however reliably replicated—depends for its meaning on the context supplied by theory and accepted knowledge . . . the quantitative findings are compatible with a wide range of explanatory accounts."[4]

To understand what might "lie behind" even the relatively limited relationship between economic development and even just the size of the CSO sector, let alone the other dimensions, it is therefore necessary to turn to theories that address the civil society sector and its determinants more directly. As noted previously, two such theories have been particularly prominent in the field, one of them focusing on certain *sentiments* thought to be congenial to the emergence of civil society organizations and to be present more in some societies than in others and the other on the *preferences* of consumers and producers of certain types of goods or services. Let us look first at the sentiment theories, since they have been around longer, and then take up the preference theories that have taken center stage more recently.

Sentiment Theories

Perhaps the most popular explanation of the growth and development of the civil society sector focuses on the *sentiments* thought to propel people to support or take part in civil society organizations. Two broad lines of thinking lie behind such theories, one of them essentially secular in character and the other sacramental or religious.

The secular line of thought can trace its origins back to Aristotle and his concept of civic virtue—the notion that mankind's highest duty is to serve the community. Though somewhat dormant during the Dark Ages that followed the fall of the western Roman Empire, this concept was revived during the Scottish Enlightenment in the work, among others, of Adam Smith. In his *Theory of Moral Sentiments,* Smith argued that moral sentiments are the "natural sources" of social order and its institutions. Of special importance to Smith was the sentiment of *sympathy,* or what we would today call empathy or altruism. Just as self-interest forms the basis of the natural tendency of individuals to look after themselves, the moral sentiment of *sympathy* toward others was for Smith the natural foundation of a workable social order.[5] Despite the popularity of Smith's later book *The Wealth of Nations,* which posited a "hidden hand" as the control mechanism of the market system, Smith's real message was that this hidden hand of the market could only operate under the prior condition that the moral sentiment of sympathy, of caring for the other, was already present in society.

This notion of a secular conception of civic virtue driving individuals toward associations, community, and charitable good works has surfaced in contemporary times in notions of civic republicanism, communitarianism, citizenship theory,[6] and, more broadly, James Coleman's concept of "social capital"—the bonds of trust and reciprocity thought to enable democratic polities and capitalist economic systems to survive.[7] This latter concept figured centrally in Robert Putnam's important 1993 study of the factors responsible for variations in the effectiveness of regional governments in northern and southern Italy. The key factor, Putnam concluded, was the gross absence in southern Italy of horizontal social capital, of norms of generalized reciprocity, which he argued resulted in a disturbing lack of those forms of civic engagement that encourage social trust and cooperation. Although Putnam notes the institutional roots of trust, which he tracks to different historical development experiences in the north and south of Italy, he nonetheless argues that it is the norm of reciprocity nourished by social capital that plays the key causal role in explaining the existence or nonexistence of robust networks of civil society organizations in Italy.[8]

Edward Banfield made a similar argument in his *Moral Basis of a Backward Society,* attributing the backwardness of southern Italy to a prevalent, but dysfunctional, moral code that he termed "amoral familism," which impeded cooperation among families or clans and thus the growth of associational ties.[9] And Francis Fukuyama has generalized the argument in a book advancing a similar cultural explanation of the sources of civil society, emphasizing the cultural value of "trust." Societies exhibiting high levels of trust create self-governing associations in both business and social life, whereas low-trusting societies rely on familial ties while the management of public affairs is carried out by a centralized authority (the state). "A thriving civil society," Fukuyama therefore explains, "depends on a people's habits, customs, and ethics—attributes that can be shaped only indirectly through conscious political action and must otherwise be nourished through an increased awareness and respect for culture."[10]

Alongside, and in some sense buttressing, these secular sentiments thought to explain variations in the presence of civil society institutions are a host of sacramental or religious sentiments. Sentiments of philanthropy or altruism have long been connected to religious beliefs, and religious institutions themselves can be thought of as civil society organizations, though the extent to which they are truly non-compulsory varies greatly.[11] It was the 13th-century philosopher and theologian Saint Thomas Aquinas, however, who tied the knot most tightly between civic virtue as articulated by Aristotle and the notion that the moral duties of man derived from God. Sentiments of altruism and mercy thus became for Aquinas and those who followed him divinely inspired impulses dictated by God and embodied in religious faith.

These ideas were given an important modern gloss some six centuries later in the influential work of Max Weber, *The Protestant Ethic and the Spirit of Capitalism,* which credits a cultural impulse originating in a particular branch of Christianity, that is, Protestantism, especially its Calvinist strain, with giving rise to capitalist social and economic institutions.[12] According to Weber, market capitalism and its associated social institutions originated in the set of moral sentiments that accompanied the spread of

Protestantism. These sentiments were a radical departure from the traditional work ethic grounded in the Catholic Church's concept of "natural order." This "natural order," in which every being had its place according to its "nature," implied a work ethic emphasizing earning only as many resources as necessary to live according to the life one is accustomed to (i.e., as defined by traditional values and expectations). By rejecting the religious authority of the Catholic Church, Protestantism also rejected the concept of a "natural order." Salvation was no longer assured by submitting to the authority of the church; it was predestined by God's grace, which could not be changed by human actions, and the main concern of the believers was to look for "signs" of being "predestined" for salvation. Economic success was interpreted as such a sign. This led to a new work ethic emphasizing individualism and the accumulation of wealth instead of the mere satisfaction of natural needs, which created the ethical foundation of modern capitalism and opened the way as well to the flowering of voluntary associations.[13]

In short, the key element of this "sentiments" line of argument is that social institutions such as civil society organizations result from the development of certain values, attitudes, and norms of behavior. According to this line of thinking, societies that espouse norms and values favorable for charity, self-governance, or altruism will have stronger nonprofit and philanthropic sectors than societies in which such impulses are weaker.

Testing the Sentiment Theory

How well does this sentiment theory account for the variations we have uncovered in the size and shape of the civil society sector among countries? Fundamentally, these theories encounter two basic limitations. The first is the incomplete causal model they employ, and the second is their questionable explanatory power even given this problematic model.

So far as the first of these problems is concerned, preference theories suggest that the direction of causation flows from sentiments to institutional outcomes, but it raises the question of what caused the development of these sentiments in the first place. Without a satisfactory explanation of the causes of these sentiments, this line of thinking merely substitutes one question with another.

To be sure, some proponents of these arguments seem aware of this problem and try to address it in one way or another. Thus, Fukuyama links different levels of trust to differences in kin relations that emphasize either close family ties or openness to dealing with strangers—but this ultimately does not answer the question about the origins of these differences in kin relations. Putnam takes a different path and links at least the absence of trust in the south of Italy to particular power relations that were already in place in the 12th and 13th centuries among various social groupings, particularly landed elites and a dependent peasantry. However, moving in this direction essentially involves an entirely different causal relationship, one more consistent with the social origins theory advanced here, and renders the notion of trust, and sentiments more generally, redundant. If we can link the absence of civil society institutions to particular power relationships in premodern societies, we do not need the nebulous and difficult-to-observe sentiments to explain this absence instead.[14]

The second limitation with sentiments-based explanations is their questionable explanatory power. The problem here is that virtually every major religion emphasizes the importance of altruism and charitable giving. The "golden rule" that Jesus uttered in his Sermon on the Mount ("Do unto others as you would have them do unto you") and that Christianity sometimes claims as its own[15] was actually taken almost word for word from chapter 19, verse 18 of the Book of Leviticus in the Jewish bible, as Jesus himself is said to have acknowledged (Matthew 7:12). And scholars have found powerful evidence of this ethical norm in every known religious tradition they have studied.[16] Clearly, a factor that is so ubiquitous can hardly be counted on to explain the enormous variations that exist in the development and character of nonprofit organizations around the world. Indeed, some of the countries with the strongest religiously inspired traditions of altruism are Islamic countries, where charity, or *zakat*, is one of the revered Five Pillars of Islam. Yet Islamic societies generally have far smaller civil society sectors than other societies.[17] Likewise, Russia is known for its hospitality and generosity toward strangers, a fact confirmed by opinion polls (see chapter 14 of this book), yet the size of its civil society sector is smaller than that of most countries on which relevant data are available. On the other hand, the Dutch are sometimes portrayed as stingy and unwilling to share their financial resources, as reflected in the popular stereotype of "going Dutch" (i.e., every person pays his or her own bill). This is consistent with the fact that philanthropic giving in the Netherlands is relatively low compared to other countries.[18] Despite this, the Netherlands boasts the largest civil society sector of any country we have studied (see figure 2.7 in chapter 2 of this volume).

TABLE 3.2   Relationship between charitable giving, church attendance, and CSO sector size, 41 countries

	Relationship between	Predicted relationship	Pearson's r	Variance explained (%)
1	Philanthropy as % of GDP and size of CSO sector	+	+.48	23
2	Church attendance* and philanthropy as % of GDP	+	+.15	2
3	Church attendance and size of CSO sector	+	–.06	0

DATA SOURCES: Church attendance: World Values Survey (1991). Available at: www.religioustolerance.org/rel_ratefor.htm. CSO size and philanthropy: Johns Hopkins Center for Civil Society Studies Global Nonprofit Data files.

*Church attendance = percentage of adults who attend church at least once a week during reference period. CSO size = full-time equivalent paid and volunteer employment as a share of total EAP.

More systematic cross-sectional data raise even broader questions about the explanatory power of the sentiment theories. Thus, for example, while there is a positive correlation between altruistic sentiments (measured by the share of GDP devoted to charitable giving) and the size of the civil society sector, this relationship accounts for only 23 percent of the variation in non-profit size, as shown in table 3.2. One reason for this, as suggested above, is that giving rates do not vary much. Argentina and New Zealand, for example, have almost identical levels of charitable giving (1.1 percent of GDP), yet New Zealand has a civil society sector that is.proportionately almost twice as large as that in Argentina. Spain, Ireland, and the United Kingdom have similar levels of charitable giving (0.9 and 0.8 percent of GDP), yet the relative size of the civil society sector in Spain is barely half that in the United Kingdom or Ireland. Likewise, most other countries have rather modest levels of charity (below 0.8 percent of GDP), but the size of their civil society sectors varies substantially.

To be sure, the fact that all religions embody virtually identical sentiments of altruism does not necessarily mean that all people in all countries are equally imbued with religiosity and the sentiments that their respective religions embody. It is therefore necessary to look beyond the religious creeds to the extent of popular adherence to these creeds. Systematic cross-national data on this precise phenomenon are difficult to find, however, making it necessary to search for proxies. One such proxy on which cross-national data are available is religious practice as reflected in attendance at religious services, which for the sake of simplicity we will refer to as "church attendance."[19] As shown in table 3.2, however, variations in adherence to religious norms, at least as reflected in church attendance, do not do much better in explaining either variations in levels of charitable giving or variations in the size of the civil society sector among countries. Thus, as row 2 of table 3.2 shows, the relationship between church attendance and philanthropy, though in the expected direction, is extremely weak, accounting for no more than 2 percent of the variance in giving levels. Countries with higher levels of church attendance do not give more generously to philanthropy than countries with lower such levels. And the direct relationship between church attendance and the size of the nonprofit sector is not even in the predicted direction and is at any rate quite weak.[20]

This is not necessarily to say that religion has no influence on the scope, structure, or financing of the civil society sector, however. The problem may be that its influence does not operate primarily through variations in sentiments, as the sentiment theories suggest. Rather, it may operate more powerfully through mechanisms suggested by the social origins theory. Anheier and Salamon thus call attention to a number of other possible impacts that religion can have on the development of the civil society sector, including through its institutional structures, which can be hierarchical or more diffuse; the degree of autonomy from existing social structures it achieves; and the degree of "modularity" the religion accommodates, that is, the extent to which it requires all facets of life—social, sacramental, economic, and political—to be fused with the religion as opposed to acknowledging that humans have multiple facets of existence only some of which need to be governed religiously.[21] In other words, as will be explored in chapter 4, religious institutions can be part of the constellation of power relationships that the social origins theory posits to be the real shapers of the size and character of the civil society sector.

One powerful illustration of this alternative explanation of the real dynamics at work with regard to religion's impact on civil society development is afforded by Putnam's study of Italy. Thus, drawing on the work of historians Larner and Hyde, Putnam reports that residents of both southern and northern Italy shared a deep Catholic religious faith, yet despite the common commitment to the Catholic sentiment of altruism this supposedly engendered, southern and northern Italy developed dramatically contrary civic traditions that led, according to Putnam, to dramatically contrary patterns of civil society development.[22] The operating dynamic, in short, was not a difference in sentiments but rather a difference in power relationships, with the Catholic clerics in the south using their position to reinforce the dominant position of the prevailing landed elites, whereas those in the north were more effectively marginalized. This southern pattern was not a wholly isolated circumstance, moreover, as the 1879 encyclical *Aeterni Patris* of Pope Leo XIII reveals in its interpretation of the teachings of St. Thomas Aquinas on "the true meaning of liberty." That "true meaning," Pope Leo instructed, actually put the emphasis "on the Divine origin of all authority, on laws and their force, on the paternal and just rule of princes, on obedience to the highest powers."[23] Here was no endorsement of voluntary civil society organizations.

Preference Theories

In addition to the economic development and sentiment theories, a third widespread set of explanations for the size and shape of the civil society sector takes it cue from neoclassical economics and focuses on variations in *preferences* as the key to the emergence and growth of the sector. Two strands of such theorizing can be discerned, one of them focusing on the demand side of the equation, that is, on why clients, donors, or purchasers might prefer to patronize nonprofits in seeking to fulfill their demands for certain goods and services; and the other focusing on the supply side, that is, on why entrepreneurs come forward to found nonprofit institutions instead of for-profit businesses.

DEMAND-SIDE PREFERENCE THEORIES

Among the first attempts at fitting nonprofits into the neoclassical economic model was Burton Weisbrod's seminal theory, which is variously referred to as the market-failure/government-failure, or heterogeneity, theory.[24] The starting point for Weisbrod's approach is the classical economic theory assumption of market failure, that is, of the inherent inability of the market to supply certain goods or services. This failure arises from the fact that the market only works for goods or services whose supply is restricted to those who pay for them. But as Mancur Olson pointed out in his work on collective action, so-called public or collective goods (e.g., clean air) are available to everyone, regardless of whether they have paid for their use, creating a "free-rider problem" since no rational person would choose to pay for goods or services they can enjoy for free.[25] This leads to an undersupply of such public goods through market mechanisms alone.

In classical economic theory, the standard remedy for this market failure is government intervention (that is, public provision of the good or service in question). But Weisbrod's insight was to observe that in a democratic polity, government will only respond to public goods demands that a majority of citizens, or what he refers to as the "median voter," supports. The more heterogeneous the demand for collective goods, however, the more difficult it will be to muster majority support for government to provide the full range of public goods that some subgroups of the public will want. According to Weisbrod, this leaves considerable unsatisfied demand for collective goods. It is to meet this unsatisfied demand, he argues, that nonprofit organizations are needed. Such organizations are established and financed by the voluntary contributions of citizens who want to increase the output or quality of particular public goods. In other words, nonprofit organizations are gap-fillers: they exist to meet private demands for public goods that are not available from for-profit providers because of their free-rider character but not satisfied by the public sector because of its need for majority support.

Weisbrod's theory applies not only to basic but also to more elaborate modes of public goods provision. Its prediction that the number of nonprofit organizations will grow with the degree of diversity of a population appears to apply whether the diversity is defined not just in terms of the traditional indicators of ethnicity, language, or religion but also in terms of age, lifestyle preferences, occupational and professional background, wealth, or income. This latter feature has made this theory far more difficult to test empirically, however, because virtually every society has some degree of diversity along some dimensions.

The theory also has implications for expectations about relations between governments and nonprofits. In particular, it implies that such relationships are unlikely to exist. This is so because the market-failure/government-failure theory predicts that nonprofit organizations arise precisely in fields where government does not operate and government support is unavailable due to the lack of sufficient public demand. Indeed, Weisbrod is quite explicit about expecting nonprofits to be supported fundamentally by donative sources, and a rich literature has arisen around the question of whether government support actually "crowds out" private philanthropy and, in the process, weakens the nonprofit sector. Weisbrod has extended his model to create a "collectiveness index" for measuring the degree of "publicness" in the demand for a public good. The index takes account of how much revenue nonprofit organizations receive from voluntary donations as opposed to private fee income and public subsidies. The greater the revenue from donations, the higher the index score. Weisbrod argues that the index is a good measure of citizen demand for a specific public good not provided by government. Donors "vote" with their financial support and express their preferences for public goods not demanded by the median voter. In the process, however, the Weisbrod theory feeds a powerful social myth about the role that private philanthropy plays in the modern nonprofit sector, overlooking or downplaying the considerable evidence of robust government reliance on nonprofits to deliver publicly funded services.[26]

The demand-side preference theory also has a second strand that builds on another shortcoming of the market. As articulated by Henry Hansmann, this theory traces the existence of the nonprofit sector to situations in which information asymmetry impedes the operation of the market either because consumers lack sufficient information to judge the quality of the services they are receiving or because the purchasers of certain goods or services are not the consumers of them.[27] In such so-called contract-failure situations, purchasers cannot easily know whether the good or service was worth the cost, breaking a link that is crucial to market operations. In such situations, some proxy for the normal control mechanism of consumer sovereignty is needed, and that proxy is the *trust* that nonprofits enjoy because they are prohibited from distributing profits to their managers or investors. This "non-distribution constraint" reassures consumers that nonprofit providers are not cutting corners or reducing quality and therefore induces them to turn to nonprofit providers over for-profit ones in such situations.[28] Although Hansmann's theory can be stretched to apply to government purchasers as well as individual ones, he does not take this step and thus also leaves us bereft of a theoretical reason for expecting what our data clearly show—that the expansion of government involvement is powerfully associated with the growth of civil society organizations.

SUPPLY-SIDE PREFERENCE THEORIES

In contrast to the heterogeneity and trust-related theories, which emphasize aspects of the demand for services, a second set of preference theories focuses on the supply side of the nonprofit market. In practice, of course, these two sets of theories are quite compatible. Supply-side theories do not take issue with the demand-side argument that societal heterogeneity, by limiting the governmental supply of public goods, leaves an unsatisfied demand for public goods of the sort that nonprofits could supply. Where they take issue with the demand-side theories is in the assumption that potential public-goods entrepreneurs will automatically come forward to form nonprofit, as opposed to for-profit, entities to deal with the resulting demand side inadequacies. According to these supply-side theories, the emphasis that the demand-side theories place on the demand for collective goods and free-rider problems limiting for-profit response to this need, while important, misses two critical points: first, that the founders of nonprofit organizations may not be interested in profits in the first place since their "production function" may lie elsewhere, in maximizing non-monetary objectives; and second, that the provision of services may not at all be the real, underlying reason for the creation of such organizations but rather merely a means for achieving some other ultimate objective.[29] Thus, according to James, what motivates non-profit entrepreneurs to create nonprofit organizations delivering food, health care, or social services may well be that they perceive such organizations to be good ways to attract believers or adherents to their faith or cause.[30] This means that the constraint on the distribution of monetary profits under which nonprofits operate is not a serious barrier to such entrepreneurs, since the pursuit of profit is not their central organizational objective; promoting their faith or their cause is.

This reasoning points to the importance of religion and other value bases and ideologies as the drivers leading entrepreneurs to form nonprofit organizations. Indeed, James suggests that "moral entrepreneurs"—or "ideologues" in Rose-Ackerman's terms[31]—are the source of the supply of nonprofit entrepreneurs, and the same religious competition that demand-side theories point to in explaining the unsatisfied demand for collective goods that gives rise to the demand for nonprofit organizations works in the supply-side theories to explain why moral entrepreneurs come forward to create them. Such theories thus agree with the demand-side theories that cultural or religious diversity leads to the growth of nonprofit organizations, but not alone for the reason that the demand-side theories suggest. The difficulty of securing political agreement on the appropriate bundle of collective goods to produce, and the free-rider problem constraining for-profit providers, may be necessary conditions for the growth of the nonprofit sector in such diverse settings—but they are not sufficient. What is necessary in addition is the impetus that diversity breeds for religious and other organizational entrepreneurs to form nonprofit organizations in order to attract more adherents to their faith or cause.

Though coming from opposite sides, however, these supply-side theories line up well with their demand-side cousins on one important hypothesis: both sets of theories postulate an inverse relationship between the expansion of government activity and the growth of the nonprofit sector. For the demand-side theories, such government expansion reduces the unsatisfied demand for collective goods and thus reduces the demand for nonprofit organizations; for the supply-side theories, the same government expansion reduces the gap that supply-side religious or ideological zealots can exploit for their recruitment efforts. In both cases, higher levels of government spending are expected to reduce the size of the civil society sector.

Testing the Preference Theories

How well do these preference theories account for the variations in civil society sector size and shape that we have identified in our data? In the absence of solid empirical data on the scope and character of the civil society sector, it has been hard to reach solid conclusions. This has allowed these theories to hold sway on the basis of fairly limited empirical testing and their logical consistency with classical economics. Thus, for example, some adherents profess to see the United States as a "living example" of Weisbrod's theory, since the country has vast numbers of nonprofit organizations and a diverse mixture of religious, political, ethnic, and racial backgrounds.[32] But such easy conclusions can be misleading. For one thing, it is important to recognize that the demand-side theories, and hence the supply-side correlates that depend on them, assume the existence of democratic political systems—and a particular form of democratic system to boot, namely, a bipartisan, winner-take-all electoral system, such as that in the United States. This form of democracy is not conducive to cooperation among diverse interest groups to form a mutually beneficial consensus and thus is more likely to result in a "government failure" to fund public goods that benefit only a relatively small portion of the electorate. But, to say the least, not all countries are democracies. And not all democracies operate bipartisan electoral systems that create winner-take-all outcomes. To the contrary, Lijphart has shown that the multiparty parliamentary systems that exist in many developed countries, such as much of Western Europe, are based on building a consensus among diverse interest groups by providing government funding for their multifaceted arrays of needs.[33]

Beyond this, heterogeneity is an extremely ubiquitous phenomenon, making it almost impossible to falsify a hypothesis based on it. Virtually every society embraces a degree of heterogeneity, whether based on differences of religion, age, geography, economic circumstance, social position, gender, political persuasion, or tastes for a wide assortment of social, cultural, or artistic values. With this much heterogeneity to choose from, gaining an empirical test of the preference theory explanation of nonprofit differences can easily become either a fool's errand or an exercise in tautology.

Certainly, when solid cross-national empirical data are brought to bear to test the preference theories, the results are far from persuasive. Because the demand-side theories have attracted the most attention, we turn first to them, beginning with the dominant market-failure/government-failure theory and then turning to the contract failure theory.

TESTING THE MARKET-FAILURE / GOVERNMENT-FAILURE PREFERENCE THEORY

Early tests of the market-failure/government-failure variant of the demand-side preference theories were, at best, inconclusive. Drawing on an initial phase of data from the CNP Project, Salamon and Anheier found cross-national evidence for this variant of the preference theories, but only for some countries.[34] What is more, they found that the underlying dynamic at work was different from the one that this theory postulates. Thus, for example, the Netherlands has both a sizable civil society sector and religious differences that were sufficiently sharp to come close to triggering a civil war in the early part of the 20th century. But the connection between these two phenomena did not follow the path that the market-failure/government-failure theory outlines. As will be explored more fully in chapter 5, instead of an inability of the democratic government to offer a sufficient supply of collective goods to meet citizen demands because of opposition among heterogeneous religious communities, the rival religious groups were able to reach a compromise and muster government support for what they both, separately, wanted: a publicly supported school system, but one in which the schooling was delivered through nonprofit organizations so that parents were left free to choose among Catholic, Protestant, or secular schools. In other words, far from an inverse relationship between government spending and the growth of the nonprofit sector, a direct relationship surfaced instead. Yet this outcome finds no place in the market-failure/government-failure theory.

With the more extensive body of data on the scope, scale, and structure of the civil society sector available for analysis here, moreover, this theory encounters even more difficulties. As suggested earlier, the market-failure/government-failure form of the preference theories posits a causal relationship among four key variables. According to this theory: (1) demand heterogeneity for public goods causes (2) limitations on government's ability to supply enough public goods to fill everyone's preferences, which in turn causes (3) citizens to raise funds or other forms of support themselves through philanthropy, which leads to (4) the growth of the civil society sector.

If this theory were correct, we would thus expect the following five relationships to hold:

1) The greater the heterogeneity of a population, the lower the level of government provision of collective goods;
2) The lower the government provision of collective goods, the larger the level of philanthropy;
3) The larger the philanthropy, the larger the nonprofit sector;
4) The larger the government provision of collective goods, the smaller the nonprofit sector; and
5) The greater the heterogeneity of a population, the larger the nonprofit sector.

To test these relationships, we relied on a number of measures of these different variables. Thus population heterogeneity was measured as: (i) the share of the population made up of nonmajority ethnolinguistic minorities; and (ii) the share of the population made up of religious minorities. The level of government provision of collective goods was measured as government social welfare spending as a percentage of the gross domestic product. The size of the civil society sector was measured as (i) the CSS full-time equivalent workforce as a percentage of the economically active population and (ii) the amount of aggregate civil society organization revenue as a share of GDP.

As it turns out, the empirical tests suggest a number of significant breaks in the causal chain suggested by this theory. To be sure, as noted in table 3.3 below, at least one of our two measures of diversity—the extent of ethnolinguistic

TABLE 3.3   Testing the preference theory explanations of CSO sector development, 41 countries

	Relationship between	Expected relationship	Actual	
			r	R² (%)
1	Religious diversity and gov't social spending as % of GDP	−	−.11	1
2	Ethnolinguistic diversity and gov't social spending as % of GDP	−	−.64	42
3	Gov't social spending as % GDP and philanthropy as % of GDP	−	+.07	1
4	Religious diversity and size of CSO workforce	+	+.12	1
5	Ethnolinguistic diversity and size of CSO workforce	+	−.32	10
6	Philanthropy share of GDP and size of CSO workforce	+	+.48	23
7	Philanthropy share of CSO revenue and size of CSO workforce	+	−.49	24
8	Gov't social spending as % of GDP and size of CSO workforce	−	+.50	25
9	Gov't social spending as % of GDP and CSO revenue as % of GDP	−	+.34	11

Data sources: Religious and ethno-linguistic diversity: CIA World Factbook, www.cia.gov /library/publications/the-world-factbook. Government social spending as % of GDP: OECD, www.oecd.org/social/expenditure.htm. Philanthropy share of CSO revenue: Johns Hopkins Center for Civil Society Studies Global Nonprofit Data files.
    *Size of CSO workforce = FTE paid and volunteer workers as share of economically active population. Religious and ethnolinguistic diversity = share of population other than largest religious or ethnolinguistic group in population.

diversity in the population of our 41 CNP countries—is negatively correlated with our measure of government spending on public goods, as the market failure theory predicts. What is more, it accounts for an impressive 42 percent of the variance in such spending. However, the other major measure of diversity, and the one that has been featured in most past research—namely, the share of minority religious adherents among the population—while also negatively related to public goods spending, is far less robustly related to it and therefore barely accounts for 1 percent of the variance explained.

More to the point, the other links in this causal chain fail to hold. Thus, as line 3 of table 3.3 shows, there is little evidence that lower government social welfare spending is associated with higher philanthropy, as the preference theories suggest. If anything, the relationship goes the other way, though

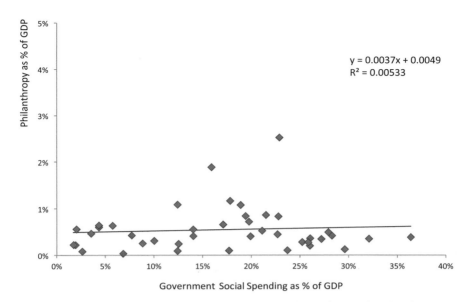

FIGURE 3.2. Relationship between government social spending and philanthropy, 41 countries. *Sources:* Government social spending, OECD (www.oecd.org/social /expenditure.htm) and Johns Hopkins Center for Civil Society Studies Global Nonprofit Data files; Philanthropy, Johns Hopkins Center for Civil Society Studies Global Nonprofit Data Files. *Note: r=.07.*

it is not strong enough to move the needle one way or the other, as figure 3.2 above reveals.

With that link broken, the others come apart as well. Thus, as shown in lines 4 and 5 of table 3.3, the hypothesized direct relationship that the market-failure/government-failure theory postulates between population diversity and the size of the civil society sector does not find support. Religious diversity is at least positively related to the size of the civil society sector, but quite weakly, and accounts for barely 1 percent of the variance. As line 5 of table 3.3 shows, ethnolinguistic diversity—which was related to public-goods spending in the way this theory predicted—turns out to be negatively related to the size of the CSO workforce, which is the opposite of what this theory predicts. Philanthropy, measured as a share of the GDP, is positively related to the size of the CSO sector, as predicted; but, as figure 3.3 shows, the scale of this impact is rather slight given the relatively modest variation in this particular variable. And when we measure philanthropy as a share of nonprofit revenue instead of as a share of the GDP, the relationship

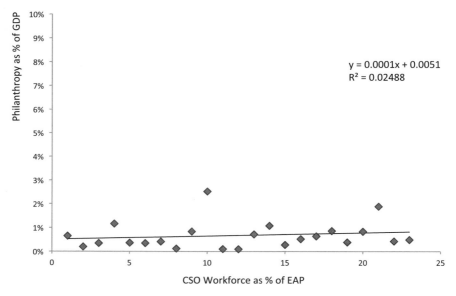

FIGURE 3.3. Relationship between philanthropy and the size of the civil society workforce. *Source:* Johns Hopkins Center for Civil Society Studies Global Nonprofit Data Files.

turns out to be negative, as line 7 of table 3.3 and figure 3.4 show. This casts a long shadow on the argument, advanced by the preference theories, that the key to the growth of the nonprofit sector is the philanthropy generated by dissatisfied consumers seeking public goods that the "median voter's" control of government is keeping government from providing.

The final critical link in the causal chain constructed by the market-failure / government-failure preference theory also fails to hold. In fact, it fails miserably. This is the link between government public goods spending and the size of the civil society sector. According to the market-failure theory, this relationship should be inverse: higher levels of government public goods spending should be associated with smaller civil society sectors, and vice versa. This is so because, according to this theory, it is the failure of governments to provide sufficient public goods that gives rise to nonprofit organizations. But as lines 8 and 9 of table 3.3 reveal, the data do not support this hypothesis. To the contrary, the data support just the opposite conclusion. A strong relationship does exist between the level of government public goods provision (measured here as the share of the GDP that goes for government social welfare protections) and the size of the civil

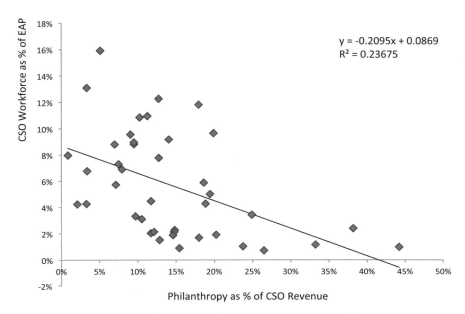

FIGURE 3.4. Relationship between philanthropy as a share of CSO income and size of CSO workforce. *Source:* Johns Hopkins Center for Civil Society Studies Global Nonprofit Data Files.

society sector, but it goes in the opposite direction from what this preference theory predicts: instead of falling as the level of government social welfare expenditures increases, the size of the nonprofit sector actually increases (figure 3.5). And this result holds whether the scale of the civil society sector is measured in terms of its workforce or its revenue, as table 3.3 shows.

TESTING THE CONTRACT FAILURE PREFERENCE THEORY

The explanatory power of the contract failure version of the preference theories is more complicated to test than the market-failure/government-failure version, at least with the aggregate data we have so far been considering. To be sure, this version of the preference theories is tied to some of the same limitations that apply to the market-failure/government-failure theory: it only really becomes relevant in those situations in which, for whatever reason, the state has not acted and a decision is therefore needed about whether to trust a nonprofit or for-profit provider. The trust theory conveniently

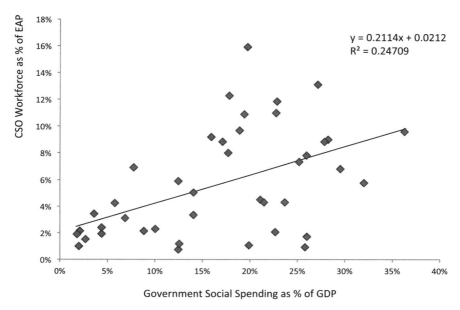

$$y = 0.2114x + 0.0212$$
$$R^2 = 0.24709$$

FIGURE 3.5. Relationship between government social spending and the size of the CSO workforce. *Sources:* Government social spending, OECD (www.oecd.org/social/expenditure.htm) and Johns Hopkins Center for Civil Society Studies Global Nonprofit Data Files; CSO, Johns Hopkins Center for Civil Society Studies Global Nonprofit Data Files. *Note: r = +.50.*

treats this threshold condition as wholly exogenous to its concerns, but that does not mean it is nonexistent.

In addition, within the more narrow range of issues it considers, the contract failure theory operates at a different level: its unit of analysis is not the civil society sector in the aggregate but particular subfields, that is, those in which the normal mechanisms of the market do not work, either because of severe information asymmetry or because the consumer of a service is not the purchaser and is therefore not in a position to bring to the purchase decision a voice informed by experience with actually consuming the good or service in question. To evaluate this theory it is therefore necessary to move to a different level of analysis and focus in on particular subfields considered to pose these trust issues especially sharply.

Since the United States is one of the few advanced countries in which consumers are likely to face choices between for-profit and nonprofit provision of trust-sensitive services in a setting where detailed field-level data are now available, it may be useful to examine experience there. Two fields in which the circumstances portrayed by the trust theory are most likely to arise are child day care and elderly care. In both, the consumer of services is not likely to be the purchaser. What is more, in many cases the consumer may not be in a position to provide a clear report on either the quantity or quality of services received. These would therefore seem prime arenas for nonprofit dominance, according to the trust theory.

In fact, however, these happen to be two fields in which for-profit provision has long been dominant in the United States. Elderly home care, for example, was one of the earliest human service fields that for-profits entered in a massive way in the United States, beginning in the 1950s. As of 2007, close to 80 percent of all nursing homes were for-profit as a consequence, and though the for-profit homes tend to be smaller in size, they still account for two-thirds of the employees and just over two-thirds of the revenues.[35] What is more, trust concerns to the contrary notwithstanding, for-profit entry into this field has become progressively more intense over time.

Nonprofits retain a stronger foothold in the social service field, but in the one portion of that field that most securely fits the contract failure theory, child day care, a similar story prevails. With 70 percent of the facilities, it is the for-profits that dominate this field, not the nonprofits.[36] If, as seems to be the case, the classical market mechanisms do not operate in these two fields, it does not seem to be the trust afforded by the nondistribution constraint on nonprofits that is guiding consumer choices.

TESTING THE SUPPLY-SIDE THEORY

Since the supply-side theory relies on the government failure theory to explain the emergence of opportunities for "moral entrepreneurs" to attract followers by providing public goods that the government failed to fund, the absence of any conclusive evidence to support the government failure theory outside the United States also weakens supply-side theories. At the same time, it is possible that moral entrepreneurs may find opportunities other than those resulting from inadequate government funding of public goods to attract adherents, so there is reason to test the supply-side theories on their own terms as well. To do so, we concentrate on the factor that, according to this theory, is most likely directly to affect the supply of moral entrepreneurs, religious diversity, on the theory that this breeds competition and prompts organizational entrepreneurs to create service-providing nonprofit organizations in order to attract adherents to their respective religious faiths.[37] Research to date has found some relationship between the religious heterogeneity of a population and the number of civil society organizations in a country. The problem, however, is that the number of nonprofit or civil society organizations in a country is a notoriously unreliable variable due to the widely divergent definitions of such organizations, the idiosyncrasies of registration requirements in various countries, and the failure to purge registries even where they do exist.[38] By contrast, when we measured the relationship between the extent of religious heterogeneity and the workforce size of the civil society sector as reported in table 3.3, line 4, we found a positive, but very weak, relationship—suggesting limited empirical validity to this version of the preference theory as well.

Conclusion

How can we explain this inability of the prevailing sentiment and preference explanations of the size and shape of the civil society sector to account for the actual size and shape of this sector that has come into focus through our empirical research? To be sure, the logic of these explanations is compelling, as is the fit with other, mostly economic and philosophical, theories. But something is clearly missing.

It is our hypothesis that this missing ingredient may be the macroeconomic environment and the power relationships that it inevitably establishes. In a word, the prevailing theories may be "under-socialized," to use the term introduced by Mark Granovetter and cited earlier: they fail to take into account the broader societal context in which individual choices have to be made.[39] A likely reason for the trust theory's failure to predict correctly the balance between nonprofit and for-profit providers in arenas that would seem to fit this theory's predictions, for example, is its exclusive focus on individual consumer preferences and choices while ignoring key external factors that may have constrained that choice. Those factors include a wide range of social, economic, and political forces, from access to capital, to changes in family structure and dynamics, to public welfare policies and powerful political ideologies and interests.

Similarly, the market-failure/government-failure theory takes as given that democratic political systems and free market economic systems are present and functioning everywhere. After all, voter and consumer preferences cannot operate the way this theory assumes if voter preferences are achieved through coalitions of minority interests or if no true free elections or free markets operate. Not only does this put countries with controlled elections and controlled or archaic markets outside this theory's analytical reach, but also it leaves out many developed democracies that have evolved what Lijphart terms "consensus democracy,"[40] which differs from the winner-take-all, "median voter" image embodied in the government-failure theory by making provision for proportional representation of minority interests. This is important because proportional representation of minority interests makes it possible to overcome the tyranny of the median voter by building consensuses among various interest groups and thereby generating support for a much broader array of public goods than the hypothesized median voter might want. This may explain why the inverse relation between government social welfare spending and the size of the civil society sector predicted by the preference theory turns out to be so powerfully refuted by the available cross-national data.

Beyond this, the preference and sentiment theories address only one aspect of nonprofit activities: the provision of marketable goods or services designed to supply collective goods or relieve tangible problems. They have little to say, however, about the important nonservice activities in which nonprofits are also involved, such as promotion of cultural values, policy advocacy, protection of individual or group rights, or collective interest representation.

In a sense, the preference and sentiment theories bring an incomplete frame to the analysis of what gives rise to civil society organizations. Not only does this leave key actors off the stage but also it assigns shrunken roles to many that are introduced. Thus, the sentiment theories put religions on center stage in explaining the civil society sector, but only to display their message of charity and altruism. Since it turns out that every religion has a virtually identical message of charity and altruism, however, it becomes impossible to explain the considerable variations in the size and character of this sector using this aspect of this player's message alone. Overlooked in these theories is all the other baggage that religions bring to the performance. Religions are also institutions that connect to other elements of society. The institutions can be hierarchical or federal, and their connections to other elements of society can serve to uphold wealth and authority or undermine it. In short, religion is also a source of social power.

So, too, the supply-side theories have an important message about the nonpecuniary motivations of those who found civil society organizations.

But the range of such motivations they have tended to focus on have been religious in character and service-oriented in function. Far less attention has been paid to the motivations of those forming civil society organizations to disrupt established structures of power and influence, to push for human rights, to promote the environment, or to suppress these same impulses. Yet this, too, is part of the civil society story.

While the supply-side theory in its classic incarnation as a corollary of the market-failure/government-failure theory fails to find support in the available data, however, this theory still contains an important insight about what motivates the formation and support of civil society organizations. That insight does not shine through, however, so long as the supply-side theory is tethered to the demand-side theory's emphasis on the nonprofit sector's role as a producer of collective goods. What the supply-side theory emphasizes instead is that those who come forward to create nonprofit institutions are often, indeed perhaps most often, not motivated primarily by material objectives but by nonmaterial ones related to values, social rights, professional or occupational interests, and, we would add, empowerment.[41] In other words, the mechanism at work in bringing forth civil society organizations may have as much to do with the mobilization of social power as with the production of material benefits, something that the preference theories, as classically drawn, tend to overlook. As such, the supply-side theory may provide a convenient bridge to the social origins theory that we take up in the next two chapters.

In short, the dominant theories of civil society or nonprofit organizations fall short of providing a sufficient explanation for the wide variation in key features of the civil society sector. A central reason seems to be that their narrow focus on the value systems, preferences, and choices of individual actors causes them to lose sight of the macrosocial conditions that constrain or shape choices regardless of what individual preferences or the most efficient means of their attainment may be. This makes these theories vulnerable to the charge economist John Kenneth Galbraith leveled at neoclassical economics, that its "most damaging feature" is the way it "remove[s] power—the ability of persons or institutions to bend others to their purposes— . . . from the subject."[42]

This suggests the need for a different body of theory to explain the significant variations in the scope, structure, functions, and financing of the civil society sector that we have uncovered, one that brings power into the picture. It is to the articulation and testing of such a body of theory that we therefore now turn.

Notes

1. Lipset 1980, 31.
2. For a discussion of these other approaches and their overall results, see Rueschemeyer, Stephens, and Stephens 1992, 13–20. As Rueschemeyer et al. conclude: "One massive result of these studies [of the relationship between economic development and democracy using cross-sectional statistical methodologies] still stands: there is a stable positive association between social and economic development and political democracy" (1992, 29).
3. The measure of economic development used here was per capita gross domestic product (GDP), which is a reliable measure of economic development available for virtually all countries. It represents the sum of the value added by all producers who are resident in a nation divided by the population of that nation. Data on this variable were secured from United Nations Statistics Division sources at: http://unstats.un.org/unsd/snaama/dnllist.asp.
4. Rueschemeyer et al. 1992, 29.
5. Smith 1759.
6. Sandel 1996, 317–351; Kymlicka 2002, 208–283, 283–326; Etzioni 1993.
7. Coleman 1990, 300–321.
8. Putnam 1993.
9. Banfield 1958.
10. Fukuyama 1995, 5.
11. Bellah et al. 1985; Wuthnow 1991.
12. Weber 1958.
13. Although this is the most popularized version of Weber's views on capitalist development, in his later writings on the subject Weber de-emphasized the doctrinal aspect of Protestantism and focused on the role of religious organizations in creating the institutional prerequisites for capitalism. The dissolution of monastic orders under Protestantism removed an obstacle to the secularization of monastic organizations and opened the way for economic pursuits (Collins 1986). In the terms introduced here, this later line of thought would replace a sentiments explanation with a social origins explanation.
14. While Putnam provides a convincing social origins explanation of the absence of sentiments of reciprocity in the Italian south, he does not carry this mode of analysis into his discussion of the north, leaving us without such a convincing social origins explanation of what produced a different outcome there.
15. Blackburn 2001, 101.
16. Spooner 1914, 310–312.
17. Rahman 1987, 309; Salamon, Sokolowski, and Associates 2004.

18. Dutch philanthropy is about three times lower than that in Israel and the United States and about half that in Canada and Argentina.

19. We use the term "church attendance" as a shorthand for attendance at any religious service. Church attendance was measured through the World Values Survey (1991) and was defined as the percent of adults who attend a religious service at least once a week during a survey reference period.

20. We are aware that bivariate correlations of the sort deployed here are often not decisive in explaining a causal relationship because of the possible presence of other intervening variables that may be the real cause, making the apparent bivariate relationship spurious. However, such multiple regression techniques are mostly needed to avoid false positives, i.e., results that attribute a mistakenly high relationship to a particular variable that is a proxy for another. But here the bivariate correlations yield little or no statistically significant relationships between the proxy variables we devised for the concepts embodied in our sentiment theory. Almost inevitably, therefore, the introduction of additional factors would simply rob the hypothesized variables of even more explanatory power by shifting what little explanatory power these variables have to one or more of the potential control factors.

21. Salamon and Anheier 1997a, 11–17. Modularity is a measure of the extent to which a religion, or any body of doctrine, acknowledges spheres of existence outside of the religious one as opposed to viewing every aspect of life infused with religious implications such that no sphere is free of religious control. See Gellner 1995, 42. Islam and Catholicism generally rank low on this measure, and Protestantism, as Weber showed, ranks fairly high.

22. John Larner 1980, cited in Putnam 1993, 22; Hyde 1973, 49, 57, 119, cited in Putnam 1993, 122–123, 127, 130.

23. Downloaded at www.papalencyclicals.net/Leo13/l13cph.htm.

24. Weisbrod 1977.

25. Olson 1965.

26. In his seminal *Democracy in America*, Alexis de Tocqueville articulates an argument about the causes of America's sizable civil society sector that contains echoes of this demand-side economic theory, albeit in completely different terms. The central puzzle that de Tocqueville sought to unravel in his travels through America in the early 19th century was how America was able to avoid descending into tyranny given the excessive individualism and substantial equality that characterized the country. What he discovered was that Americans invented civil society organizations out of necessity to overcome this excess of individualism. In other words, de Tocqueville saw civil society organizations not as vehicles through which to pursue differences but as vehicles to overcome them in pursuit of common goals. Unable to compel anyone to address any issue of common concern, de Tocqueville thus notes, America's individualistic citizens "would fall into a state of incapacity, if they do not learn voluntarily to help each other" (de Tocqueville 1835, 1840).

27. Hansmann 1987.

28. *Ibid.*, 29.

29. Krashinsky 1986; Ben-Ner and Van Hoomissen 1993.

30. James 1987.

31. Rose-Ackerman 1996.

32. Yamauchi 2004.

33. Lijphart 1999.

34. Salamon and Anheier 1998.

35. Salamon 2012a, 132.

36. *Ibid.*, 174.

37. James 1993; Chang and Tuckman 1996.

38. A recent examination of nonprofit organization registries in India, for example, uncovered over 3 million nonprofit organizations on the books of India's registration offices scattered across the country. But when interviewers set out to locate these organizations, only 400,000 could be found.

39. Granovetter 1985.

40. Lijphart 1999.

41. On the role of professional and occupations interests in motivating the formation of civil society organizations, see Sokolowski 2000.

42. Galbraith 2001, 135.

CHAPTER FOUR

Explaining Civil Society Development II

The Social Origins Theory

LESTER M. SALAMON *and* S. WOJCIECH SOKOLOWSKI

> [T]he search for explicative laws in natural facts proceeds in
> a torturous fashion. In the face of some inexplicable facts you
> must try to imagine many general laws, whose connection
> with your facts escapes you. Then suddenly, in the unexpected
> connection of a result, a specific situation, and one of those
> laws, you perceive a line of reasoning that seems more
> convincing than the others . . . . But until you reach the end
> you never know which predicates to introduce into your
> reasoning and which to omit.
>
> —UMBERTO ECO, *THE NAME OF THE ROSE*, 366

Introduction: Bringing Power In

In the preceding chapter we examined several theories attempting to explain
the cross-national variations in the dimensions of the civil society sector that
have emerged from our empirical work and found them largely inadequate to
the task. We suggested that a major reason for this may be that these theories
are "undersocialized," that is, that they take too little account of the macrosocial conditions that constrain or shape choices regardless of individual
preferences or the most efficient means of their attainment.

In point of fact, choices about whether to rely on the market, the civil
society sector, the state, or kinship networks in the provision of key human
services are not simply made freely by individual consumers or service providers adhering to norms of altruism or operating in an open market and
perfectly functioning democratic political system, as the preference and sentiment theories seem to imply. Rather, research into human behavior has
shown that such choices are heavily constrained by existing social, economic,
and political structures resting on foundations inherited from the past and
shaped by complex interrelationships among social strata and social institu-

tions.[1] These outcomes are therefore heavily affected not simply by sentiments and preferences but also by the exercise of political, social, and economic power. In other words, the warm, fuzzy world of charity and civil society activity is hardly immune from the fundamental insight of Anthony Giddens that "[p]ower is to social science what energy is to thermodynamics."[2] It determines whether there is movement and, if so, in which direction. Against the backdrop of this discussion of sentiments and preferences we therefore turn in this chapter to an alternative body of explanation that brings power full-square into the story.

But what aspects and forms of power are most likely to be involved? Fortunately, as mentioned in the introduction, we are not completely at sea in identifying some likely suspects. Rather, scholars who have grappled with the intriguing and complex question of what accounts for different historical patterns of social, political, and economic development have provided us with a number of promising clues about the factors that might be involved and the outcomes likely to result. Three strands of such theorizing in particular seem most relevant.

In this chapter we first review these three alternative strands of theorizing and then lay out the implications they hold for the development of an alternative "social origins theory" of civil society development and for the patterns of civil society development it brings into view.

Three Promising Strands of Theorizing

SOCIAL ORIGINS THEORY AND ECONOMIC CLASS RELATIONSHIPS

Perhaps the most persuasive of these strands of theory is the one associated with the work of Barrington Moore, Jr., a Harvard sociologist whose book *Social Origins of Dictatorship and Democracy* has significantly reshaped thinking about the factors responsible for what Moore identified as three distinct "routes to the modern world"—democratic, fascist, and communist.[3] The key drivers of these alternative routes, Moore argues, are the different patterns of socioeconomic class relationships that exist in different societies during the critical period of industrial development. Unlike conventional Marxian analyses of class relationships, however, Moore extends his analytical focus to class relationships in the rural countryside, subtitling his book "Lord and Peasant in the Making of the Modern World" to underline the point.

In Moore's analysis, whether countries evolve into democracies, fascist states, or communist dictatorships—or wallow in poverty—depends fundamentally on the particular constellations of relationships that emerge among landed elites, the rural peasantry, urban workers, commercial and industrial middle-class elements, and the state. Where landed elites establish exploitative forms of agriculture requiring repressive systems of labor control and the governmental apparatus to enforce them, the prospects for the growth of a market economy and democratic political institutions are limited. Depending on other circumstances, two other outcomes are more likely. The first is "a revolution from above" leading to authoritarian and militaristic regimes. This occurs if modernizing elites in the state administration or the military react to foreign threats or pressures from below by abolishing the old order and the landed elites supporting it and establishing modernizing, but still authoritarian, regimes to push through programs of rapid industrialization. Such developments occurred, according to Moore, in Germany, Japan, and, according to subsequent scholarship, also in Turkey, Egypt, and Peru.[4] The alternative, Moore argues, is prolonged economic stagnation that either persists, as in India, or, under the proper circumstances, triggers a communist revolution, as in China.

For democracy to emerge, Moore suggests, the hold of landed elites and labor-repressive agriculture has to be broken, the "peasant problem" solved, urban commercial and industrial elements strengthened, and some reasonable balance established between the working classes and these middle-class elements.[5] This can occur through revolution, as in 18th-century France; through the conversion of landed elites into capitalist farmers through a shift to export-oriented agriculture, as in England; or in a variety of different ways. But the basic shift in class relationships remains the same regardless of the form through which it is achieved.

BRINGING IN THE POLITICAL

This central, and almost exclusive, role of socioeconomic class in the social origins explanation of different paths to the modern world has, in turn, stimulated a second line of theorizing that takes the class-based analysis to task for paying insufficient attention to political institutions, including the state and political parties. Thus, Evans et al. argue that class-centered, or macroeconomic, explanations of political outcomes are incomplete without considering the role played by the state, which they argue has considerable, albeit varying, autonomy from class and other interest group pressures.[6] Dietrich Rueschemeyer et al. develop this line of argument more fully by combining the analysis of class relationships à la Moore with an analysis of the impact of political institutions, particularly political parties and transnational state relations, on political and economic outcomes.[7] Focusing on a wide range of European and Latin American countries, this group of analysts points to strong political party systems as crucial factors in the emergence of democracy in a number of Latin American countries, since such systems made it possible to mediate and moderate conflicting class interests between traditionally dominant landed elements and the emergent urban middle class that grew to prominence through Latin America's expanding export-oriented economy.[8] A similar line of argument can be found in Skocpol's explanation of different welfare policy outcomes in the United States and Western Europe, though here more emphasis is placed on the structure of government itself.[9] In the United States, she argues, a fragmented governmental structure, a relatively weak federal bureaucracy, and intensive competition between major political parties that often relied on patronage to mobilize popular support, coupled with strong women's civil society organizations, led to the implementation of decentralized social policies limited to targeting narrowly defined constituent groups (such as war veterans or working women). In Europe, by contrast, the much stronger role of the central government was a key factor, in addition to pressures from organized labor, in the implementation of universal, state-funded social welfare policies.

ALTERNATIVE WELFARE REGIMES

A third line of theorizing of potential assistance in our search for explanations of the observed variations in civil society characteristics around the world emerges from research into post–World War II government social welfare policies. This research has led to the conceptualization of various distinctive patterns of welfare regimes. Richard Titmuss, for example, offers a tripartite classification of such regimes, which he characterizes as "residual," offering minimal social assistance consistent with traditional liberal ideology; "institutional," striving to assure adequate living conditions to the entire population; and "industrial-achievement," providing benefits conditioned on employment status and earnings.[10] Gøsta Esping-Andersen introduces another classification, characterizing different welfare state regimes as

Free Market?

"liberal," or minimalist; "corporatist," or responding to a wide assortment of engaged institutional actors; and "social democratic," or universalistic and rights-based.[11]

Putting It All Together: An Expanded Social Origins Theory of Civil Society Development

Although these various theoretical frameworks go to great lengths to explain the role of power relations in shaping modern institutions, they tend to view the civil society sector, at best, as a tangential independent variable that helps to explain broader political outcomes (e.g., the formation of political parties and the consequent structuring of political institutions) while paying less attention to the factors that shape the civil society sector itself. Indeed, one of the striking realities of the welfare state literature is its virtual disregard and neglect of the civil society sector, even though the welfare state in many of its classic European incarnations really took the form of a "welfare partnership" instead, as the data reported in chapter 2 made clear.

To what extent, therefore, can these theoretical frameworks help us explain the presence, shape, and role of the civil society sector itself? Our argument here is that they are enormously helpful, that the same factors that have been used to explain the appearance of democracy, fascism, communist revolutions, persistent underdevelopment, and diverse welfare regimes can provide powerful insights into the central research question guiding this book—namely, what explains the tremendous variations in the size and contours of the civil society sector in different countries? The theoretical approach we propose here draws most fundamentally on Barrington Moore's insight by arguing that these variations, and the patterns to which they give rise, can be traced ultimately to different power arrangements among key socioeconomic classes during critical turning points in national development. For this reason we call our approach the "social origins of civil society," or SOCS, theory.

Our methodological approach to building and testing the social origins theory of civil society involves the following three steps. First, we outline the causal model that identifies the social forces that we suggest are likely to shape the dimensions of civil society. Second, we identify different configurations or patterns of these social forces and develop hypotheses that link these configurations to different constellations of civil society outcomes. Finally, we test these hypotheses against the available data. In the present chapter we take up the first two of these steps. Then, in chapter 5, we present the tests.

COMPONENTS OF A CAUSAL MODEL OF CIVIL SOCIETY DEVELOPMENT

The key contention of the SOCS theory is that the dimensions of the civil society sector are shaped by power relations among different social groupings and institutions. But what are those social groupings and institutions? To answer this question we make extensive use of the well-known social science concept of socioeconomic class, but in its Weberian manifestation more than in its Marxist one. Like Weber, we treat a socioeconomic class as a group of people who not only have a similar relation to economic resources (such as similar roles played in the production of economic outputs) but also occupy a similar social position or status.[12] These socioeconomic classes, their various components or "fractions,"[13] and various organizations affiliated with them are defined here as social actors. As such, they possess two important attributes—a certain level of common interests, whether clearly recognized and articulated or not, and a certain capacity to act on these interests. One measure of that capacity to act is the collective power of a social actor, that is, the capacity to prevail when confronted by opposing efforts of other social actors.[14]

The types of socioeconomic classes that exist in a society depend on the types of economic activities that prevail in that society, which, in turn, depend on the level of economic development. In premodern societies where agriculture is the dominant form of economic activity, *the main socio-economic classes* include the *nobility and landowning classes*; the *agrarian laboring classes* that, depending on the geopolitical context, take the form of free peasants, serfs, or slaves; the *intermediate classes* consisting of small numbers of craftsmen, merchants, and professionals; the *state*, including ruling figures (e.g., monarchs), office holders, and the military; *kinship groups*, such as tribes, clans, or extended families; and *organized religion*, including priests, clerics, preachers, monks, and so on. In modern times, where industry is the dominant form of economic activity, some of these premodern classes lose power or disappear while new socioeconomic classes emerge, often in complex and interconnected forms. In necessarily simplified form, the resulting new class composition includes owners of capital and industrial establishments (the bourgeoisie), factory and farm workers (the working class), skilled professionals (doctors, lawyers, engineers, teachers, etc.), semi-professional occupations (technicians, office employees, etc.), the self-employed (small shopkeepers, craftsmen, artists, etc.), and professionalized civil servant and military elements.

Although we see in social class power an important driver of civil society development, we also recognize that power is not automatic. To Moore's emphasis on social class power we therefore add a second element in the form of Rueschemeyer et al.'s and Skocpol's emphasis on a set of essentially political factors that determine how effectively various social classes actually take advantage of their potentials. The power of social actors depends, in other words, on several factors beyond the sheer numbers or economic weight of the social grouping. Also important are a variety of factors that can *amplify,* or alternatively *filter and reduce,* social class power and influence. Such factors can include the extent to which the class is conscious of its common interests, is mobilized and organized to advance those interests, has effective leadership, has links to potential allies, wraps its positions in culturally effective messages, and is not internally divided along racial, religious, or ethnic lines. The presence or absence of these various factors can enhance a class's relative position or limit the ability of the class to play its potential historical role.

Also, like Skocpol and Rueschemeyer et al., we acknowledge that government is itself a key social actor. Contrary to the conventional Marxist analysis that views government mainly as the "executive committee" of the dominant socioeconomic class, the institutions of government can play their own significant role in shaping power relations in society. However, government is not a single actor but an assembly of different actors—including different branches (legislative, executive, and judiciary), different departments, law enforcement (the police), the military, and the political parties—sometimes acting in coordination and sometimes acting independently or even against each other. These different government actors may represent diverse interest groups in society as well as the interests of their own members. For that reason, we consider government to be a separate social actor rather than a mere representative of other socioeconomic classes.

In calling attention to the important impact that socioeconomic classes and the organizations and agencies that represent or oppose their interests have on the development of the civil society sector, we do not suggest that these actors operate in a social vacuum. Rather, we recognize that they are embedded in the rich fabric of social norms, cultural values, religious beliefs, and ideologies. The relationship between social groupings and these cultural values is interactive, however. On the one hand, the norms and values can constrain even powerful social groupings. At the same time, whether particular values or norms gain support or legitimacy can be influenced by their consistency with group interests. Max Weber recognized this latter point in his concept of "elective affinity," the tendency of social actors to lean toward cultural norms and values that align with their predispositions and group interests.[15] Thus, according to Weber, Protestant religious doctrines emerging in 15th- and 16th-century Europe gained ground in important part because they were more aligned with the economic interests of wealthy merchants than the traditional Catholic teaching renouncing worldly possessions.

Although the importance of social values and cultural beliefs was emphasized by the sentiment theories discussed in chapter 3, these theories treated them as free-floating influences without observable causal links to particular social groupings or specific institutional outcomes. By contrast, the theoretical model proposed here acknowledges these causal links. Thus, the long-standing Catholic doctrine of subsidiarity, holding that social issues ought to be addressed by the social unit closest to the family, including, of course, the parish, provided a convenient template for conservative elements to use in resisting worker pressures for expanded state-provided social welfare protections in 19th-century Germany and ultimately led to channeling what protections were provided through safe, religiously affiliated, nonprofit organizations. Hence was borne a pattern we will later term "welfare partnership."

From the third strand of theory introduced above, that reflected in the work of Esping-Andersen and other theorists of the welfare state, as well as from Moore, we take the important additional insight that the resulting relationships produce outcomes that are not scattered or random. Rather, they are patterned. They produce characteristic constellations of features that Esping-Andersen terms "regimes" and that we will refer to as characteristic "patterns" of civil society development.

Finally, throughout all three of these prior strands of theory runs another important insight that also figures prominently in our SOCS theory: that the patterns formed by the power relations among these social classes as they work themselves out during critical turning points in societal development persist over extended periods, even though the forces that initially produce them may no longer be in existence. The mechanism responsible for this

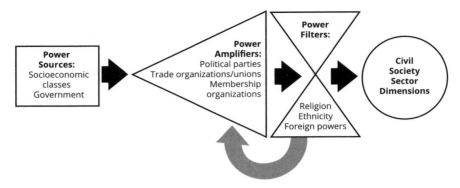

FIGURE 4.1. Social and institutional forces shaping civil society dimensions: the social origins model.

persistence is referred to in social and economic literature as "path dependence." Path dependence is observed in a wide range of social and economic phenomena, from geographical concentrations of industry,[16] through trajectories of economic development,[17] to political reforms and systemic transitions.[18] Path dependence results from the fact that once certain institutional arrangements are put in place, it is easier and less expensive to expand on these arrangements than to create entirely new arrangements from scratch.[19]

In short, as depicted in figure 4.1, our social origins theory of civil society development holds that power relationships among identifiable social classes and actors, mediated by a variety of power amplifiers and filters, stamp onto societies distinguishable patterns of civil society development that persist over extended periods.

IDENTIFIABLE CONFIGURATIONS OF POWER RELATIONSHIPS AND THEIR HYPOTHESIZED EFFECTS ON CIVIL SOCIETY

But what types of such configurations are possible, and what constellations of social actors, amplifiers, or filters are responsible for them? To answer this question, we begin with the observation that, although the types and number of socioeconomic classes in a country vary from one period or geographic region to another, it is possible, at least for analytic purposes, to group them crudely, using a concept known as "structural equivalence," into three broadly defined categories defined by the relative power and social positions of the classes that occupy them: the high-, intermediate-, and low-status classes.[20] Depending on historical circumstances, different social groupings may fit into each of these three structurally equivalent categories, though historically certain patterns have been most common. The high-status group has thus tended to be populated by the nobility and landowning classes, by commercial or industrial elites, or by both. The intermediate level has most commonly been occupied by craftsmen and merchants, skilled professionals, the professional military, or government officials. Finally, the low-status group has long been occupied by agrarian laboring classes, landless rural masses, factory workers, or service workers.

At various points in time, however, these roles and relationships can shift significantly, and it is these shifts that we suggest affect the size, shape, and contours of the civil society sector, often for long after the shifts occur. For heuristic purposes, however, it is possible to discern three broad configurations of power relations among these structurally equivalent status groups. In the first configuration, which we term "hegemonic," the high-status groups exercise virtually absolute dominance over all other groups. In the second configuration, which we term "contested dominance," the power of the high-status group is to some degree challenged by lower-status groups. Finally, in the third possible configuration, which we term "pluralism," power is dispersed among high-, intermediate-, and low-status groups. Of course, there are possible variations within each configuration caused by historical, social, economic, and political circumstances, but the main insight suggested by this framework is that power relations among socioeconomic classes in different countries fall into a relatively small number of patterns, and those patterns of power relations, in turn, can result in a correspondingly constrained set of patterns of civil society sector development.

More specifically, based on this classification and the insights of Moore, Rueschemeyer et al., and Esping-Andersen, it is possible to postulate at least five types of social class power relationships, which vary according to which social class and social actors, or combination of these, holds dominant power in a society. The SOCS theory associates each of these social class power relationships with a likely pattern of civil society characteristics. As summarized in table 4.1, the particular civil society characteristics that are driven by these different social class power relationships vary somewhat, so that it is necessary to distinguish between the defining features of a particular civil society pattern and the potentially variable ones. Thus, for example, discussed in the rough order in which they appear historically, what we term the "Traditional Pattern" of civil society is associated with what was once

TABLE 4.1 Patterns of power relations and their hypothesized effects on the civil society sector

Pattern	Type of power constellations	Hypothesized effect on civil society	Hypothesized dimensions of civil society sector				
			Workforce size	Volunteer share of workforce	Dominant function	Government share of revenue	Philanthropy share of revenue
Traditional	Dominance of nobility/landowners *Traditionalism*	Labor repressive practices to maintain exploitative mode of production restrict growth of civil society; prevalence of clientelistic dependency, kin ties	Small	Large	Service	Small	Large
Liberal	Dominance of bourgeoisie *Individualism*	Economic productivity and political liberalization promote civil society growth, but limited by sole reliance on charity; liberal doctrine limits government role	Large	Large	Service	Relatively small	Relatively large
Welfare partnership	Countervailing power of landed and industrial elites confronting growing working class *Moralism*	Pressures from rising working class lead to growth of government-funded social spending delivered through "safe" (religious-based) civil society orgs.	Large	N/A	Service	Very large	N/A

Social democratic	Effective worker mobilization yields pluralist sharing arrangement with intermediate classes	Worker power leads to support for government-funded and -delivered welfare services and robust civil society sector focusing on expressive functions and advocacy	Large	Large	Expressive	N/A	N/A
Statist	Modernizing elites launch "revolution from above" in support of militarization and accelerated industrialization	Restrictions on freedoms to facilitate industrialization policies limits space for civil society development	Small	Small	N/A	Small	N/A

the most prevalent social class power arrangement in world history. This relationship is characterized by the dominance of the nobility and landed elites, who exercise hegemonic influence over the social, economic, and political life of a society or country. This hegemonic position is necessary to sustain an essentially exploitative mode of mostly agrarian production, which requires a variety of labor-repressive measures and strong clientelistic relationships. In this environment, the emergence of any form of organization of the subaltern social groupings faces serious obstacles because it poses a threat to elite hegemony. Therefore, the traditional pattern of civil society projected to emerge in this circumstance is small in scale, oriented to service functions, supported largely by the paternalistic charity of the dominant classes, and not uncommonly used by the landed or other economic elites to reinforce patterns of dependence. This is the pattern that Putnam describes so vividly operating in the south of Italy in the 14th century—curtailing the liberties of large segments of society and severely restricting the development of a meaningful civil society sector for literally centuries thereafter.[21] Indeed, one keen observer found the basic circumstances intact five centuries later, depicting the social relations of Sicily as of 1876 as follows: "Every local notable in his jurisdiction of power was the head of a network of persons of the most diverse social conditions, who depended on him for their economic survival and social prestige and who furnished him legal support in terms of electoral suffrage and illegal support in the recourse to violence in defense of his particular interests, in a rigorously hierarchical relationship of para-feudal dependence."[22]

Durable as this traditional pattern has proved to be in many places, however, it is vulnerable to both economic and ideological shifts, particularly since, as Acemoglu and Robinson demonstrate, it is associated with extreme inequality, overall poor economic performance, and widespread poverty.[23] As other social classes gain power and influence, they can challenge the hegemony of landed interests and seek political and economic changes. This occurred, for example, in England beginning in the 17th century as the growth of commerce fueled the emergence of a wealthy class of merchants and industrialists who sought relief from the restrictions of feudal privilege and of landed dominance and who fortuitously benefited from the shift in the agriculture sector toward an export-oriented product (wool) that eliminated the need for a large and dependent rural peasantry and prompted the enclosure movement that rid the countryside of surplus labor. Armed with new liberal economic ideas calling for limits on big government and Protestant social values privileging thrift and blaming the poor for their indigence, these new elites looked to free enterprise in the economic sphere and reliance on private charity in the social sphere as their goal. We hypothesize that these developments give rise to a distinct "Liberal Pattern" of civil society development characterized by the emergence of various professional organizations but, in a climate of liberal hostility to government spending and long-standing traditions of deference by lower-status groups to privileged elites, an otherwise constrained civil society sector depending heavily on upper- and middle-class generosity to minimize the extremes of social distress while otherwise holding firm to principles of individual responsibility.

A third pattern emerges where industrialization and the partial liberalization of social relations leads to the substantial growth of a working class and of organizations representing its interests, but not to the point of displacing the dominant position of landed, industrial, or commercial elites. Confronted with stronger pressures from organized workers than those characteristic of circumstances that give rise to the liberal pattern, social elites in this situation face a number of options. One of the most common is to reduce the pressure by taking steps to splinter the working class elements along religious, ethnic, or racial lines. The effort to wean workers away from socialist-oriented unions and parties by establishing safer Catholic-oriented such entities in late-19th-century Europe is one illustration of this tactic.[24] But another reaction, typified by the social welfare innovations of Chancellor Otto von Bismarck in late-19th-century Germany, is to buy off worker protest with state-sponsored social welfare protections—but channel these protections through "safe," religiously affiliated, private voluntary organizations. We hypothesize that this produces its own characteristic pattern of civil society development, which we characterize as the "Welfare Partnership" pattern. This pattern leads to a substantial civil society sector, mostly focused on service activities instead of protest and advocacy, heavily subsidized by the state but safely held in check by conservative religious or other institutions.

Yet a fourth pattern can occur where the power of landed elites is weakened, whether by war, internal conflicts, or other factors, opening the way to industrialization and the emergence of a more pluralistic configuration of power relations engaging new professional and commercial elites and an energized and sizable working class. Where these latter lower-class elements remain unified and able to exert substantial influence on their own behalf, or with the aid of civil servants mobilized by concerns about social distress, we hypothesize the possibility of another distinctive pattern of civil society development, which we term the "Social Democratic Pattern." Unlike under the welfare partnership model, where services are delivered through conservatively oriented religious charities that can co-opt and mute worker protest, in this social democratic pattern social welfare services are treated as a right of all citizens—not a gift bestowed by charitable institutions—and are delivered directly by governmental institutions subject to popular control by citizens. Worker political power, in this pattern, promotes an open political system with considerable freedom to form civil society organizations, but these organizations function mostly in expressive fields—arts, culture, recreation, sports, and advocacy for rights—and draw heavily on volunteers rather than paid staff.

A fifth constellation of social class and social actor power relationships arises where premodern landed elements retain power into the modern era and prolong economic stagnation that threatens the country's sovereignty and national pride. In such settings, intermediate elements consisting often of military leaders, senior civil servants, urban professionals, or modernizing revolutionaries—fearing threats from more economically developed powers or mobilized by radical modernizing ideologies—take over state institutions in order to push through programs of rapid industrialization and modernization. Nineteenth-century Japan offers an example of this pattern when an offshoot of the country's samurai warrior caste, embarrassed by the forced entry of the US navy in the 1850s, joined with some political leaders to seize power through what was known as the Meiji Restoration, disrupted the power of the feudal lords, and pursued rapid industrialization, militarization, and ultimately a war for control of natural resources. Early-20th-century Russia provides another example, though here it was an ideological clique that managed to seize control in a moment of war-induced weakness of both the military and traditional elites.

To keep popular forces at bay and make it possible to channel whatever surplus is produced into modernization rather than consumption, such modernizing elites often find it necessary to limit personal freedoms and particularly restrict the growth of civil society organizations that could challenge governmental dominance and disrupt the rapid modernization agenda through demands for greater political voice and better living standards. The hypothesized result is thus a "Statist Pattern" of civil society development characterized by a fairly small nonprofit sector, with little volunteer engagement, operating in a narrow range of essentially service fields.

Conclusion

In short, the SOCS theory argues that it is possible to discern in the historical record of recent human history at least five different constellations of social class and actor relationships, each associated with a particular, hypothesized pattern of civil society development characterized by a particular set of defining features. These constellations and their associated civil society patterns either took shape during the process of modernization and have largely survived into recent times due to the phenomenon of path dependence or were fixed in premodern times in societies where modernization has been largely delayed, except in narrow oases of urban modernity.

To be sure, these five constellations are ideal types, and particular details may differ, as suggested by the concept of structural equivalence. But the key thrust of the social origins theory is that the shape of the civil society sector in a society can be predicted, with more or less precision, from the constellation of social class and actor power relationships that the society exhibits. The test of this theory is thus the extent to which these predictions can be verified in the empirical record. To do so, such a test must address three interrelated questions:

- First, can the five hypothesized patterns of civil society development suggested here be observed in the actual empirical data we have assembled, and, if so, how extensively visible are they?

- Second, if they can be observed, can the hypothesized causes of these patterns—the five constellations of power relations as mediated by the identified filters and amplifiers—be found to be operating as hypothesized in the countries falling into the various patterns?

- Finally, can the SOCS theory also explain any countries that do not fit any of the patterns identified and therefore demonstrate its capacity to make sense of the inevitable shifts in underlying social and economic realities?

It is to these questions that we turn in the next chapter.

Notes

1. Zukin and DiMaggio 1990b.
2. Giddens 1987, 7, 17.
3. Moore 1966.

4. Timberger 1978.

5. Brenner (1982) brings a similar line of argument to explain differences in the institutional development of continental Europe and England, arguing that these differences can be traced to different power relations between the landed gentry and the peasantry in the Middle Ages. These power relations made it necessary for landed elements to rely heavily on the state to control the peasantry in Europe, whereas English landlords utilized market-type relationships to advance their interests instead.

6. Evans, Rueschemeyer, and Skocpol 1985.

7. Rueschemeyer, Stephens, and Stephens 1992.

8. Ibid.

9. Skocpol 1995.

10. Titmuss 1974.

11. Esping-Andersen 1990.

12. For a discussion of Max Weber's conception of social class, see Collins 1986, 125–130.

13. The term "class fraction" has been introduced by Bourdieu (1984) to refer to socially distinct segments of a socioeconomic class identified primarily by social and cultural characteristics.

14. Giddens 1987.

15. Weber 1958. See also Howe 1978.

16. Krugman 1991.

17. Gerschenkron 1992.

18. Hausner, Jessop, and Nielsen 1995.

19. A good illustration of path dependence is the persistence of the imperial measuring system in the United States, whereas almost all other countries adopted the metric system. The imperial system was the basis for the development of measurement standards when the industrial revolution in the United States took off, and changing these standards to the metric at a later time proved too difficult politically and economically.

20. The concept of structural equivalence, used widely in analyses of social structure, refers to the fact that different individuals or groups may play similar roles or occupy similar positions in different social arrangements. For more detail, see Sailer 1978.

21. Putnam 1993, 121–134.

22. Quoted in Putnam 1993, 145.

23. Acemoglu and Robinson 2012.

24. See, for example, the 1891 encyclical *Rerum Novarum*, which warned Catholic workers to be wary of trade unions that "are in the hands of secret leaders, and are managed on principles ill-according with Christianity and the public well-being; and that they do their utmost to get within their grasp the whole field of labor, and force working men either to join them or to starve. Under these circumstances," Pope Leo XIII advised, "Christian working men must . . . form associations among themselves and unite their forces so as to shake off courageously the yoke of so unrighteous and intolerable an oppression" (Pope Leo XIII 1891, para. 54).

CHAPTER FIVE

Testing the Social Origins Theory of Civil Society Development

LESTER M. SALAMON *and* S. WOJCIECH SOKOLOWSKI

We must discipline our tale by careful counting.
—ROBERT PUTNAM, *MAKING DEMOCRACY WORK*, 148

T HE PREVIOUS CHAPTER LAID out an alternative explanation for the variations in civil society development visible in the data we have generated on over 40 countries throughout the world. The heart of that explanation is the suggestion that the size and contours of the civil society sector are fundamentally shaped by particular constellations of social class relationships as they are amplified or filtered by a variety of essentially contextual factors at critical moments in the evolution of societies and that once shaped, these features survive over extended periods as a result of the phenomenon of "path dependency." Out of this analysis came the hypothesis that at least five distinctive patterns of civil society structure could be expected in our data, manifested in different defining combinations of civil society size, reliance on volunteers, functions, and funding structure.

This is not to say that only five such patterns are possible. Social reality is too unpredictable and variable to expect any such finite "end of history." Indeed, as we will see, a number of new patterns may already be visible on the horizon. An important test of the social origins theory may therefore be its ability not only to identify and explain existing patterns but also to discern any new such patterns and to account for them with the same set of factors that comprise the theory's existing core drivers. But, clearly, the initial five patterns must be identifiable in the data for the theory to have even surface validity.

The purpose of this chapter is to subject this social origins theory of civil society development to such empirical testing. As already hinted, such a test must proceed in three steps:

- First, to establish that some or all of the patterns of civil society development outlined in the theory can, in fact, be discerned in the cases we have so far examined;

- Second, to determine whether the hypothesized causal factors that the theory associates with each of these patterns can be verified in the historical record; and

- Third, to ascertain whether the theory can account not only for the cases that fit the theory but also for the ones that appear not to.

Let us proceed, therefore, to the first of these tasks.

Testing the SOCS Theory I: Assessing the Presence of the Hypothesized Patterns

A first task in assessing the validity of the social origins of civil society (SOCS) theory is to determine whether the patterns of civil society development hypothesized by the theory do in fact appear in the data we have assembled. To answer this question objectively, we had to establish operational criteria for sorting countries in terms of the dimensions of the civil society sector hypothesized in our theory. Those dimensions were: (i) the sector's overall size measured by the share of each country's economically active population (EAP) that is working in the civil society sector; (ii) the volunteer share of that workforce; (iii) the extent to which this workforce is engaged in service as opposed to expressive functions; and (iv) the share of the sector's financial support coming from government, private fees, and philanthropy, both individual and institutional. As reflected in table 4.1, however, the different civil society patterns vary in terms of which of these dimensions are truly defining for them.

In establishing these criteria we divided the values on each dimension among the population of cases into quartiles and quintiles, using the top and bottom quintiles or quartiles as rough proxies for values such as "large" or "small." We then applied these criteria to each of the 41 countries on which we have suitable data to identify those countries that have the combination of values predicted in the previous chapter as characteristic of the various patterns (see table 4.1). Thus, to fall into the "traditional pattern" a country would have to have *all* of the following: (a) a relatively small civil society workforce; (b) a large share of this workforce in service activities; (c) mostly private sources of financial support; and (d) a relatively high share

TABLE 5.1   Incidence of documented patterns of civil society development,
41 countries

Pattern	Number of cases			
	In scope	Borderline	Out of scope	Total
Traditional	6	1	—	7
Liberal	4	1	—	5
Welfare partnership	6	2	—	7
Social democratic	3	1	—	4
Statist	7	2	—	10
Subtotal	26	7	—	33
Out of scope			8	8
Total	26	7	8	41

of volunteers in its workforce. A failure to meet any of these conditions would disqualify a country from being assigned to this pattern. Where the quartiles or quintiles did not provide a clear enough split among high or low ratings on a particular variable, we made slight variations in these cut-off points to make sure no country fell into more than one model while making it possible that countries could logically fall into none of the specified models. This latter condition was necessary to make sure that we had a truly testable proposition that could logically be disproved.

Table 5.1 reports the overall results of this analysis. What it shows is that 26 of the 41 countries, or about 63 percent, could in fact be identified as falling clearly into one, and only one, of the hypothesized patterns. An additional 7 countries, or another 17 percent, were at least on the borderline of one of the patterns. This means that 33 of 41 countries (80 percent of the cases under investigation) met, or came very close to meeting, the characteristics ascribed to one of the civil society patterns hypothesized by our theory. This constitutes initial strong evidence of the predictive power of this theory.

Testing the SOCS Theory II: Assessing the Validity of the Hypothesized Causal Factors

The next step in assessing the validity of the social origins theory of the civil society sector is to determine whether the countries fall into these five patterns for the reasons that the SOCS theory says they should, that is, because of the hypothesized patterns of power relations. To determine this, we look at each of the patterns in turn, beginning with the historically earliest and working our way to the historically more recent. Because it is obviously impossible to recount the histories of all 41 countries within the confines of a single book, let alone a single chapter, our analysis is limited to the much more modest task of examining a few representative cases for each pattern and comparing and contrasting these cases in terms of their different civil society outcomes and different power constellations to assess causal connections, an approach known formally as Mill's method of difference.[1] While this cannot be considered a definitive proof of the theory, it will nonetheless establish the empirical plausibility of the claims posited by it. In part II of this book, we then bring this theory to bear in a more limited way on an additional set of countries newly added to this project on which data are published here for the first time.

THE TRADITIONAL PATTERN

We begin this discussion with what could be considered the default scenario—the "traditional pattern" of civil society development. Table 5.2 lists six countries whose civil society sectors exhibit all the features hypothesized for the traditional pattern: a small civil society workforce, a relatively large

TABLE 5.2   Countries falling into the traditional pattern of civil society development

| Country | Defining features | | | |
	Workforce % of EAP (%)	Volunteer share of workforce (%)	Service share of workforce (%)	Government share of revenue (%)
Predicted values	≤4.5%	≥34.8%	service>expressive	<32.1%
Kenya	2.1	39.1	59.0	4.8
Pakistan	1.0	44.6	76.9	5.9
Peru	2.1	38.2	94.9	18.1
Philippines	1.9	62.0	56.9	4.5
Tanzania	1.9	75.2	51.2	26.9
Uganda	2.4	59.3	67.8	7.1
6-country average	1.9	53.1	67.8	11.2
41-country average	5.7	40.6	59.1	35.3
Borderline: India	1.5	56.0	82.8	36.1

share of volunteers in the civil society workforce, a large share of the CSO workforce in service activities, and a low share of government support in CSO revenues. Also included is one borderline country—India—that exhibits three of the four key features but has one outlier, very likely a product of the artifact of how international aid is treated in the data, as will be discussed in more detail below. Included in this resulting array of countries are three African countries, three Asian countries (with India included), and one South American country.

According to the SOCS theory, the explanation for the development of a traditional model of civil society can be found in the success of those who benefit from traditional institutions to preserve their power and influence into the modern era. This can occur because of the strength of these premodern social forces, such as a monarchy or a landed elite; because of inherent weaknesses or divisions within the ranks of those who might have an interest in contesting these elements (e.g., the rural laborers, the bourgeoisie, or the industrial working class); because of the power of organized religion to prop up and legitimize premodern power relations; or because of the presence of external actors (e.g., colonial powers) that stand to gain from the persistence of the premodern traditions and relationships and consequently support the existing elites.

The inclusion of several African countries in this model underlines the important point that the limited scale of private civil society organizations in such settings does not mean that social institutions are lacking in such areas. Rather, the social institutions in these settings take a different form, resting often on family or kinship ties and on what Weber termed "traditional authority."[2] This is often accompanied by rich networks of social bonds and strong sentiments of solidarity.

But if it is a mistake to overlook the importance of these informal, premodern institutions, it is also a mistake to romanticize them. Like all social arrangements, these often come with a price, and that price can be the perseverance of social relationships that limit opportunities and constrain choice. As Moore reminds us, to maintain traditions and a value system, "human beings are punched, bullied, sent to jail, thrown into concentration camps, cajoled, bribed, made into heroes, encouraged to read newspapers, stood up against a wall and shot, and sometimes even taught sociology. To speak of cultural inertia is to overlook the concrete interests and privileges that are served by indoctrination, education, and the entire complicated process of transmitting culture from one generation to the next."[3] Indeed, such premodern relationships can lead to clientelistic relationships and patterns of dependence that breed distrust, as reflected in Putnam's depiction of social realities in southern Italy.[4] What this suggests is that the persistence of a traditional system, for good or ill, must be explained.

India is a particularly illustrative example of this pattern. Until very recently, the Indian subcontinent remained under the hold of conservative elites in the countryside who maintained tight control over a dependent peasantry and resisted efforts to usher in significant industrialization. The durability of this pattern was due to three sets of factors: first, the social system put in place under the Moghul empire, which was characterized by a pattern of rapacious squeezing of the Indian peasantry by the *zamindars* or rural landowners; second, the power of India's caste system, which splintered the rural peasantry and thereby limited meaningful, organized pressures from below; and finally, and decisively, the British system of indirect colonial rule, which relied on the same *zamindars,* or their successors, to secure the taxes from the peasantry needed to sustain the colonial presence. Although the export-oriented agricultural economy that the British fostered, and the legal system the British established, gave rise to an Indian middle class, it was a cramped middle class, dependent on the British colonizers, who controlled much of the surplus being created and shipped it back home rather than investing it in India's industrial development.[5]

To be sure, the British colonial system left room for the emergence of the kind of institutional forms that existed in Britain, including voluntary organizations supported by charity. But many of these basically served the needs of the expat colonial officials, though it also spurred the growth of indigenous voluntary associations designed to promote education, economic development, self-governance, and national independence, leading to the formation of the Indian National Congress in 1885. While these activities established the framework for a sizable civil society sector, however, the limited scale of the Indian middle classes and the continued hold of traditional elements kept access to these organizations confined to a narrow band of Indian society. Indeed, with the landed elements in the employ of the British as tax collectors and money-lenders, and little prospect for alliances with working-class elements, the lawyers, bureaucrats, and merchants who composed the Indian middle class had little choice but to ally with the lower social strata and with essentially traditional sources of authority as they sought to free themselves from the confining embrace of the British.

This alliance was cemented with the rise of Mahatma Gandhi as the dominant figure in the independence movement after World War I. Rather than preaching the virtues of rapid modernization, Gandhi essentially urged a return to the simplicity of an idealized village existence—but one shorn of some of its most objectionable features, such as untouchability. He thus made it possible, in Moore's terms, to "galvanize the country into opposition against the British without threatening vested interests in Indian society."[6]

This pattern persisted into the post-independence period. The Western, democratic, national government of India put in place following independence and persisting to this day is in many respects a veneer that obscures the fact that real power resides at the state level, where dominant rural groups have remained fundamentally in control.[7] As a consequence, although the Indian government moved soon after independence to abolish the most visible aspects of the caste system and establish universal suffrage, traditional social institutions—including informal aspects of the caste system—persist. Indeed, with 75 percent of the population still residing in rural areas, life for most villagers retains many similarities to Moghul times. In many regions, land remains in the hands of dominant castes that exploit the low-ranking landless laborers and artisans. A national government, committed since the 1960s to encouraging civil society development, has made little headway, since the overall levels of government social spending are heavily constrained and since much of the responsibility for implementation lies at the state level, where conservative elites remain very influential.[8]

Pakistan, which became a separate country in 1947, did not fare any better in this respect. Slow industrialization kept the number of urban industrial classes relatively limited while wealthy landowners maintained their grip in the countryside.[9] Moreover, continuing political instability, external threats resulting in repeated declarations of martial law (1956 and 1977), and military control of society more generally suppressed the development of the civil society sector.

As a result, the civil society sector in the Indian subcontinent remains small by international standards and well within the contours of the traditional pattern. Pakistan squarely fits the traditional pattern, while India is considered a borderline case of this pattern. India meets two out of the three criteria defining the traditional pattern—small size and a relatively large volunteer share of the workforce—but the level of government financial support of CSO activities (36 percent of CSO revenue) is slightly above the cutoff value (32 percent) defining this pattern. This somewhat larger-than-expected share of government support is at least partly an artifact reflecting the influence of bilateral and multilateral development-agency funding, but it is also very likely a signal that India may be on a road leading away from the traditional pattern—an issue that will be discussed in more detail later in this chapter.

A similar pattern, though with its own peculiarities, evolved in Kenya, another country falling into the traditional pattern. Prior to the arrival of the British, Kenyan society was characterized by small rural communities engaged in subsistence agriculture and organized along tribal lines, though regularly disrupted by incursions from Arab slave-traders operating out of Zanzibar. Landownership patterns remained in communal form until the arrival of the British in the late 19th century. Although the British established a system of indirect colonial rule that relied heavily on a small class of native elites, this was augmented by a pattern of direct colonialism in the person of European settlers, who received land grants from the British authorities, set themselves up as a landowning elite in the lucrative coffee-growing regions, and reduced the native population to tenant status on settler-owned land. Over the subsequent decades, the landowners increased their pressures on the natives working their lands while further encroaching on native access to landownership, creating a large class of landless peasants and increasing migration of the rural poor to the cities.

As in India, traditional tribal and kin-based divisions kept the rural poor and their urban brethren badly fragmented. Some significant civil society organizations did emerge, such as the kin-based Kikuyu Central Association representing the landless masses in the coffee growing regions, trade unions based in Nairobi and Mombasa that later merged into the East African Trades Union Congress, and the loyalist and reformist Kenya African Union, which also had an urban base. But growing economic hardship and regular suppression of these native organizations led to demands for economic reforms and greater political representation. When these were resisted, the so-called Mau Mau uprising broke out in the early 1950s, as landless peasants joined forces with radical elements in the Nairobi labor movement to push for land reform and political freedom. While this might have led to a communist-style modernizing revolution, the British, along with reformist elements in the native population, brutally suppressed this uprising and then initiated a series of reforms that essentially co-opted the opposition, paving the way for independence and the electoral victory of the reformist Kenya African National Union led by Jomo Kenyatta.

Like Gandhi in India, Kenyatta pursued a moderate course, reaching back to traditional tribal concepts of self-help and social solidarity embodied in the concept of *harambee*, or "pooling together," to mobilize local populations to build schools, health facilities, community centers, and infrastructure. However, this did little to damp down traditional ethnic and kin-based rivalries, and the resulting factional strife and instability led to the suppression of civil society organizations under Kenyatta and his authoritarian successor, Arap Moi. More importantly, these policies, plus the slowness of the modernization process, kept in place the traditional social institutions rather than promoting growth of the civil society sector.

THE LIBERAL PATTERN

Four countries fall squarely into the "liberal" pattern hypothesized by the SOCS theory, and one (Switzerland) ends up in this pattern's borderline status, as shown in table 5.3. This pattern features a relatively large nonprofit sector supported extensively by private sources—such as market sales, philanthropy, and volunteer work—and relatively less so by government. The United States and the United Kingdom, at least up through the post–World War II era, are countries that most clearly reflect this pattern, though Australia and New Zealand strongly resemble it as well.

TABLE 5.3   Countries falling into the liberal pattern of civil society development

	Defining features				
Country	Workforce % of EAP (%)	Volunteer share of workforce (%)	Service share of workforce (%)	Government share of revenue (%)	Philanthropy share of revenue (%)
Predicted values	>/=6.8%	>/=26.7%	service > expressive	=/<45.2%>	>/=9.1%
Australia	8.8	33.5	57.3	33.5	9.5
New Zealand	9.6	66.7	46.2	24.6	20.0
United Kingdom	11.0	53.0	50.1	45.2	11.3
United States	9.2	32.4	66.2	30.0	14.1
4-country average	9.6	46.4	54.9	33.3	13.7
41-country average	5.7	40.6	59.1	35.3	14.4
Borderline: Switzerland	6.9	37.2	55.0	34.5	7.9

The SOCS theory hypothesizes that the liberal pattern is most likely to develop in circumstances where landed elites enter the modern era in a weakened state, where urban middle-class elements are in the ascendance, and where the working class is weakened by social, racial, or ethnic divisions. And as it turns out, each of these elements finds clear reflection in the social histories of both England and the United States. In the case of England, the central features are as follows:

1. English agriculture underwent a significant transformation in the 16th and 17th centuries as a dominant agricultural elite turned toward an export-oriented agriculture built around wool that made it necessary to force the peasantry off the land through the enclosure movement. This transformed the landlords into capitalists and reduced the need for a strong, repressive state to keep rural peasants from gaining power.
2. Commercial activity gave rise to a strong urban middle class that sought freedom from Crown control of the economy and was able to break the hold of royal power with the aid of landed capitalist interests in the parliament during the civil war of 1642–1651.
3. The country's working class was divided by regional (Welsh, Scottish, Irish, etc.) and religious (Catholic vs. Protestant) divisions and imbued with a powerful ethos of deference that kept it from mounting a serious assault on dominant urban and landed middle classes until emboldened by the United Kingdom's participation in two world wars.[10]
4. The emergence, following the break with the Catholic Church, of a Protestant religious tradition established a strong ethos of individualism and personal responsibility, which contrasted sharply with the ethos of social solidarity that characterized what became the welfare partnership countries of continental Europe.
5. The powerful bourgeoisie fundamentally opposed any expansion of social protections through the state, which would have increased its tax burden. This position was reinforced by the Protestant religious tradition of self-reliance preached to the country's workers.[11]

The upshot, as predicted by the SOCS theory, was the emergence of a liberal civil society sector pattern, in which nonprofit organizations were allowed to emerge, but without the benefit of substantial state support. The less well-off were consequently left to the mercies of private charity and lopsided direct negotiations with employers until soldiers returning from two world wars finally rebelled politically and insisted on a different social contract.

A slightly different set of circumstances produced a similar set of power relationships in the United States. Formed as a result of the full colonization of New World lands by the British, the American colonies reproduced British political institutions favoring protection of private property and democratic governance, which in turn created the foundations for a strong commercial and industrial middle class. Small-farm agriculture, at least in the northern colonies, prevented the development of a strong landed elite. Though such an elite did emerge in the plantation economy of the South, it was defeated in the Civil War, though its vestiges survived into the 20th century and impacted the development of the nonprofit sector in the South in ways that the social origins theory predicts—limiting civil society development significantly until the civil rights movement of the 1960s finally broke landed elite power.[12] Working-class pressures were also muted in the United States due to intense racial, ethnic, and religious rivalries reinforced by ethnic-based political party "machines" that together kept the working class internally divided.[13] This combination of a strong middle class, weak landed elites, and divided working class resulted in highly limited state involvement in social protections and left the poor largely dependent on well-meaning philanthropists up until the Great Society breakthrough of the mid-1960s. This constellation of elements is precisely what the social origins theory predicts would produce a liberal pattern of civil society development.

This pattern has remained fundamentally in place, moreover, despite some dramatic subsequent developments. Two events provided opportunities for the expansion of the role of the state in the provision of social welfare. The Great Depression, which temporarily stunned the powerful industrialists, opened the door for a greater role of the state in providing a social safety net through the New Deal. However, the US federal structure, deeply reflected in the country's political party system, allowed Southern landed interests and conservative Midwestern farmers and industrialists to blunt the social reforms initiated by the New Deal, so that they did not extend beyond old-age insurance and limited support to fatherless children.[14] The second break with this historic pattern occurred with the rise of the civil rights movement and the urban violence of the 1960s, which opened the political window for the 1960s War on Poverty and Great Society expansions of government social welfare protections. However, arising as it did from the disadvantages affecting a particular racial group, this protest was weakened by regional and racial divisions and did not have political power sufficient to establish anywhere near as extensive a range of public social welfare programs as are found in other advanced capitalist democracies. What emerged instead, therefore, was an amalgam of a welfare partnership and liberal pattern—with expanded public sector support channeled through existing nonprofit institutions and a resulting extensive expansion of the country's civil society sector—though a sector still more heavily dependent on philanthropy and fees, and less heavily supported by government, than its European welfare-partnership counterparts.[15]

Switzerland is considered a borderline case because it exhibits all the features of the liberal pattern—large size, significant volunteer share of the CSS workforce, and relatively low share of government financial support—but it falls short of meeting the philanthropy share of revenue by only 1.2 percentage points (7.9 percent rather than the 9.1 percent of CSS revenue predicted for this pattern). As will be discussed in more detail in chapter 7, Switzerland was dominated by forces favoring liberal pro-business policies and small government. The high level of industrialization in the 19th century strengthened the role of the bourgeoisie, while labor remained weak and divided along religious lines. This started to change after World War I, as membership in labor unions increased. This shift in power relations in favor of organized labor occurred gradually, without any major upheavals, and was characterized by generally collaborative relations between labor and government, but it eventually led to a policy shift that adopted elements of the welfare partnership pattern after World War II, thus departing somewhat from the strictly liberal model that used to dominate the country.

THE WELFARE PARTNERSHIP PATTERN

Six of our 41 countries exhibit the characteristics we have identified as hallmarks of the "welfare partnership" pattern of civil society development, and two others reach the borderline of this pattern, as shown in table 5.4. Distinctive features of this pattern consist of a rather large civil society sector workforce that is mostly engaged in service functions and is heavily supported by government.

The social origins theory suggests that this model is associated with situations in which fairly strong landed or industrial middle-class elements

TABLE 5.4   Countries falling into the welfare partnership pattern of civil society development

Country	Workforce % of EAP (%)	Service share of workforce (%)	Government share of revenue (%)
		Defining features	
Predicted values:	>4.5%	>50% service	>/=50%
Belgium	13.1	85.2	68.8
France	9.0	62.0	62.8
Germany	6.8	54.8	64.8
Ireland	10.9	80.3	74.5
Israel	11.8	81.7	63.6
Netherlands	15.9	64.4	62.6
6-country average	11.2	71.4	66.2
41-country average	5.7	59.1	35.3
Borderline: Chile	5.0	55.8	45.2
Borderline: Canada	12.3	68.0	48.5

begin to encounter serious pressures from lower socioeconomic classes and look to state and associated religious institutions to broker some kind of compromise. The compromise characteristic of this pattern is the provision of state-funded social welfare protections delivered through "safe," church-dominated or otherwise tame nonprofit service organizations. The predicted, but paradoxical, result is the growth of both government social welfare protections and civil society—an outcome that the preference theories miss.

This constellation of factors certainly seems to fit the realities of class, social, and political relationships in Germany—one of the six countries squarely falling into the welfare partnership pattern. The Prussian state that pushed for the unification of all German lands in the second half of the 19th century was controlled by an eastern landed aristocracy (the *Junkers*) and western heavy industry magnates (the so-called rye and iron marriage). Faced with a growing labor militancy that threatened the expansionist policies of the Prussian state, Chancellor Otto von Bismarck resorted to political authoritarianism coupled with social programs aimed at buying off the working class and weaning it from socialism.[16] This was done by tying benefits to the workplace and by delivering social assistance through church-based social institutions supportive of the conservative regime. The result was a state-dominated social welfare system that nevertheless maintained a sizeable religious presence. This arrangement was further legitimated by the Catholic doctrine of subsidiarity as the guiding principle of social policy. According to this doctrine, social protections should always be sought first from the social institution closest to the problem—the family, the parish church, or local charitable institutions—and only as a last resort from the state.[17]

The role of political parties and civil society organizations as vehicles for political mobilization of class-based interests greatly intensified after World War I. Germany's defeat, which weakened the power of the military and the Hohenzollern monarchic system, combined with the successful proletarian revolution in Russia in 1917, provided a powerful impetus for working-class political mobilization. However, the labor movement in Germany was fraught with factionalism. While the majority, affiliated with Social Democrats or the Catholic Center party, stressed the defense of the newly established parliamentary democracy against reactionary attacks and gradual social and economic reforms, radical factions represented by Communists and a variety of other social movement organizations pressed for an overhaul of political and economic institutions following the example of Russia. At the same time, the reactionary elements affiliated with the landowners, industrialists, and the military established a network of paramilitary organizations to terrorize their political enemies, especially the radical left. This extreme partisanship intensified class conflicts instead of mediating them and destabilized the parliamentary system in the aftermath of the Great Depression, paving the way for the Nazi takeover in 1933.[18] This represents a sharp contrast to the social democratic pattern in Sweden, discussed in the following section, in which parties representing the urban working and middle classes, as well as the farmers, were united in the pursuit of reformist goals.

After the Nazi defeat in World War II, Germany was split into two separate states. The Western Allies, which controlled the Federal Republic of Germany, returned the country to a parliamentary democracy and the welfare partnership model of the pre-Nazi era. The Soviet-controlled German Democratic Republic, which before the war had been the stronghold of the landowning aristocracy (*Junkers*) and the Hohenzollern military caste, adopted a Soviet-style Communist system. In East Germany, the power of the Junkers and the remnants of the military caste were thoroughly destroyed by the Soviet-backed Communist government. However, following the Soviet withdrawal in 1991 and the resulting dissolution of the German Democratic Republic, the eastern states were absorbed by the Federal Republic, and

West-German institutions—including the civil society sector—were transferred wholesale to this part of the country.

In the Netherlands, a rather different sequence led to a similar result.[19] The Netherlands came into existence as an independent state during the 16th-century religious wars unleashed by the Protestant Reformation, and its population was split between a Protestant majority and a Catholic minority. After the separation of church and state during the Napoleonic wars, Catholics resisted the expansion of universal secular education and demanded separate confessional education for their children following the teaching of the encyclical *Quanta Cura*. The Calvinists put forth similar demands.

This conflict and competition between two major organized religious groups had two profound consequences for the institutional layout of the social service delivery system. First, each of these religious denominations created a separate system of schools and social-support organizations exclusively serving their respective co-religionists. Second, this religious "pillarization" divided organized labor into two different, often hostile, camps, thus preventing the formation of a strong and united labor movement, as emerged in Sweden, where organized religion was weaker.

Dutch working-class militancy grew with industrialization, especially in the urban industrial areas in the northern and western parts of the country, giving rise to a third pillar of social-democratic-leaning people. This militancy was opposed not only by the country's urban middle class but also by the Catholic Church, which maintained an especially strong foothold in the southern part of the country, where Spain once exercised control. In fact, the Dutch Catholic hierarchy, hostile not just to socialist worker organizations but to Protestant labor unions as well, forbade Catholic workers from participating in these organizations and undertook to provide conservative, Catholic alternatives to existing workers' organizations. As a consequence, despite the absence of landed elites, which elsewhere (e.g., in neighboring Germany) were a major force weighing in to curb labor militancy, the working class played a much weaker role in the formulation of social policy in the Netherlands than in other European countries with a similar class structure (e.g., Sweden). Thus, when the leadership of the Social Democratic Labor Party, inspired by the revolutionary outbreak in Germany in 1918, called for a revolution, conservative elements were easily able to fend off the more radical features of labor demands with a series of co-optation efforts beginning with the creation of a universal system of public education.

This effort encountered resistance, however, from the two competing religious communities—both of which had established their own educational systems and both of which resisted the idea of secular, as opposed to value-based, education paid for through general taxes. This dispute came to a head in 1919 in what became known as the "battle of schools," which was ultimately settled in classic Dutch fashion—with a compromise, and a compromise that would set the mold for the future evolution of Dutch social welfare policy. At issue was the funding of the private, mostly religious, schools as the state expanded its own system of tax-supported public education. Following a heated controversy, Protestant, Catholic, and social democratic political parties were able to reach an understanding known as the "pacification" under which the state would pay for universal schooling through what is essentially a voucher system, giving parents the choice about the type of school their children would attend—private Catholic, private Protestant, or public secular—but providing the same amount per pupil to whatever school was chosen. This compromise on education was considered so important that it was even included in the constitution.[20]

More important for our purposes, this decision set the mold for further expansions of state-funded social welfare protections in the Netherlands as successive Dutch governments responded to growing labor militancy following World War I and into the post–World War II period using the same pattern of state finance but extensive private nonprofit delivery. The upshot was a "welfare partnership" pattern of civil society development—with an enormous civil society sector mostly engaged in service provision and funded massively with government resources.

In the process, the Dutch case provides a strong counterfactual to the preference arguments advanced in the market-failure/government-failure theory discussed in chapter 3. Where that theory attributes the growth of the nonprofit sector to the *absence* of public funding of collective goods caused by the diversity of demand for such goods and the resulting "failures" of the market and the state to respond, here just the opposite dynamic was at work. Because of the political and power relationships that were at work as portrayed by the social origins theory, it was the expansion of public funding that led to a robust nonprofit sector. Pressured to expand social welfare services in a conflict-laden environment, successive Dutch governments cleverly extended the funding for such services to the nonprofit organizations serving the various factions, thus averting protracted political conflict and mobilizing widespread support for the programs.

Chile is a borderline case because it meets two criteria of the welfare partnership pattern—large size and dominance of service over expressive activities. Although it falls short on meeting the minimum government support feature defining this cluster (at least 50 percent of CSS revenue), the level of government financial support of CSS activity is extraordinarily high for a Latin American country—45 percent versus 13 percent on average in the remaining five Latin American countries covered in our data (Argentina, Brazil, Colombia, Mexico, and Peru). As will be discussed in more detail in chapter 11, this lower-than-expected level of government support is a residual result of the neoliberal policies forced upon the country by the military dictatorship of General Augusto Pinochet. However, before Pinochet's coup, Chile was a parliamentary democracy where the political party system mediated the conflict between the lower classes and the elites by embracing welfare partnership policies very similar to those observed in Western Europe.

Canada is another borderline case because the level of government financial support of CSS activity (about 49 percent) falls one percentage point below the threshold defining the welfare partnership pattern (50 percent). This adoption of welfare partnership policies in Canada may be attributed to government efforts to mediate a somewhat different type of conflicting interest threatening the national unity of that country—that between the Francophone population of Quebec and the Anglophone population in the remaining provinces.

THE SOCIAL DEMOCRATIC PATTERN

The fourth pattern of civil society development identified in our data is the "social democratic" pattern. Only three of our target countries exhibited this model, suggesting the difficulties attending its development. A fourth country stands on the borderline of this model, however.

As table 5.5 shows, this pattern is characterized by a fairly sizable nonprofit workforce, mostly composed of volunteers and heavily oriented toward expressive functions. Austria and several Nordic countries exhibit this pattern most vividly.

What the SOCS theory claims is that this pattern tends to emerge in situations where the power of both landed elites and the bourgeoisie has been effectively neutralized by that of the lower classes, leading to the expansion of government funding of public welfare services and the delivery of these

TABLE 5.5 Countries falling into the social democratic pattern of civil society development

| Country | Workforce % of EAP (%) | Defining features | |
		Volunteer share of workforce (%)	Service share of workforce (%)
Predicted values:	>4.5%	>/=56%	<50% service
Austria	7.8	72.2	48.7
Norway	7.3	62.2	37.9
Sweden	9.6	73.7	29.9
3-country average	8.2	69.4	38.9
41-country average	5.7	40.6	59.1
Borderline: Finland	5.7	53.8	40.9

services by the government, rather than by private, nonprofit institutions as in the welfare partnership model.

Sweden is perhaps the classic example of the social democratic pattern. Its relatively large, but volunteer-dominated, civil society workforce focusing mostly on expressive functions clearly exemplifies this model. And it fairly powerfully exhibits the social conditions hypothesized by the SOCS theory to lead to this outcome.

Prior to industrialization, Sweden was governed by a centralized, but nonrepressive, monarchy and had a weak landed aristocracy, an emerging urban bourgeoisie, and a free peasantry. Due to the fact that the peasantry was engaged in nonagricultural production—including metalworking in often-collectively-owned works and mining of iron and copper ores, which was encouraged by government policy—it had relatively greater social standing and self-governance than its counterparts in other European countries.[21] With the progress of industrialization, conflicts between employers and labor intensified. The labor movement, influenced by socialist ideas, developed a highly centralized organization connected to the Social Democratic Workers Party and pursued reformist rather than revolutionary objectives.[22] This, in turn, strengthened the expressive elements of the emerging civil society sector and transformed them into a powerful force for further change.

Also contributing to the growing power of the labor movement were the absence of labor-repressive modes of production, the ethnic and cultural homogeneity of the Swedish population, and the earlier establishment of a state religion, which avoided the divisive influence that organized religion (especially the antagonism between the Catholic Church and Protestantism) had on organized labor in neighboring states. In addition, the reformist tactics adopted by working-class leaders allowed them to work closely with reform-oriented civil servants, who formulated a series of far-reaching proposals for social welfare services, strengthening the similar demands coming from the labor movement.[23] The electoral victory of social democrats in 1932 in alliance with the Agrarian Party therefore opened the way to the enactment and implementation of broad-scale, state-sponsored, social welfare protections provided as a matter of right by reform-minded civil servants. The civil society sector willingly ceded its service functions in a number of key fields to state agencies but retained important expressive functions in such fields as culture, recreation, and protection of citizen rights.

Additional evidence supporting the crucial role of the dominant position of the working class for the emergence of the "social democratic" pattern comes from contrasting Sweden with Italy, Portugal (chapter 16), and Spain. These three Mediterranean countries experienced strong conflicts during their initial period of industrialization in the beginning of the 20th century between highly militant labor and entrenched landed elites and bourgeoisie. However, unlike in Sweden, where organized industrial and agrarian labor faced little resistance from the bourgeoisie and landowning classes, in Italy, Portugal, and Spain organized labor met strong resistance from conservative landed elites and elements of the bourgeoisie to the point where these interests were willing to support military coups leading to the fascist dictatorships of Mussolini, Salazar, and Franco—which had disastrous effects on the civil society sectors of these countries.[24]

It also worth pointing out, however, that the dominance of the working class alone is a necessary but not a sufficient condition for the development of the social democratic pattern. We also need to examine the role of the amplifiers of class interests (figure 4.1) in articulating and prioritizing class interests and pursuing them in the political arena. In the case of Sweden, the main amplifier of working-class interests was labor unions strongly influenced by socialist goals of providing collective security arrangements, which resulted in a political push for the welfare state.[25] Evidence supporting this crucial role of class interest amplifiers comes from contrasting Sweden with other countries where organized labor, although strong at times, failed to produce outcomes observed in Sweden. Like Sweden, New Zealand and

Australia had strong organized labor and Labour-Party-controlled governments, yet these amplifiers of working-class interests pursued a different set of policy objectives emphasizing collaborative arrangements with the private sector in the delivery of public welfare benefits and paying less attention to collective security arrangements (chapters 8 and 9). This set of policies kept the civil society sector in their time-honored role of service delivery rather than crowding it out into leisure and expressive activities. As a result, one of the key defining characteristics of the social democratic pattern that differentiates it from the liberal pattern—the dominance of expressive functions instead of service ones—failed to develop, and both countries strongly resemble countries in the liberal pattern.

Finland is a borderline case because it meets two criteria defining the social democratic pattern but is just two percentage points below the cutoff level on the volunteer share of the workforce (54 versus 56 percent). Despite that, the CSS workforce in Finland is still dominated by volunteers—a feature that exclusively defines the social democratic pattern but is conspicuously absent from any other pattern. Furthermore, power relations in Finland resemble those in Sweden due to the fact that, until the 19th century, Finland was a part of the Swedish empire.

THE STATIST PATTERN

Finally, seven countries exhibit the hypothesized features of the statist pattern of civil society development, in which virtually all facets of civil society activity are constrained. Thus, as shown in table 5.6, in this pattern the overall size of the sector is limited, the volunteer share of the CSS workforce is small, and the government support of the sector's activities is low.

According to the SOCS theory, this outcome is likely to develop where economic development has been held back—typically by conservative landed elites who benefit from the exploitative agrarian mode of production—leading to economic stagnation and military threats from more advanced powers. This external threat provides motivation for intermediate class elements such as military officers, intellectuals, professionals, or reformist elements in the state bureaucracy to execute a "revolution from above," seizing control of the state administration and launching a program of state-centered rapid industrialization and modernization. This can occur because of conflicts among the elites, defeat in war or other humiliating events that trigger defensive reactions by key actors, foreign intervention, or other crises.

TABLE 5.6 Countries falling into the statist pattern of civil society development

Country	Workforce % of EAP (%)	Defining features Volunteer share of workforce (%)	Government share of revenue (%)
Predicted values:	=/<4.5%	=/<38%	=/<36%
Brazil	3.3	18.5	5.7
Colombia	2.3	24.0	14.9
Mexico	3.1	32.7	11.0
Poland	0.9	21.2	24.1
Russia	1.2	36.3	15.2
Slovakia	1.0	27.7	22.1
Spain	4.3	34.8	32.1
7-country average	2.3	27.9	17.9
41-country average	5.7	40.6	35.3
Borderline: Romania	0.7	56.6	6.5*
Borderline: Korea, Rep. of	4.2	40.4	35.5

*Excluding transfers from EU and other developed countries.

Late-modernizing countries may be particularly prone to this outcome since key modernizing elites, frustrated by their countries' relative economic backwardness, perceive an urgent need for modernization, yet the socioeconomic classes that are the likely agents of modernization—industrialists and the industrial working class—have not yet fully made their appearance. In the absence of such actors, the state assumes the role of modernizing agent through administratively-controlled programs aimed at boosting industrial infrastructure and production.[26] To succeed, however, such elements must constrain consumption by "squeezing" workers and peasants to generate investment capital, which is likely to provoke popular unrest. Consequently, such regimes tend to suppress any potential sources of organized opposition to their programs—especially labor unions, advocacy groups, and political parties—and often create skeletal pro-government organizations to mobilize popular support for their policies. This, in turn, stunts the development of the civil society sector.

Japan—not allocated to any pattern due to very recent developments that moved it in the welfare partnership direction by the time we collected our most recent data—offers an especially striking example of this configuration of power relations up through the mid-1990s. Faced with the threat of foreign intrusion following the arrival of an American fleet in the second half of the 19th century, and emboldened by disaffections among the country's warrior samurai class, modernization advocates among Japanese elites pulled off a "revolution from above" aimed at abolishing the feudal order and restoring imperial rule in Japan. This enabled Emperor Mutsuhito (who assumed the name Meiji) to implement what is known as the Meiji Restoration, involving a modernization of Japanese society and economy, destruction of the country's feudal structure, and development of an army and military might. The instrument for this bold initiative was not a hegemonic social class but the state apparatus itself, thus establishing a tradition of state dominance over the economy and society that has survived until relatively recently.[27]

To achieve this, however, it was necessary to limit the independent power of the landowners and urban bourgeoisie, resist pressures from below for social welfare protections, and constrain the growth of citizen organizations that might pose a threat to state power. This was achieved by denying legal status to any citizen organization that did not receive specific authorization to exist from the relevant branch of the national bureaucracy. The upshot was a highly constrained nonprofit sector operating in close coordination with the state despite the considerable industrialization of the Japanese economy. Only in the wake of the Kobe earthquake of 1995, which shook public confidence in the capability of the state apparatus, did Japan open the way for a more vibrant civil society sector, and even then it did so only partially.

Japan clearly followed the statist pattern of civil society development until the 1970s. The activities of the sector were limited to a handful of foundations, sponsored by large corporations, and small social movement organizations. This started to change only in the 1970s, when Japan's process of catching up with the West was virtually completed. Due to an increasing internationalization of Japan's economy and the globalization of many social and environmental issues, among others, the space for nonprofit organizations widened. Both public and private expectations of what civil society organizations can and should do in modern Japanese society have grown considerably, resulting in a very substantial increase of public support for the sector.[28]

Similar developments were evident in late-19th- and early-20th-century Russia, which squarely falls into the statist pattern. As discussed in more detail in chapter 14, vestiges of labor-repressive feudalism survived in Russia well into the 20th century, limiting industrial growth.[29] The defeat of the Russian army in World War I opened an opportunity for a revolutionary movement, which led ultimately to the Bolshevik takeover. The Bolsheviks destroyed the remnants of the country's feudal structure and further centralized control of the economy to facilitate rapid industrialization.[30] Although the revolution created a momentum for citizen activism—which led to the emergence of a plethora of self-help and cultural groups—the subsequent Stalinist regime suppressed these activities to preempt potential opposition and replaced them with government-controlled mass membership organizations aimed at promoting citizen loyalty to the regime. This model was subsequently "exported" to other Eastern European countries after the USSR's victory in World War II. After Stalin's death, the civil society sector experienced a slow revival, which accelerated after the radical political reforms initiated by Gorbachev in the late 1980s but was then subsequently constrained by the authoritarian regime of Vladimir Putin.

Two continents away, similar patterns of power relations surfaced in Latin America. Mexico (chapter 15), another country where the statist pattern is evident, provides perhaps the clearest case—though similar developments are evident elsewhere in the continent. Like most other Latin American countries, Mexico was a Spanish colony and inherited the Spanish feudal system in which the nobility and Catholic clergy played prominent roles. An extended period of internal strife triggered by the mid-19th-century war of independence led to the fragmentation of the economic elites and the emergence of the state as a mediator among different elite groups. The power of the state was further enhanced by the political reforms of Benito Juarez in the 1860s that curbed the power of the Catholic Church and consolidated the government's control of the military.[31] This enabled the military-dominated National Revolutionary Party (later renamed the Institutional Revolutionary Party, or PRI) to seize power in 1911 and use the state apparatus to promote economic change, including a major land reform and efforts to promote industrialization. To cement its political position and forestall opposition from below, the PRI incorporated organizations representing subordinate classes into the structure of a single party, thus co-opting and undermining any opposition to its rule and leaving little room for an independent civil society sector.[32]

The effect of the developmental state's administrative control on civil society sector development can be demonstrated by contrasting Mexico and Chile (chapter 11). Both countries share a similar history as Spanish colonies that gained national independence in the 19th century, and both had strong landed aristocracies that grew under Spanish rule. In Mexico, the power of the landed gentry was severely reduced during the struggle for national independence, leading to state dominance of economic and social affairs. In Chile, by contrast, the landed gentry managed to preserve their power during industrialization. As a result, the situation in Chile resembled that in Germany, where landowners and industrialists were locked in a prolonged struggle with the rising working class, and political parties and their offshoots played a key role in maintaining a political balance between these conflicting class interests. Chile thus developed a large—by Latin American standards—civil society sector that falls closer to the welfare partnership pattern observed in Western European countries than it does to patterns found elsewhere in Latin America. By contrast, the single-party rule that emerged in Mexico produced a small, state-controlled civil society sector characteristic of the statist pattern.

There are also two borderline cases in this pattern: Romania and the Republic of Korea. Both meet two defining criteria of the statist pattern—small size and low government support—but fall above the cutoff line on the volunteer share of the workforce. The Republic of Korea experienced a spike in volunteer activity around 2003, when the data were collected. In 1997, volunteers accounted for only about 27 percent of the CSS workforce, well within the range defining the statist pattern. Romania has one of the lowest rates of volunteering among all countries covered by this study, about 2 percent of the adult population compared to an international average of 10 percent.[33] The reason why volunteering accounts for about 57 percent of the Romanian CSS workforce is likely to be a statistical artifact resulting from a very conservative method of estimating paid CSS employment,[34] which yielded a very small number of employees—about 38,000 workers or 0.3 percent of the economically active population—that likely underestimates the actual number. However, both countries pursued statist economic development policies in the second half of the 20th century to overcome their economic backwardness, the factor that the SOCS theory claims to be the leading cause of the statist pattern of CSS development.

SUMMARY

The evidence reviewed here thus offers substantial validation for the social origins theory of civil society development, the notion that it is possible to explain a considerable portion of the variation in the different dimensions of the civil society sector around the world by reference to historic patterns of power relationships among social classes during crucial turning points in national development. Certain configurations of power relationships open the way to robust civil society development, and others severely constrain it and shape it in sometimes awkward ways. The size of the sector, what shape it takes, and what role it plays thus indeed seem to depend heavily on the particular, definable structures of power relationships in society highlighted by the social origins theory.

Testing the Social Origins Theory III: Explaining the Outliers

Ultimately, the real test of a theory must be not only its ability to explain the aspects of reality that seem consistent with it but also the hints it can provide about the causes of aspects that seem inconsistent with it. Before we rest content with the conclusion reached in the previous section, therefore, it is necessary to look more closely at the cases that did not fit into any of the patterns predicted by our theory.

As reported in table 5.1, of the total of 41 cases, 26, or 63 percent, fit neatly into the hypothesized patterns predicted by our theory for all of the hypothesized dimensions of civil society development we focused on—a highly satisfactory outcome for a theory attempting to explain so complex a set of social phenomena. Of the remaining 15 cases, moreover, seven, or another 17 percent, were "near misses" that fit the hypothesized patterns on all but one dimension. And the misses were really near. Thus, Switzerland missed lining up squarely in the liberal pattern by 1 percentage point of the targeted philanthropy share of civil society revenue. Canada similarly missed the welfare partnership model by 1 percentage point of the targeted government share of civil society revenue. In two other cases, Finland and Romania, the misses were 2 percentage points off the targeted volunteer share of the civil society workforce for their respective hypothesized pattern. In two other cases the misses were byproducts of statistical artifacts—the fact that Indian nonprofits received substantial support from international development agencies that was clocked in as government support and the apparent gross underestimate of the size of the CSS workforce in Romania that had the effect of overstating the volunteer share of that workforce. In each of these cases, moreover, we were able to show that the social origins that the

SOCS theory predicted would cause a country to exhibit the just-missed pattern were in fact present. In short, it seems reasonable to claim these seven near-miss cases as further confirmations of the explanatory power of this theory, thus boosting the explanatory power of the SOCS theory to 80 percent of the cases examined.

This leaves eight cases that are "clear misses" rather than "near misses." How can we interpret this?

One possible explanation could be that our theory simply does not account for these cases. This would obviously suggest some limitation to the theory. Even so, a theory that accounts for 80 percent of the cases studied would still be worthy of considerable respect, particularly given the complexity of the underlying social reality it is attempting to explain.

But there is another possibility. Notwithstanding the power of path dependence, social reality is always in flux. Expecting countries to be locked in rigid patterns of social and economic relationships among social classes, ethnic or religious groups, and political factions forever is clearly unrealistic. The real test of the power of this or any other theory is thus whether it can also explain the trajectory of any outliers that might be in the midst of transitions and any hybrids that may have formed, and do so in terms of the premises outlined in the theory. To the extent this is possible, it will demonstrate the dynamic quality of this theory and, potentially, even its predictive power. In the balance of this chapter we therefore turn to this task.

Table 5.7 identifies the eight outlier countries that miss fitting any of our initially hypothesized patterns on at least two dimensions. These countries have been split into two groups. The first group consists of countries that the social origins theory would lead us to expect to fall into the statist or traditional pattern based on their historical patterns of social and economic relationships. Yet none of them seems to manifest the civil society features that our theory suggests should result using the criteria we set. The second set all exhibit unexpected combinations of dimensions that suggest some type of semipermanent hybrid character. Thus, Denmark displays many of the attributes of a social democratic pattern, but both the government share of its civil society revenue base and the volunteer share of its civil society workforce are below the norms we identified for this pattern. Italy and Argentina similarly have unexpected combinations of attributes. To what extent can our theory provide clues to what is going on with these two sets of cases?

TABLE 5.7   Countries not assigned to any of the five patterns, grouped by apparent pattern of evolution

Country	Features				
	Workforce % of EAP (%)	Volunteer share of workforce (%)	Service share of workforce (%)	Government share of revenue (%)	Philanthropy share of revenue (%)
Delayed democratization					
Hungary	2.0	19	60	52	12
Czech Republic	1.7	16	69	65	18
Portugal	4.5	27	63	40	11
Japan	8.0	19	79	38	1
South Africa	3.4	49	52	42	25
Hybrid					
Denmark	8.8	44	51	40	7
Italy	4.3	43	59	36	3
Argentina	5.9	46	54	17	19
41-country average	**5.7**	**40.6**	**59.1**	**35.3**	**14.4**

DELAYED DEMOCRATIZATION

One significant commonality shared by the first group of countries may provide an important clue to the answer to this question: they all underwent a discontinuous systemic social or political transformation in very recent years. Such discontinuous shifts are precisely the turning points that the social origins theory predicts can shift the kinds of social class and institutional power relationships that the theory postulates are responsible for shaping the size, functions, and financing of the civil society sector. Given that the timing of these shifts was such that their full effects were only partly visible by the time the data reported here were collected, it should come as no surprise that the full consequences of these shifts would not yet be visible in our data. Far from refuting the SOCS theory, therefore, these outliers may further confirm it—particularly if we find in the record of these transformations hints that the kinds of shifts in social class and institutional power relationships identified as crucial in this theory actually operated and had the effects predicted.

In the cases of the Czech Republic and Hungary, this certainly seems to be the case. The transformative development for these two countries was, of course, the collapse of the Soviet Union and the end of the Communist regimes that the Soviet Union imposed on these societies. Of special importance from the perspective of the social origins theory, however, is that what transpired in these two countries was more than a regime change. Also involved were significant changes in power relations among key social actors and institutions.[35] This was due in important part to the influence of the European Union, the International Monetary Fund, and other actors that helped encourage a reasonably transparent privatization process leading to the emergence of an industrial, commercial, and professional middle class; to legal and political changes that promoted the growth of an independent civil society sector; and to a significant narrowing of the power of the state in both economic and political affairs. As a consequence, the Soviet-era statist pattern of civil society development has given way to a pattern that has begun to resemble the welfare partnership model common in the dominant European Union countries. Although the remnant of this former statist pattern is still visible in the relatively small CSS workforce reflected in table 5.7, other features of the civil society sector in these countries—such as the substantial growth of governmental support for civil society—signal a move in a different direction.

Further supporting the SOCS theory argument that it is shifts in underlying power relations among key social actors, and not simply regime change, that produces lasting alterations in the pattern of civil society development is the experience in some other former Soviet Union countries, including Russia. Although all Soviet bloc countries underwent a political transformation, in not all of them was this accompanied by a significant narrowing of the power of the state—a key requirement for the statist model to be disrupted. Unlike in Hungary and the Czech Republic, where new social forces were able to put in place laws and procedures to constrain the power of the state, in Russia the power of the state remained virtually intact—certainly after Vladimir Putin succeeded Boris Yeltsin. As a consequence, the contours of the CSS in the Czech Republic and Hungary underwent changes that moved it away from the statist pattern and toward the welfare partnership one widespread in the European Union, whereas the CSS in Russia still falls squarely into the statist pattern, though certain winds of change are also in evidence there.[36]

A very similar shift in power relations occurred in Portugal (chapter 16) but at an earlier date. Portugal came under the sway of the statist pattern in the 1920s, when growing political unrest triggered by the dissolution of the ancient regime led to the rise of the authoritarian Salazar regime, which placed severe constraints on the civil society sector. This authoritarian rule persisted until 1974, when it was ended by a military coup, the so-called Carnation Revolution staged by left-wing military elements dissatisfied with the increasing burden of colonial wars. The Carnation Revolution created a shift in power relations in favor of the urban middle class, which resulted in a push toward greater integration of Portugal into Europe and eventual accession to the European Union. As a consequence, the civil society sector—severely suppressed under the Salazar regime—started to develop and gravitated toward the welfare partnership model dominating the European Union. The only dimension that sets Portugal apart from the welfare partnership pattern is its relatively low government share of CSS revenue (40 percent)—very likely a sign that its transition is still under way.[37]

By contrast, neighboring Spain—which also was under an authoritarian statist rule until 1975—underwent a slower political transformation after the death of the authoritarian dictator Francisco Franco. Unlike Portugal, Spain became a constitutional monarchy, and the military remained hostile toward the fledging democratic system. Democratic rule was firmly upheld only after a failed coup attempt by a group of military officers in 1981. This suggests that the power relations that developed under the Franco regime did not change as dramatically as their counterparts did in Portugal. Consequently, the Spanish CSS was still within the boundaries of the statist pattern in 1995 when the data analyzed in this study were collected.[38]

These cases thus suggest a sixth pattern of civil society development, which we label the "delayed democratization" pattern. This pattern includes countries that in the past pursued the statist model of economic development but underwent a systemic transition, resulting in their departure from the statist path in the direction of an opening to democracy and to civil society. In all three of the cases discussed to this point, the transition seems to be in the direction of what we have termed the welfare partnership model, but the transition is not yet complete. Delayed democratization may thus be a transitional state and not an endpoint.

The two other countries listed in the first cluster of localities in table 5.7—Japan and South Africa—also seem to fit this delayed democratization pattern, though the direction of ultimate change is a bit more uncertain. As we noted earlier, Japan has long been a clear example of a statist pattern of economic and social development, characterized by the domination of the state over all aspects of civil society.[39] This pattern was partially interrupted after the country's defeat in World War II by the American occupation of Japan, which sought as one of its key objectives the dismantling of the power of the centralized state through a set of liberalization policies that included the promotion of civil society.[40] A second impulse disrupting the statist pattern came from the Kobe earthquake, which shook public faith in the all-powerful state and opened greater space for independent civil society activity. Not yet clear, however, is whether Japan is transitioning toward a welfare partnership model or more of a liberal model. The sizable scale of the country's civil society sector suggests the former, but the limited level of government support suggests the latter. A key determinant is likely to be the strength of citizen opposition to a state that has recently been seen as faltering in its response to recurrent crises and economic stagnation.

Finally, South Africa is a particularly interesting case of a delayed democratization transition pattern illustrating the key role of power relations in the shaping of CSS development. Dutch colonization, starting in the mid-17th century, introduced farming and slavery to the area. In 1795 the British took over the Cape. Rapid economic growth in the 1880s brought a massive influx of immigrants. Each of these ethnic, cultural, and religious groups developed organizations to serve its own interests, but these groups rarely joined together to fight for common interests. The formation of the Union of South Africa in 1910 and continued industrialization spurred a large-scale labor movement that resulted in new labor legislation granting trade union rights to all ethnic groups except Africans. This split the labor movement, and the civil society sector more generally, along racial lines.

Following the Anglo-Boer wars, the victorious British authorities consolidated their control of the former Boer colonies under a single state, the Union of South Africa. Instrumental in this process was the exploitation of racial divisions and exclusion of non-White populations—which eventually led to the implementation of the apartheid regime in 1948 and extension of welfare protection for Whites only. As a consequence, Blacks formed separate self-help groups based on more traditional forms of social organization, such as burial clubs and informal savings clubs (*stokvels*), as well as trade unions and clandestine political organizations resisting the apartheid regime. This result was a special hybrid case of two different CSS patterns coexisting side by side— welfare partnership for the Whites and the traditional pattern for the Blacks. After a prolonged struggle of the African resistance movement and increased international pressure aimed at isolating the apartheid regime, the apartheid laws were finally rescinded in 1991, followed by far-reaching democratic reforms that significantly shifted the power balance in favor of the Black population. As a consequence, the shape of the CSS sector in South Africa also started to change, gravitating toward the welfare partnership model that in the apartheid era was limited to the White minority. However, a uniquely South African feature of that development is a relatively high level of business philanthropy that shows up in the relatively high 25 percent of South African CSS revenue coming from philanthropy, presumably some form of compensation by businesses for the discriminatory practices against Blacks under apartheid.[41]

HYBRIDS

The remaining three countries—Argentina, Denmark, and Italy—appear to be semi-stable hybrid patterns. To what extent is this outcome explicable in terms suggested by our theory? Denmark provides a useful test case. As one of the Nordic countries, Denmark has historically fit the social democratic pattern common elsewhere in the region, with social conditions that mirror those in the other countries considered here.[42] But in the 1990s, elements with neoliberal leanings gained increased influence in the political arena and put a brake on further expansions of state-delivered social welfare benefits.[43] Instead, these elements successfully pushed through reforms that shifted more of the burden of social welfare provision from the state to nonprofit groups, producing a mixture of social democratic and welfare partnership features,[44] as detailed more fully in chapter 13.

Italy can also be considered a semi-stable hybrid case. Here, however, it is the sharp socioeconomic fault line dividing the north and the south in this country, as evidenced, among others, by Putnam,[45] that has produced this result. In the process, Italy points up a limitation that runs throughout our analysis: all of our data treat countries as meaningful analytical units. To be sure, we have had occasion to note the impact of internal divisions that take a geographic form in a variety of places—such as the mostly Protestant north and Catholic south in the Netherlands, the French-speaking Catholic province of Quebec in Canada compared to the largely Protestant and English-speaking rest of the country, and the historically sharply divided North and South in the United States. But all of our data report national, rather than regional, averages, thereby potentially obscuring significant regional differences.

Italy brings this limitation into particularly sharp relief. In a real sense, Italy is the locus of two distinctly different patterns of civil society development, each associated with its own constellation of social-class and institution-based power relationships. While the industrialized north historically represents the liberal pattern emphasizing a strong role of civil society but somewhat limited state support, as befits a middle-class-dominated class structure, the rural south is still dominated by vestiges of traditional social institutions and the widespread clientelism characteristic of the traditional pattern. With these two realities merged in our data, it is no wonder that Italy does not cleanly fit any of our models but rather stands out as a stable hybrid.

Finally, Argentina also has a turbulent history that left behind a highly confusing mixture of organizational residues. Throughout most of the 20th century, Argentina oscillated between Peronist populism and military dictatorship that did not leave any clear and lasting single pattern of CSS development.[46]

Conclusion

The evidence reviewed here thus lends substantial credence to the social origins theory of civil society development as a way to explain the different patterns of civil society development evident in the 41 countries on which reliable empirical data have become available. This theory goes beyond the prevailing explanations of civil society development stressing the presence or absence of various sentiments or preferences by emphasizing the embeddedness of civil society institutions in prevailing power relationships in society as these relationships take shape during crucial historical periods and then persist over time. The theory points us to enduring commonalities in the development of civil society sectors in the historical records of widely divergent societies, making it possible not only to detect common patterns descriptively but also to explain analytically how and why they emerge. In the process, this theory suggests a number of implications for our understanding of the civil society sector more broadly and for its possible future evolution in regions and countries beyond those examined here. It is to these broader implications and our final conclusions that we therefore now turn.

Notes

1. For further detail on this method, see Ragin and Becker 1992.
2. Weber 1978, 215.

3. Moore 1966, 486.

4. Putnam 1993.

5. Moore 1966, 355.

6. *Ibid.*, 373.

7. Rosen 1967, 102.

8. Heitzman and Worden 1996; Singh 1996.

9. Mohmand and Gazdar 2007.

10. Berger and Broughton 1995, ch. 5.

11. Moore 1966, 3–39; see also Brenner 1982.

12. Salamon 1972.

13. Rueschemeyer, Stephens, and Stephens 1992; Skocpol 1992.

14. Skocpol 1995; Salamon 2012a.

15. Salamon 1995, 82–90.

16. Halperin 1964; Moore 1966, 34–38.

17. Sachße 1994; Backhaus-Maul and Olk 1994; Anheier and Salamon 2006.

18. Halperin 1964.

19. Heerma van Voss 1995; Kramer 1981.

20. Brandsen and Pape 2015.

21. Hoppe and Langton 1994.

22. Berger and Broughton 1995.

23. Heclo 1974.

24. Berger and Broughton 1995; Drake 1996; Rueschemeyer, Stephens, and Stephens 1992; Sokolowski 2011.

25. Berger and Broughton 1995.

26. Gerschenkron 1992.

27. Moore 1966, 228–291; Timberger 1978.

28. Amenomori 1993.

29. Gella 1988.

30. Gerschenkron 1992.

31. Rueschemeyer, Stephens, and Stephens 1992, 199–204.

32. *Ibid.*, 200.

33. Salamon, Sokolowski, and Associates 2004, table A.2.

34. This method relied on estimated shares of nonprofit employment in service industries where nonprofits typically operate.

35. Hausner, Jessop, and Nielsen 1995.

36. Linz and Stepan 1996. A similar development took place in other Eastern European countries that joined the European Union—Poland, Romania, and Slovakia. However, the data on those countries presented in this study were assembled in 1995, very early in the transformation process. As a result, these countries still fell into the statist pattern. On the other hand, the data for the Czech Republic and Hungary were assembled in 2004 and 2003, respectively. The data on Russia were assembled in 2008. For further evidence of this disparity between Central European and other former Soviet Union nations, see Cook 2015. On recent developments suggesting some movement toward a welfare partnership model in Russia in response to popular

dissatisfaction with state-provided social welfare services, see Salamon, Benevolenski, and Jakobson 2015.

37. Franco 2005; Franco et al. 2006; Linz and Stepan 1996.

38. Linz and Stepan 1996; Preston 1987; Tusell 2011.

39. Timberger 1978.

40. Cohen and Passin 1987.

41. Kruger 1969; Omer-Cooper 1988; Swilling et al. 2004; Wilson and Thompson 1969.

42. Wollebæk and Selle 2000; Svedberg and Grassman 2001.

43. Villadsen 2004.

44. Pestoff 1995.

45. Putnam 1993.

46. Romero 2002.

CHAPTER SIX

Conclusion and Implications

LESTER M. SALAMON *and* S. WOJCIECH SOKOLOWSKI

A S THE PREVIOUS CHAPTERS SHOW, the social origins theory of the civil society sector carries us considerably far down the road toward explaining the diverse size, shape, functions, and support structure of the civil society sector around the world, and does so considerably better than the existing theories that have been deployed up to now. What the analysis here reveals is that while the civil society sector may be a conduit for altruistic sentiments and personal preferences, the size of the sector and the shape that it takes depend heavily on the broader structures of power relationships in society. Restoring considerations of power to the center of analysis of civil society thus emerges as a central imperative if we are to understand the path that civil society development takes.

Of course, this corroboration in a number of representative cases does not represent a definitive proof. Further inquiry is needed to provide additional evidence and to test alternative explanations and causal relations. Data on countries not covered by this study may yield new evidence that will require modifications or even substantial revisions of the social origins of civil society (SOCS) theory.

As it stands, however, the social origins theory goes beyond the prevailing explanations of civil society development stressing the presence or absence of various *sentiments* or *preferences* by emphasizing the embeddedness of civil society institutions in prevailing *power relationships* in society as these relationships evolve over time. In the process, this theory proves able to explain developments that these other theories cannot. One of them is the robust growth of the civil society sector in countries with generous public welfare programs. Another is the relatively small size of the sector in countries where government public welfare programs are minimal or virtually nonexistent. And yet others are the peculiar variations in the functions carried out by the sector, the revenue sources on which it relies, and the levels of volunteer participation it engages from place to place.

Also of particular interest within this reframed explanation of civil society development is the significant connection that emerges between the growth of the civil society sector and the strength of labor movements and their political extensions. This connection is often missed in public perception, as civil society and organized labor are often seen as two separate social institutions pursuing wholly disparate, if not mutually antagonistic, goals. But the contribution of the labor movement to the development of the civil society sector is significant and takes two different forms. In the first place, organized labor has created a wide array of self-help groups and clubs serving the needs of the working class. And in the second, organized labor's demands have often leveraged government policies that create favorable conditions for general civil society sector growth. This observation brings us back to the observation of Kwame Nkrumah, cited in chapter 2, that helped explain our emphasis on the organizational core of civil society. As Nkrumah put it: "We must organize as never before, for organization decides everything."[1]

A final implication of the analysis here is the realization that civil society institutions, broadly conceived, can function not only as sources of protection and support for those at the bottom of the social and economic pyramid but also as convenient excuses for evading more robust forms of assistance to those in greatest need or, worse yet, as instruments for suppressing more radical forms of social and political activism. In its heyday, the liberal pattern of civil society development functioned very much in the former way, while the early development of the welfare partnership pattern had elements of the latter—and there is a danger that recent appearances of this pattern in Russia and China could evolve in the same way.

The SOCS theory seems able to explain not only why some culturally different and geographically distant countries fall into the same patterns of civil society development but also why certain others deviate from the initially hypothesized patterns. The key to this explanation for both sets of countries is the analysis of the dynamics of power relations among key social actors, socioeconomic classes, and institutions representing or mediating their class interests.

The real promise of the social origins of civil society theory may ultimately lie elsewhere, however. For if this set of factors can explain what has happened in the past, it may also be capable of yielding reasonable hunches about what might be lurking on the horizon if present trends continue.

Stated differently, the SOCS theory can not only explain the past but also help forecast the future. This can offer valuable insights into possible outcomes in rapidly changing parts of the world. For example, what might the SOCS theory suggest about likely developments of the civil society sector in such turbulent regions as Central and East Asia or the Middle East? In Central Asia, a number of former Soviet republics seceded from the Russian Federation, forming new sovereign countries and potentially opening new space for civil society development. At the same time, China instituted a series of reforms that radically liberalized its economy. A rather different development occurred in the Middle East. Following the example of Turkey, many Middle Eastern countries instituted statist regimes in the 1950s and 1960s to promote rapid modernization of their traditional societies and economies, but, unlike Turkey, most of them failed to achieve that objective due to a combination of international and domestic factors. This failure to produce the promised results undermined the legitimacy of the statist regimes and fueled growing popular dissent, manifested by the Arab Spring and, in other places, by fundamentalist religious movements.

Despite their fundamentally different natures, developments in both of these sets of regions spurred renewed interest in the potential of civil society, creating a wave of optimism about its future in Asia and the Middle East. Yet the SOCS theory suggests a much more sober, and perhaps more realistic, view of the situation. Despite far-reaching political transformations, the power relations in many of the countries in these parts of the world have not been transformed that much. In the newly independent states of Central Asia and in China, the state still holds the hegemonic power it did throughout the second half of the 20th century. In the Middle East, the military exercises hegemonic power in countries ruled by both secular regimes, like Egypt, and by fundamentalist theocracies, like Iran or Saudi Arabia. The SOCS theory would therefore predict that the civil society sector in these countries will continue to face constraints and is likely to remain caught in the statist pattern—with its characteristic features of small size, limited volunteer participation, and low government support—for the foreseeable future. On the other hand, the collapse of the central state in countries like Libya, Syria, or Iraq is likely to perpetuate the traditional pattern of civil society development, or perhaps a fundamentalist variant of it characterized by tight control by clerical authorities, private philanthropy as a major, but confining, revenue source, and a growing reliance on religiously based charitable organizations that utilize access to human services as a vehicle of social control and religious mobilization.

But prescient as it might be about future outcomes in the absence of changes in prevailing structures of power, the SOCS theory is also available as a guide to the steps needed to alter the current trajectories. If by bringing a fresh set of insights into our understanding of the important social phenomenon represented by the global civil society sector, this book succeeds in bridging the gap that has long existed between the study of civil society and the study of the broader dynamics of social reality with which it is so intimately intertwined, it will have served its purpose well. This, at any rate, would be our hope.

Note

1. Nkrumah 1973.

PART TWO

Further Detail—Ten "New" or Newly Updated Countries

LESTER M. SALAMON, S. WOJCIECH SOKOLOWSKI,
MEGAN A. HADDOCK, *and* ASSOCIATES

In this part of our volume we take up a task that has been the focus of prior volumes reporting on the results of the Johns Hopkins Comparative Nonprofit Sector Project:[1] namely, to present an in-depth and focused portrait of the scope and shape of the civil society sector in countries newly added to the project or for which updated data have newly become available through implementation of the United Nations *Handbook on Nonprofit Institutions in the System of National Accounts* or other means.

Given the analytical thrust of the present volume, however, we have extended the discussion of the empirical results in the ten countries newly added to the project's reporting through this volume by identifying the pattern of civil society development that is evident in each of these countries and exploring at least briefly how well the social origins theory developed in the body of the book seems to account for these patterns. Since some of these are countries on which earlier data were available, the discussion of these countries also allows us to assess the ability of the SOCS theory to explain not only what now exists but also what accounts for any significant changes that become evident. As in the body of the book, we take up the countries in the order in which the models they embody appeared historically, beginning, in this case, with countries that exhibit key features of the liberal pattern and then proceeding in turn to examine countries exhibiting the welfare partnership, social democratic, and statist patterns. And as will become clear, some of these countries seem to be in transition from one pattern to another in ways that the social origins theory can help us understand.

CHAPTER SEVEN

Switzerland

A Liberal Outlier for Europe

BERND HELMIG, MARKUS GMÜR, CHRISTOPH
BÄRLOCHER, GEORG VON SCHNURBEIN,
BERNARD DEGEN, MICHAEL NOLLERT, S. WOJCIECH
SOKOLOWSKI, *and* LESTER M. SALAMON

SWITZERLAND AFFORDS AN OPPORTUNITY to demonstrate how the social origins theory can unravel what appear, on first glance, to be unexpected patterns of civil society development. We might expect Switzerland, as a German-speaking nation in Western Europe, to exhibit a pattern of civil society sector development similar to that in Germany and much of the rest of Northern Europe—a welfare partnership model characterized by a large civil society sector heavily financed by government and engaged mostly in service activities. Viewed through the lens of the social origins theory, however, Switzerland emerges into view as perhaps the only country in Continental Europe that exhibits key features of the liberal pattern—a pattern that is more commonly encountered in the Anglo-Saxon countries. In particular, although it has a sizeable civil society sector, this sector is still smaller than that in the welfare partnership countries, with a substantially lower level of government support, higher volunteer involvement, and greater focus on expressive functions. How do we explain this unique structure of the civil society sector in Switzerland compared to its Western European neighbors? More importantly for our purposes here, to what extent does the social origins theory point us toward a plausible explanation?

The social origins theory attributes the emergence and persistence of the liberal model of civil society development to situations in which commercial and industrial elements are exceptionally strong and encounter limited pressure from labor. As this chapter shows, this is indeed the situation found in Switzerland. The relatively weak position of labor and the strong political influence of commercial and industrial employers and their associations, coupled with general prosperity, a fragmented political structure, and a strong tradition of citizen self-management, were the key social forces behind the development of a liberal model of civil society in Switzerland. Although elements of the welfare partnership pattern made their appearance in the 20th century, a full-scale welfare partnership model similar to that found in Germany and other European countries did not materialize. And this was due to precisely the social factor that the social origins theory points us toward: the absence of the more acute working-class pressure found in those other countries during the critical industrialization period.

To explore these phenomena, this chapter first outlines some of the salient features of the Swiss civil society sector as it has become visible through our data and then assesses the extent to which the social origins theory can explain the pattern that has emerged.

Dimensions of the Swiss Civil Society Sector

SIZE OF THE WORKFORCE

The civil society sector is a considerable component of the Swiss economy. As of 2005, Swiss civil society organizations employed over 180,000 full-time-equivalent (FTE) workers, which represents about 4.5 percent of total employment. In addition, these organizations engaged over 1.6 million volunteers who contributed on average about 155 hours of their time per year. This translates into another 107,000 full-time-equivalent jobs, bringing the total workforce of Swiss civil society organizations to 287,500 FTE workers or 6.9 percent of the country's economically active population (EAP).

Figure 7.1 gauges the size of the Swiss civil society sector's workforce against that of four major Swiss industries: agriculture and fishing, manufacturing, construction, and transportation. In Switzerland, the size of the civil society workforce is second only to manufacturing (671,000 employees) and exceeds employment in the construction (294,000), transportation (241,000), and agriculture and fishing (160,000) industries.

The civil society sector in Switzerland is quite sizable in relation to other countries. Measured as a share of the EAP, the 6.9 percent workforce of the Swiss civil society sector ranked substantially above the 5.7 percent average for the 41 countries for which such data are available, as figure 2.1 demonstrates.

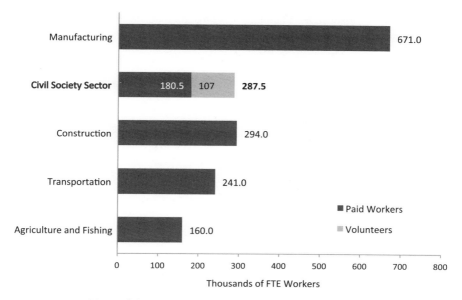

FIGURE 7.1. FTE workforce, civil society sector vs. selected industries, Switzerland, 2005.

TABLE 7.1 Civil society sector workforce as share of EAP, Switzerland vs. country clusters and 41-country average

Cluster	Workforce as a share of EAP (%)
Switzerland	**6.9**
41 countries	*5.7*
Traditional	1.9
Liberal	9.6
Welfare partnership	11.2
Social democratic	8.2
Statist	2.3

At the same time, Switzerland's civil society workforce is proportionately considerably smaller than the average for its European welfare-partnership neighbors, which, at 11.2 percent of the economically active population, is proportionately 60 percent higher than Switzerland's, as table 7.1 shows. Switzerland is thus closer to the liberal model in this regard.

TABLE 7.2 Volunteer share of CSS workforce, Switzerland vs. country clusters and 41-country average

Cluster	Volunteers as a share of CSS workforce (%)
Switzerland	**37.2**
41 countries	*40.6*
Traditional	53.1
Liberal	46.4
Welfare partnership	29.1
Social democratic	69.4
Statist	27.9

VOLUNTEER PARTICIPATION

Over 26 percent of Swiss adults engaged in some form of volunteer work as of 2005, contributing over 250 million work hours to civil society organizations in that year alone. As noted above, this translates into more than 107,000 full-time jobs, which represents 3.3 percent of the economically active population. Volunteer time thus accounted for about 37 percent of the entire civil society workforce.

The volunteer share of the civil society workforce in Switzerland is somewhat below the 41-country average of 41 percent, as table 7.2 demonstrates. This puts Switzerland well above the welfare partnership average along this dimension but somewhat below the average for countries exhibiting the liberal pattern.

SERVICE AND EXPRESSIVE ACTIVITIES

Most (55 percent) of the Swiss civil society sector workforce (paid and volunteer) is engaged in service activities, especially social services (26 percent) and health care (20 percent). Expressive activities employ 43 percent of the workforce, with culture, sports, and recreation alone accounting for 29 percent (table 7.3).

This distribution of the workforce between service and expressive activities in Switzerland is quite close to that found, on average, in the liberal country cluster but diverges sharply from the pattern in the welfare partnership countries, as table 7.4 shows.

TABLE 7.3   Distribution of Switzerland's CSS workforce,
by field, 2005

Field	Share (%)
Service fields	55
Education and research	7
Social services	26
Health care	20
Economic development	2
Expressive fields	43
Culture, sports, and recreation	29
Religion	5
Advocacy	7
Professional associations, labor unions	2
Environmental protection	1
Other fields	2
Philanthropic intermediaries	0
International	1
Not elsewhere classified	1
N	287,491

TABLE 7.4   Distribution of CSS workforce by type of function, Switzerland
vs. country clusters and 41-country average

Cluster	Share of CSS workforce, by type of function* (%)		
	Service	Expressive	Other
Switzerland	55	43	2
41 countries	59	37	4
Traditional	68	24	8
Liberal	55	36	9
Welfare partnership	71	25	4
Social democratic	39	59	2
Statist	50	47	4

*Figures may not add to 100% due to rounding.

REVENUE SOURCES

The total revenue of the civil society sector in Switzerland was over 10 billion Swiss Francs (US$8.6 billion) in 2005. More than half of that amount
(nearly 58 percent) came from fees (table 7.5). The second-largest source of
revenue was government, which accounted for nearly 35 percent, while private philanthropy provided the remaining 8 percent. The government share

TABLE 7.5   Sources of Switzerland's CSS revenue by field, 2005

Field	Government (%)	Philanthropy (%)	Fees (%)
All fields	35	8	58
Service fields	41	5	54
Health care	45	3	52
Education and research	29	1	70
Social services	45	9	46
Economic development	24	4	72
Expressive fields	13	16	71
Environmental protection	15	20	65
Culture, sports, and recreation	22	14	64
Religion	0	43	57
Professional associations and labor unions	5	2	93
Advocacy	11	6	83
Other fields	21	24	56
Philanthropic intermediaries	1	10	89
International	33	47	20
Not elsewhere classified	22	1	77

of CSS revenue is also relatively low across all fields of activity, but even at its highest (45 percent in health care and social services) it is not a dominant revenue source in Switzerland. While private philanthropy is a relatively minor source of support to the sector as a whole, it is the dominant source in international activities (47 percent) and a major source in religion (43 percent) and environmental protection (20 percent).

The government share of civil society revenue in Switzerland, at 35 percent, falls far below that found in the welfare partnership countries of Europe and within the range that defines the liberal pattern (45 percent of total revenue or less). However, the philanthropy share of that revenue, at 8 percent, falls slightly below the range defining the liberal pattern (9 percent or more) making Switzerland a near miss along this one dimension. Nonetheless, the distribution of civil society sector income in Switzerland is quite similar to averages found in the liberal country cluster, where, on average, government payments account for 33 percent, fees for 53 percent, and philanthropy for 14 percent of the total, as table 7.6 shows.

TABLE 7.6 Shares of CSS revenue by source, Switzerland vs. country clusters and 41-country average*

Cluster	Government (%)	Philanthropy (%)	Fees (%)
Switzerland	35	8	58
41 countries	35	14	50
Traditional	11	24	65
Liberal	33	14	53
Welfare partnership	66	8	26
Social democratic	38	10	52
Statist	18	18	64

*Figures may not add to 100% due to rounding.

SUMMARY

In short, the civil society sector in Switzerland shares many features with countries that exhibit what we have termed the liberal model of civil society development. This makes Switzerland an exception among the countries of continental Europe, which tend to fall into the welfare partnership or social-democratic patterns. Given the cultural proximity of Switzerland to neighboring Germany, and the similar roles that organized religion played in the history of both countries, the sentiment model (discussed in chapter 3) would predict that both countries would also share the same trajectory of civil society development, resulting in the emergence of a welfare partnership model. To what extent can the social origins theory explain the alternative outcome that has emerged?

Explaining the Swiss Pattern of Civil Society Development

The answer, it seems, is quite effectively. Viewed through the lens of the social origins theory, the liberal model outcome in Switzerland makes perfect sense since the power relations among socioeconomic classes visible in Switzerland align closely with those that the social origins theory finds likely to produce precisely this outcome. Specifically, this includes a weak landed aristocracy, the fostering of a strong tradition of local self-government by merchants and industrialists in the cantons to limit control or interference with business by a centralized state, a resulting ideological hegemony of liberal ideas emphasizing limited government, and a relatively weak and divided labor movement unable to mount an effective push for extensive public welfare programs. Taken together, these factors all conspired to produce the structure of class power favoring urban merchants and industrialists that the social origins theory links to the liberal model.[2]

THE RISE OF MERCHANT POWER

A key factor in the emergence of a liberal model of civil society in Switzerland occurred during the end of the Middle Ages when the Swiss confederacy defeated the Habsburg forces and gained independence from the Holy Roman Empire. The dominance of the urban areas of Lucerne and Zurich in the confederacy led to a gradual decline of the landed aristocracy and the ascent of urban classes. The country was fragmented along political and religious lines, with local jurisdictions (*cantons*) having a significant level of sovereignty. This opened the way for the emergence of guilds, which may be considered the forerunners of modern civil society organizations in Switzerland. The main purpose of the emerging guilds was the protection of business and professional interests through self-regulation of the market, but they also performed many social functions, including maintaining social solidarity and providing a social safety net for their members.

The era of the Enlightenment and increased secularization of Swiss society created new opportunities for the establishment of civic associations formed by merchants, members of the professions, and regional elites. These associations included scientific and educational societies, public-benefit organizations promoting social or educational reforms or providing relief for the poor, economic societies aiming to link theoretical knowledge with practical improvements in agriculture or in trades, and political societies engaged in the study of history, the promotion of republican civic education, and the reform of the military system. These societies took on a transitional role between traditional corporations and civic organizations.[3] Another organizational form that developed in this time period was freemasonry, which was instrumental in maintaining elite solidarity. Its members belonged to different status groups (noblemen, patricians, or commoners) that practiced a highly ritualized friendship in regular gatherings.

THE HELVETIC REPUBLIC PERIOD

This comfortable localized pattern of merchant and industrialist control was partially shaken by the Napoleonic Wars, when French troops occupied Swiss territory and established a centralized state called the Helvetic Republic, which lasted from 1803 to 1813. Although these efforts led to the emergence of a single Swiss state, central authority remained relatively weak, and the cantons retained a substantial level of sovereignty. Despite its short life, however, the Helvetic Republic had a dramatic impact on corporate bodies of all kinds. At its beginning, the republic tore open deep rifts in society, which divided even relatively democratic organizations. Corporations, guilds, and similar corporate bodies, for example, lost their importance, and the power base of the old elites was uprooted as well. New organizations emerged to alleviate adverse conditions created by the battles waged on Swiss territory by Russian, Austrian, and French armies. Relief organizations were founded in Basel, Zurich, and Bern, among others. The Helvetic Republic also stimulated the establishment of civil society organizations operating on a nationwide level.

INDUSTRIALIZATION, LIBERALIZATION, AND THE GROWTH OF CIVIL SOCIETY

The high level of industrialization in the 19th century allowed the Swiss industrial and merchant classes to re-establish their position and reinstate liberal policies limiting the role of government and placing reliance on a strong civil society to address social issues. This liberal political climate, encouraged by the wave of social revolutions that shook Europe in 1830, brought to power the Swiss Liberals in the most important cantons and led ultimately to a new constitution in 1848 that opened new opportunities for the further liberalization of the economy and society. This, in turn, encouraged the rapid growth of civil society organizations, with an estimated 30,000 societies established in that time period.[4] Industrialization, and the weakening of traditional social networks it produced, also spurred the growth of mutual associations, whose main role was provision of a social safety net to their members. In the absence of state-provided services, mutual associations gained significance by the early 20th century, with more than 500,000 members.

Although industrialization brought with it the creation of a sizable Swiss working class, for a variety of reasons this class was not able to pose the kind of challenge to middle-class power that its counterparts in Germany or Austria—let alone Sweden and Denmark—mounted. For one thing, although the passage of the 1874 constitution expanded the authority of the federal government and enabled the state to assume a more active role in alleviating the social pressure caused by industrialization, the powerful doctrine of citizen self-management (known as *Milizverwaltung*), firmly embedded in Swiss public services, kept the scope of government intervention relatively modest and reliant on private associations that played a significant role in public policy.

Also working to blunt the force of working-class opposition was the robust power in Swiss economic and political life at both the federal and cantonal levels of business associations, such as the Swiss Chamber of Commerce and Industry, the Swiss Association of Machinery Manufacturers, and the Swiss Society of Chemical Industries.

Finally, the labor movement, which emerged in the second half of the 19th century, was initially limited to skilled craftsmen such as typographers, cabinetmakers, carpenters, stonemasons, dressmakers, and shoemakers. With industrialization, labor unions spread to other occupations, and workers formed their own association, the Swiss Federation of Trade Unions (*Schweizerischer Gewerkschaftsbund*). But labor remained fragmented and weak, separated by religious divisions growing out of the Reformation and the teachings of John Calvin as well as more recent ideological and status divisions. This is evidenced by the emergence of the separate Catholic labor unions under the umbrella of the Christian Social Federation of Swiss Trade Unions formed in 1907. Membership in labor unions and affiliated cultural associations (such as sporting or musical societies) was linked to religious and ideological denominations, although the extent of pillarization did not reach the level observed in the Netherlands (described in chapter 10).

After World War I, membership in labor unions further increased, but labor demands concentrated on negotiating collective bargaining agreements with employers and did not include more radical policy goals. The relationship between labor and government was generally collaborative, as federal authorities consulted on their policies with labor representatives. However, mutual aid societies linked to different religious denominations continued to play a key role in providing a social safety net (e.g., unemployment or old age insurance), so that demands on the government to provide the kind of comprehensive social welfare policies found in other Western European countries, such as Germany, were muted.

The general economic prosperity of Swiss society after World War II created a favorable environment for liberal economic policies favored by the commercial and industrial bourgeoisie and designed to keep government in a rather limited role. These liberal tendencies were strengthened in the 1980s, when neoliberal influences intensified pressure toward the privatization or commercialization of many state functions.[5]

In sum, the relatively weak position of labor, the strong political influence of employers and their associations, general prosperity, and the strong tradition of citizen self-management that grew out of these factors were the key social forces behind the development of a liberal model of civil society in Switzerland. While elements of the welfare partnership pattern of government and nonprofit cooperation in providing social services did emerge in the 20th century, the limited scope of public welfare in Switzerland prevented the formation of a full-scale welfare partnership model similar to that in Germany and other Western European countries.

Conclusions

The civil society sector is a sizeable component of the Swiss economy today and an important provider of human services. By European standards, it receives relatively small levels of government support and relies mainly on fee income. These features of the Swiss civil society sector correspond closely to those defining the liberal country cluster, though the level of private philanthropy and volunteering in Switzerland falls somewhat below the liberal norm.

The origins of this pattern can be found in Swiss history, especially the weak position of the aristocracy, the early rise to significant influence of urban merchants and industrialists, and the resulting stunted growth of centralized state authority. The ideological hegemony of the bourgeoisie, the resulting strong tradition of local self-governance, and the relative affluence of Swiss society further advantaged private solutions to social and economic problems over state action.

Industrialization—which in other European countries created intense class conflicts and struggles that were the force behind the implementation of welfare partnership or social democratic solutions to social problems—took a rather different turn in Switzerland. Industrialization, instead, created a working class that relied more on self-help and direct collaboration with employers than on the state in arranging collective security. At the same time, divisions along religious, ideological, and status lines fragmented and weakened the labor movement.

Switzerland can thus be considered a test case for two of the theoretical models discussed in previous chapters of this book. The sentiment model would predict a similar civil society development trajectory in Switzerland as in neighboring Germany, which shares with Switzerland quite similar cultural and religious sentiments. The social origins model, which looks into the structure of power relations among social and economic groupings from a historical perspective, however, accurately predicts a liberal model of civil society development in Switzerland given the strong position of the commercial and industrial bourgeoisie coupled with a small state and the relatively weak position of labor. The Swiss experience presented in this chapter thus lends substantially more credence to the SOCS explanation of diverging patterns of civil society development than it does to the alternative sentiments theory.

Notes

This study was made possible thanks to the effort of a broad group of researchers at the University of Fribourg under the direction of Prof. Dr. Bernd Helmig as part of the Johns Hopkins Comparative Nonprofit Sector Project. Historical material cited here draws heavily on Helmig et al. 2011.

1. Salamon, Anheier, List, et al. 1999; Salamon, Sokolowski, and Associates 2004.
2. Helmig, Bärlocher, and von Schnurbein 2009.
3. Erne 1988.
4. Helmig, Bärlocher, and von Schnurbein 2009; Kriesi 1995.
5. Korpi and Palme 2003; Nollert 2007.

CHAPTER EIGHT

New Zealand

An Unusual Liberal Model

S. WOJCIECH SOKOLOWSKI *and* LESTER M. SALAMON

NEW ZEALAND IS a challenging case for the social origins theory. Its socioeconomic class structure resembles more that of Sweden than of Great Britain, which colonized the country in the 19th century. Unlike in Great Britain, landed elites were relatively weak in New Zealand, and the country was among the most egalitarian countries in the English-speaking world. What is more, at the turn of the twentieth century New Zealand was one of the most unionized countries in the world. Organized labor was strongly influenced by socialist ideas, and the first Labour government was elected in 1935. Unlike Sweden, however, New Zealand falls into the liberal pattern of civil society development with a large civil society workforce, relatively limited levels of government support, and a high level of private philanthropy. This poses a challenge to the social origins theory that links a strong position of labor vis-à-vis other socioeconomic classes to the social democratic pattern of civil society development.

But while the social origins theory views the existence of a strong working class as a likely necessary condition for a social democratic outcome, it does not view this as a sufficient condition. Equally important are the power amplifiers, such as unions and political parties, that are needed to organize, articulate, and represent working-class interests and the potential power diffusers, such as ethnic, religious, racial, or ideological divisions, that can weaken worker unity.

In Sweden and other Scandinavian countries, such power amplifiers proved able not only to unify the urban working class but also to form broader alliances with other political elements, notably agrarian parties, and thereby generate sufficient political support to pass the comprehensive social welfare protections sought by labor interests. In New Zealand, however, after an initial, unsuccessful push for radical economic reforms, New Zealand's

Labour Party opted to pursue more modest objectives and less comprehensive social welfare protections. What is more, in the 1980s the Labour Party took a more dramatic turn to the right and introduced sweeping neoliberal reforms, known as "Rogernomics" (after Minister of Finance Roger Douglas), that drastically reduced social spending, shifted the focus of the economy from manufacturing to finance, and put heavy reliance on market competition as a policy tool. These policies were continued by the right-wing National Party in the early 1990s, resulting in the establishment of a liberal pattern in New Zealand. As will be argued in more detail later in this chapter, these political decisions of the Labour Party resulted from multiple factors, including the lack of unity between urban and rural voters, the affluence and significant prospects for upward mobility that New Zealand society offered, and, later, the pressures arising from the growing integration of New Zealand into the global economy.

But first, let us establish the contours of the New Zealand civil society sector. We can then assess whether the social origins theory can help us explain the phenomena we identify.

Dimensions of the New Zealand Civil Society Sector

SIZE OF THE WORKFORCE

The civil society sector is a sizeable component of the New Zealand economy. As of 2004, the latest year for which data are available, civil society organizations in New Zealand employed nearly 67,000 paid full-time-equivalent (FTE) workers, representing over 3.3 percent of total employment. In addition, these organizations engaged the equivalent of another 134,000 FTE volunteer workers, bringing the total workforce of civil society sector organizations in New Zealand to over 200,000 FTE workers, or about 9.6 percent of the country's economically active population (EAP).

Figure 8.1 gauges the size of the civil society sector's workforce in New Zealand against that of four major industries: agriculture and fishing, manufacturing, construction, and transportation. As this figure shows, at 200,000 FTE workers, the civil society workforce in New Zealand is second in size only to that of manufacturing (over 295,000 employees) and exceeds employment in construction (153,000), agriculture and fishing (150,000), and transportation (121,000).

The civil society sector in New Zealand is sizable not only in relation to other components of the national economy but also in relation to civil society

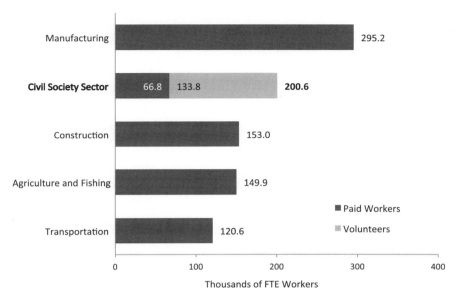

FIGURE 8.1. FTE workforce, civil society sector vs. selected industries, New Zealand, 2004.

sectors in other countries. The workforce of the civil society sector in New Zealand (at 9.6 percent of the EAP) ranks among the highest, significantly exceeding the 41-country average of 5.7 percent of the EAP (see table 8.1).

This characteristic of New Zealand's civil society sector falls within the range defining the liberal country model (6.8 percent of the EAP or more). As shown in table 8.1, the size of the civil society sector in New Zealand is identical to the liberal pattern average of 9.6 percent.

VOLUNTEER PARTICIPATION

As noted above, volunteers in New Zealand contributed the equivalent of 134,000 full-time jobs to civil society organizations, which accounts for about two-thirds (67 percent) of the civil society workforce (33 percent are paid employees).

This share of volunteer input in New Zealand is significantly higher than the 41-country average of 41 percent (table 8.2) and closer to the average for the social-democratic cluster (70 percent) than to the liberal one with which it otherwise shares many features.

TABLE 8.1   Civil society sector workforce
as share of EAP, New Zealand vs. country
clusters and 41-country average

Cluster	Workforce as a share of EAP (%)
New Zealand	**9.6**
41 countries	5.7
Traditional	1.9
Liberal	9.6
Welfare partnership	11.2
Social democratic	8.2
Statist	2.3

TABLE 8.2   Volunteer share of CSS workforce,
New Zealand vs. country clusters and 41-country
average

Cluster	Volunteers as a share of CSS workforce (%)
New Zealand	**66.7**
41 countries	40.6
Traditional	53.1
Liberal	46.4
Welfare partnership	29.1
Social democratic	69.4
Statist	27.9

SERVICE AND EXPRESSIVE ACTIVITIES

In New Zealand the share of the CSO workforce engaged in service and expressive activities as of 2004 was split almost equally (46 and 45 percent, respectively), as table 8.3 shows.[1] The field with the largest share of employment is culture, sports, and recreation, which employs about 25 percent of the sector's entire workforce. Advocacy, another expressive function, accounted for an additional 16 percent of sector employment, bringing the total in expressive functions, once religion and professions are added, to 45 percent. Service functions, led by education and research and social services, accounted for an almost identical 46 percent of the workforce.

TABLE 8.3 Distribution of New Zealand's CSS workforce, by field, 2004

Field	Share (%)
Service fields	46
Education and research	16
Social services	16
Health care	8
Economic development	7
Expressive fields	45
Culture, sports, and recreation	25
Religion	3
Advocacy	16
Professional associations and labor unions	1
Environmental protection	0.3
Other fields	9
Philanthropic intermediaries	0.2
International	0.2
Not elsewhere classified	8
N	200,605

TABLE 8.4 Distribution of CSS workforce by type of function, New Zealand vs. country clusters and 41-country average

Cluster	Share of CSS workforce, by type of function* (%)		
	Service	Expressive	Other
New Zealand	**46**	**45**	**9**
41 countries	59	37	4
Traditional	68	24	8
Liberal	55	36	9
Welfare partnership	71	25	4
Social democratic	39	59	2
Statist	50	47	4

*Figures may not add to 100% due to rounding.

In this respect as well, the New Zealand civil society sector diverges from the average for other liberal-cluster countries. Thus, as shown in table 8.4, compared to the 46-percent share of the New Zealand civil society sector (CSS) workforce engaged in service activities, the average for the civil society sectors in the liberal cluster was 55 percent. Only one other cluster of countries had a lower level of civil society workforce involvement in service functions—that is, those in the social democratic cluster.

The total revenue of the civil society sector in New Zealand in 2004 was over NZ$8 billion (US$4.9 billion), of which government payments accounted for 25 percent[2] and private donations 20 percent.[3] The remaining 55 percent of civil society sector income in New Zealand is derived from fees that civil society organizations receive for goods and services provided to beneficiaries, as shown in table 8.5.

A revenue structure like New Zealand's, which is dominated by fee income, with modest levels of government support and sizable levels of philanthropic support, is typical of countries exhibiting the liberal model of civil society development. In fact, New Zealand's level of government support, at 25 percent, is considerably smaller than the liberal average of 33 percent, as table 8.6 reveals. One reason for this relatively low government share of total CSS revenue in New Zealand is the relatively large proportion of the civil society sector involved in expressive activities, which derive 65 percent of their income, on average, from fees and philanthropy, while government support accounts for only 6 percent (table 8.5). In the key service fields of health care and social services, however, the government share of civil

TABLE 8.5   Sources of New Zealand's CSS revenue by field, 2004

Field	Government (%)	Philanthropy (%)	Fees (%)
All fields	25	20	55
Service fields	49	13	38
Health care	67	12	21
Education and research	40	8	51
Social services	48	16	36
Economic development	29	24	47
Expressive fields	6	29	65
Environmental protection	25	13	62
Culture, sports, and recreation	8	22	70
Religion	1	71	28
Professional associations and labor unions	4	2	94
Advocacy	7	8	85
Other fields	2	15	82
Philanthropic intermediaries	0	6	94
International	9	72	19
Not elsewhere classified	13	40	48

TABLE 8.6   Shares of CSS revenue by source, New Zealand vs. country clusters and 41-country average*

Cluster	Government (%)	Philanthropy (%)	Fees (%)
New Zealand	25	20	55
41 countries	*35*	*14*	*50*
Traditional	11	24	65
Liberal	33	14	53
Welfare partnership	66	8	26
Social democratic	38	10	52
Statist	18	18	64

*Figures may not add to 100% due to rounding.

society revenue stood at 67 and 48 percent, respectively, close to welfare partnership levels.

SUMMARY

In sum, New Zealand's civil society sector exhibits many of the defining features of the liberal model of civil society development, including a large civil society workforce and a revenue structure characterized by relatively limited government support and a considerable share of philanthropic giving. However, the findings presented above also reveal a sector using a relatively large proportion of volunteers and relatively heavily engaged in expressive activities, both of which bring it close to the ranges defining the social democratic pattern. This demonstrates that New Zealand is not a typical case of the liberal pattern and challenges us to see whether the social origins theory can account for this somewhat deviant case.

Explaining the Unexpected Dimensions of the New Zealand CSS

THE BRITISH COLONIAL PERIOD: PLANTING THE SEEDS[4]

New Zealand became a colony of Great Britain in 1840 as a result of the Treaty of Waitangi between the British Crown and the indigenous Māori chiefs. The treaty established British sovereignty over the island and recognized Māori ownership of their land and their rights as British subjects. The colonization of New Zealand also initially created the social, legal, and political conditions for the development of Anglo-settler paradigms of the nonprofit sector. New Zealand was a relatively late addition to the Anglo-settler world, and the "associational revolution" which had started in Britain and Europe in the late 18th century was in full swing when Europeans, mostly British, started to migrate to the colony in significant numbers. The settlers were well acquainted with voluntary associations of various kinds, although local circumstances gave a special flavor to the associational mix as it emerged in the new colony.

New Zealand drew on English common law precedent in providing a facilitative legal environment for the nonprofit sector. Historically, government regulation of the sector was relatively light-handed despite early state financial aid to parts of the sector. The first pieces of legislation were intended to simplify the titles to land held in trust for charitable purposes, to facilitate the receipt of government subsidies, and, in the case of the 1908 Incorporated Societies Act, to protect funds and property for nonprofit organizations. It was relatively easy to obtain the privileged tax status associated with charitable entities, and the few laws governing nonprofit organizations that existed were loosely enforced.

The rapid growth of the New Zealand population throughout the second half of the 19th century, together with advances in communication and transportation, also fostered the emergence of numerous voluntary associations formed by the European settlers. These included not only charitable and welfare organizations but also political associations. These developments fostered the formation of national political parties, beginning with the Liberal Party in 1887, the farmer-dominated Reform Party in 1909, and the Labour Party in 1916.[5]

Unlike in Great Britain, however, the power of landowners was kept in check by the constitution approved by the British colonial government and by subsequent expansions of the franchise under settler governments.[6] These developments created favorable conditions not only for the quick ascendance of organized labor but also for a robust growth of civil society organizations, particularly labor unions, which developed rapidly in the late 19th and early 20th centuries. The number of unions rose from 50 in 1888 to 200 in 1890, with a possible 20-fold increase in membership.[7] By 1913, New Zealand was among the most unionized countries in the world, and some 15,000 of its 70,000 unionists had an affiliation with the radical Federation of Labour,[8] which was strongly influenced by socialist ideas. Unions partnering with the Labour Party became a rapidly growing political force in

New Zealand and formed an increasingly powerful Labour group in the parliament.

LABOUR'S STRATEGIC CHOICE:
STATE-CIVIL SOCIETY PARTNERSHIPS

These structural conditions—the relative weakness of landed elites and the growing power of Socialist-influenced labor organizations—somewhat resembled those seen in Sweden's development (see chapter 5). However, there were also significant differences. The chief among them was the relative affluence of New Zealand in comparison to European countries at that time. Workers received significantly higher wages than their counterparts in Great Britain and enjoyed much better working conditions. As one observer noted: "This is a glorious country for a labouring man!!! No starvation, no fear, no poor law union, high wages, short hours, infinite grazing for cows."[9] Second, New Zealand offered great opportunities for upward mobility. The New Zealand bourgeoisie was composed almost exclusively of people who rose from the ranks of workers, farmers, and artisans. Most of them were working proprietors heavily involved in the running of farms or businesses.[10] As a consequence, the demand for social protections to ameliorate the negative aspects of capitalist development was relatively muted in New Zealand. This does not mean, of course, that there was no labor unrest, but the demands of organized labor were more limited, focusing on better working conditions and higher wages.

The event that helped shape future union activity was a major strike in 1912 by gold miners in the town of Waihi, which exposed a rift between radical and moderate factions in the nascent labor movement. The strike pitted these two factions against each other, leading to violent clashes and eventual intervention by the police that killed one radical trade unionist. In the aftermath, there was a push toward bridging this split in the labor movement, as a result of which the Socialist Party, which supported the strike, and the moderate United Labour Party, which did not, merged into the Social Democratic Party, which later was transformed into the modern New Zealand Labour Party. The merger moderated the positions of labor unions and the organizations representing them.

A similar pivotal event also helped shape the political posture of the Labour Party. After winning a relatively small number of parliamentary seats in 1919, Labour boldly introduced a so-called usehold policy measure, which sought to eliminate land speculation by nationalizing New Zealand's farmland and making it available to citizens on perpetual leases from the state. This policy proved unpopular with voters, however, which resulted in an electoral setback for the Labour Party in the 1925 election. This loss fundamentally changed the balance of power within the Labour Party and allowed the moderate factions to gain the upper hand.[11]

In the face of this setback, the Labour Party made a strategic choice to abandon the usehold policy and pursue instead a more conciliatory and partner-like relationship between the state and the private sector while implementing social protection programs. In 1938, the first Labour government passed the Social Security Act, which vastly expanded the social safety net, bringing it more in line with the welfare partnership model but not fully nationalizing health care and social services, as in countries that implemented the social democratic model. Hospital services were provided for free through a mixture of public and private providers, hence the substantial government share of nonprofit health care organization revenue identified earlier. Primary and secondary education were free in state schools, and higher education was provided mostly through public universities. Fees were charged to those attending the country's four university colleges, though after 1937, students passing (or accredited with) the national university entrance examination gained free tuition for four years. In sum, despite the expansion of public welfare programs, this policy course provided room for the private nonprofit sector in the delivery of social welfare services.

The elaboration of the welfare state was initially reinforced by World War II regulations and by a strong post-war emphasis on centralized planning. Nonprofits continued to be active in partnering with key government agencies in specialized fields, however, demonstrating how a strong state and a flourishing nonprofit sector could co-exist and complement each other. The relatively small size of the country intensified the influence of government departments but also gave an intimacy and informality to their dealings with nonprofit organizations, especially within the social service sector. Consequently, many organizations gained, and retained, government financial support that included both direct grants and contracts as well as subsidies via the national lottery, which came under the direction of the Department of Internal Affairs. For example, beginning in 1950, the Department of Health provided subsidies to religious and secular nonprofit welfare organizations willing to provide residential care for the elderly, a deliberate attempt to reduce public-sector involvement in this area. Funding from the Department of Justice in the late 1950s and 1960s similarly rejuvenated welfare organizations, such as Marriage Guidance or Prisoners' Aid and Rehabilitation, giving them a mandate to experiment and undertake new activities on the government's behalf.[12]

GROWTH OF EXPRESSIVE ORGANIZATIONS
AND MĀORI GROUPS[13]

In addition to their service functions, New Zealand nonprofit organizations also engaged heavily in a variety of expressive functions. Organizations promoting women's suffrage emerged in 1885, followed by the establishment of women's leagues and temperance organizations,[14] which led to massive national petitions in support of women's franchise.[15] Largely as a result of such activity, New Zealand became the first nation to enfranchise women in September 1893. Beyond these political activities, nationally organized recreational and sporting associations emerged in the late 19th century. These expressive associations were extremely popular and attracted tens of thousands of members.

A significant force behind the development of organizations engaged in expressive activities in New Zealand was the growing political awareness of the Māori population striving to preserve its cultural identity. Over the course of the 19th century, the Māori developed new institutions that drew upon settler political and organizational forms, though these organizations remained distinctively Māori in nature, connected by family ties and tribal affinities. These included such pan-tribal movements as the Kingitanga or King movement, formed in the late 1850s; Paremata Māori, or the Māori Parliament, established in 1882; and the Young Māori Party, which grew out of the Te Aute College Students' Association, formed in 1892.[16] The first two were formed as "parallel and equal authorities to the settler parliament," aiming for some degree of constitutional autonomy for the Māori.[17] This tendency to constructively borrow and translate settler organizational forms to meet Māori ends has continued into the 21st century.

The expansion of expressive activities accelerated in the 1970s when various social movements, such as the feminist, disabled persons, senior citizen, peace, and Māori civil rights movements, formed advocacy organizations. This expansion of expressive activities is reminiscent of the developments in the social democratic model, which the CSS in New Zealand resembles. Another characteristic element of the social democratic model observed in New Zealand is the high level of volunteer participation, chiefly as a result of the expansion of expressive activities, which absorb 57 percent of the volunteer staff effort.[18]

EXPANSION OF NEOLIBERAL POLICIES

What seems to have pushed the New Zealand civil society sector across the line from being a hybrid liberal and welfare partnership model of civil society development toward a much more overt liberal model was the rightward shift that its Labour Party took in the 1980s in response to a financial crisis resulting from a hike in the costs of government borrowing and an unfavorable shift in the exchange rate for its currency. In response, the Labour Party's Minister of Finance, Roger Douglas, pushed through sweeping neoliberal reforms, drastically cutting social spending, shifting from direct subsidies to service providers to market-based vouchers provided to beneficiaries, and instituting a series of other "new public management" reforms into the government bureaucracy.[19] This radical policy shift was possible due to a centralized political system and limited constitutional checks on the executive but was very unpopular among the rank and file. As a result, Labour lost to the center-right National Party in the 1990 election for the first time since 1935.

But ironically, the National Party continued and expanded the neoliberal policy course. As a consequence, a massive restructuring of the public service took place, undermining long-standing relationships between government departments and nonprofit organizations and removing many officials with knowledge of the voluntary and community sector. By the late 1980s, relatively short-term and fiercely negotiated purchase-of-service contracts replaced direct grants as the dominant mechanism for government funding of the nonprofit sector.[20] In the process, key features of the still-salient welfare-partnership pattern began to be squeezed out, and important features of the liberal model, such as heavier dependence on philanthropy, moved to the fore.

Conclusions

New Zealand's nonprofit sector thus started out in classic liberal fashion, embodying key features imparted by the British origins of its early settlers. In short order, however, the New Zealand civil society sector took on features more characteristic of the welfare partnership and social democratic patterns, particularly their reliance on significant government funding, before ending up in the liberal pattern, thanks to a sharp policy turn of its Labour Party toward a set of neoliberal policies in response to exchange rate challenges threatening the island nation's economy.

The social origins theory helps us understand this hybrid story by focusing attention on two significant sets of factors: first, the balance of power among key social classes; and second, the way in which various power amplifiers and power diffusers affect how social class power is organized, articulated, and translated into concrete social action. So far as the first is concerned, what is especially notable about the New Zealand case is the significant strength of organized labor. Elsewhere, this factor has often led to a social democratic pattern. But in New Zealand, labor stopped well short of such an outcome and ended up with something closer to a welfare partnership pattern instead, and even this outcome was set back on its heels in recent years by a sharp rightward turn in labor's own political party under pressure from international financial markets.

That labor's power was somewhat blunted in this way has much to do with the way its power amplifiers, its unions and its political party, responded to a set of failed initiatives early in the twentieth century. One of these was the disruptive strike that made significant elements of the labor movement skittish about direct industrial action. The other was the failed attempt to nationalize the land, which likely left the Labour Party skittish about insisting on total nationalization of social welfare provision. Also at work, in all likelihood, were the opportunities for upward mobility in New Zealand society, which may have inclined workers to accept a more gradualist approach. Labour was able to push for significant public funding of social welfare provision but not for complete government takeover of social welfare delivery; the latter was left much more fully in the hands of private, nonprofit groups. And by the 1980s, an increasingly middle-class society was willing to see some of these protections whittled away as conservative pro-business forces took over the reins of government and pushed through a sharp neoliberal agenda that put new strains on the nonprofit partner in this welfare partnership package.

Notes

This study was possible thanks to the effort of a group of researchers at the Massey University in New Zealand—Jackie Sanders, Margaret Tennant, and Mike O'Brien. The research draws heavily on this country's first *Non-Profit Institutions Satellite*

Account: 2004 produced by Statistics New Zealand in August 2007. The research was carried out following the methodology developed by the Johns Hopkins Center for Civil Society Studies and outlined in the United Nations *Handbook on Non-Profit Institutions in the System of National Accounts.*

1. Volunteer input was estimated from a time use survey that used an activity classification system different from that used for employment data. While there is some correspondence between these two systems, it was not possible to report volunteering data at the same level of detail as paid employment. However, the distinction between volunteering in service and expressive activities could be rendered with reasonable accuracy.

2. This is a conservative estimate of the government share of civil society income developed by Statistics New Zealand. This estimate undercounts the full extent of government contracts for services to civil society organizations in the health care field due to limited available data.

3. The actual share of private donations may be somewhat lower due to the peculiar treatment of membership dues in the System of National Accounts (SNA), which is the source of these data. Under SNA rules, dues are treated as fees if they are paid to business-serving NPIs but as donations if they are paid to household-serving NPIs. By contrast, the Johns Hopkins Center for Civil Society Studies methodology uniformly treats dues as fees. The size of the discrepancy due to these methodological differences is unknown at this time, but it does not alter the fact that the share of philanthropic support in New Zealand is one of the largest among Organisation for Economic Co-Operation and Development countries.

4. This section draws heavily on Sanders et al. 2008.

5. Richardson 1992; Dalziel 1993.

6. Rueschemeyer, Stephens, and Stephens 1992.

7. Roth 1973, 10.

8. Belich 2001, 145; Olssen 1988, 107, 217.

9. Quoted in Phillips 2012, 3.

10. *Ibid.,* 2.

11. http://www.teara.govt.nz/en/1966/political-parties/8, retrieved June 6, 2013.

12. Tennant 2007, 217–218.

13. This section draws heavily on Sanders et al. 2008.

14. Dalziel 1993, 55.

15. Grimshaw 1987, 117–118.

16. Durie 2005, 16.

17. Cheyne, O'Brien, and Belgrave 2005, 29.

18. Sanders et al. 2008.

19. Miller 2005; Harvey 2007.

20. Nowland-Foreman 1997.

CHAPTER NINE

Australia

A Liberal Model in Spite of Itself

MARK LYONS, S. WOJCIECH SOKOLOWSKI,
and LESTER M. SALAMON

THE AUSTRALIAN CIVIL society sector (CSS) represents a classic example of the liberal pattern of civil society development, with a large CSS workforce, a relatively small share of government support, and a pronounced presence of private philanthropy in its revenue structure. This is a somewhat challenging case for the social origins theory, however, given the country's history of relatively strong organized labor and rather weak landed upper classes, since such a set of conditions is conducive to the social democratic pattern of civil society development. How do we reconcile the development of the liberal pattern with the relatively strong position of labor in Australia's national politics?

The answer to this question lies in the social origins theory's recognition of the role that intermediaries, or power amplifiers, play in articulating and pursuing class interests. In particular, the chapter will suggest that the liberal cast to CSS development in Australia was significantly shaped by the policy course pursued by the organizations representing the labor movement. The high point of labor strength came in 1910 with the election of the first Labour government, which promptly implemented a wide range of pro-labor policy measures, including social security, old-age and disability pensions, improved working conditions including a maternity allowance, and workers compensation, among others. However, the Labour Party was internally split between radical and conservative factions, and the conservative factions split from the Labour Party and joined forces with liberal, anti-socialist, and nationalist elements, enabling the latter to control the national government in Australia throughout most of the 20th century. The remnants of the Labour Party therefore had little choice but to focus on reformist policies favoring higher wages over social protections. This contrasts with the developments in Sweden and Denmark, where labor was not only internally unified but also formed a coalition with agrarian parties to demand a wide range of social reforms consistent with the socialist ideal. Australia's position in the liberal country cluster was further solidified when the Labour Party's wage policy was eventually significantly eroded by the rise of neoliberalism in the 1980s.

Dimensions of the Australian Civil Society Sector

SIZE OF THE WORKFORCE

That the Australian civil society sector exhibits features characteristic of the liberal pattern is evident from an examination of the sector's major dimensions. In the first place, this sector is quite sizable by international standards. As of 2007, the latest year for which data are available, Australian civil society organizations accounted for 948,000 full-time equivalent (FTE) workers, or about 8.8 percent of the country's economically active population (EAP). Of these 948,000 FTE workers, approximately 631,000 were paid workers, and another 317,000 were volunteers.[1]

Figure 9.1 compares the size of the Australian civil society sector's workforce to that of four key Australian industries: agriculture and fishing, manufacturing, construction, and transportation. As this figure shows, the civil society workforce in Australia, with 948,000 FTE workers, is second only to manufacturing, which employs 1.1 million people, and exceeds employment in the construction, transportation, and agriculture and fishing industries.

The civil society sector in Australia is sizable not only in relation to other components of the Australian economy, however, but also in relation to civil society sectors in other countries. Measured as a share of the EAP, the workforce of the Australian civil society sector in 2007, at 8.8 percent, ranked well above the 41-country average of 5.7 percent (see table 9.1). But this puts Australia somewhat below her neighbor, New Zealand, at 9.6 percent, as well as below other English-speaking countries classified in the liberal pattern—Canada (12.3 percent), the United Kingdom (11 percent), and the United States (9.2 percent)—though within the range defining the liberal pattern (6.8 percent of EAP or more). As shown in table 9.1, as a share of the overall economically active population, the Australian civil society sector workforce falls between the liberal and the social democratic pattern averages (9.6 and 8.2 percent, respectively).

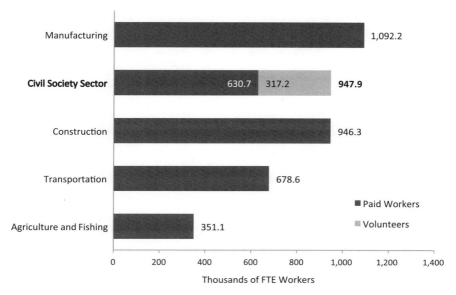

FIGURE 9.1. FTE workforce, civil society sector vs. selected industries, Australia, 2007.

TABLE 9.1   Civil society sector workforce as share of EAP, Australia vs. country clusters and 41-country average

Cluster	Workforce as a share of EAP (%)
Australia	8.8
41 countries	5.7
Traditional	1.9
Liberal	9.6
Welfare partnership	11.2
Social democratic	8.2
Statist	2.3

Though it remains somewhat smaller in comparison to other countries in the liberal cluster, it is worth noting that the civil society sector in Australia is a growing force. A comparison of the 2007 figures to those generated through the Johns Hopkins Comparative Nonprofit Sector Project in 1995 shows that the civil society workforce in Australia grew by 40 percent between 1995 and 2007 (on average, 2.8 percent annually), nearly twice as fast as the growth of total employment in the Australian economy during that same period.[2] As will be examined more fully below, this significant growth is likely a result in important part of a recent policy shift that has been pushing public welfare service delivery from government to the private nonprofit sector.

VOLUNTEER PARTICIPATION

The volunteer share of the civil society workforce in Australia, at 34 percent of the CSS workforce, is well below the 41-country average of 41 percent, as table 9.2 shows.

Such a low volunteer share of the civil society workforce in Australia is probably a result of the faster growth of paid employment in the sector caused by the public policy shift mentioned earlier involving increased government reliance on nonprofits to deliver public services. Interestingly, in 1995 volunteers accounted for 39 percent of the civil society workforce in Australia,[3] suggesting that increases in volunteer participation in the subsequent years simply did not keep up with the growth of paid employment.

SERVICE AND EXPRESSIVE ACTIVITIES

As measured by the shares of the workforce they engage, services dominate CSS activities in Australia, engaging about 57 percent of the CSS workforce

TABLE 9.2   Volunteer share of CSS workforce, Australia vs. country clusters and 41-country average

Cluster	Volunteers as a share of CSS workforce (%)
Australia	33.5
41 countries	*40.6*
Traditional	53.1
Liberal	46.4
Welfare partnership	29.1
Social democratic	69.4
Statist	27.9

TABLE 9.3 Distribution of Australia's CSS
workforce, by field, 2007

Field	Share (%)
Service fields	57
Education and research	18
Social services	25
Health care	14
Economic development	57
Expressive fields	25
Culture, sports, and recreation	20
Religion	3
Professional associations and labor unions	2
Other fields	18
N	947,923

TABLE 9.4 Distribution of CSS workforce by type of function, Australia vs. country clusters and 41-country average

Cluster	Share of CSS workforce, by type of function* (%)		
	Service	Expressive	Other
Australia	57	25	18
41 countries	59	37	4
Traditional	68	24	8
Liberal	55	36	9
Welfare partnership	71	25	4
Social democratic	39	59	2
Statist	50	47	4

*Figures may not add to 100% due to rounding.

(paid and volunteer) as of 2007, with social services representing the largest of the service fields (25 percent), as table 9.3 shows.

By comparison, expressive and other activities employ a considerably smaller 43 percent of the CSS workforce in Australia, with culture, sports, and recreation alone accounting for 20 percent. In both respects, this puts Australia's civil society sector close to the 41-country average and closest overall to the liberal pattern of the five clusters examined, even though it is above the liberal pattern in terms of the service share of the civil society workforce and below it in terms of the expressive share, as table 9.4 shows.

The total revenue generated by the civil society sector in Australia was about 76 billion Australian Dollars (US$59.8 billion) in 2007. As seen in table 9.5, fees account for 57 percent of CSS revenue in Australia, government support for 34 percent, and philanthropy for about 10 percent.[4]

This revenue structure, particularly the relatively low share of government support, puts Australia firmly within the range defining the liberal cluster of countries, as table 9.6 shows.

TABLE 9.5 Sources of Australia's CSS revenue by field, 2007

Field	Government (%)	Philanthropy (%)	Fees (%)
All fields	34	10	57
Service fields	51	3	46
Health care	47	2	51
Education and research	51	3	45
Social services	55	4	41
Expressive fields	7	13	80
Culture, sports, and recreation	7	9	84
Religion	7	38	55
Professional associations and labor unions	7	2	91
Other fields	26	20	54
Not elsewhere classified	26	20	54

TABLE 9.6 Shares of CSS revenue by source, Australia vs. country clusters and 41-country average*

Cluster	Government (%)	Philanthropy (%)	Fees (%)
Australia	**34**	**10**	**57**
41 countries	*35*	*14*	*50*
Traditional	11	24	65
Liberal	33	14	53
Welfare partnership	66	8	26
Social democratic	38	10	52
Statist	18	18	64

*Figures may not add to 100% due to rounding.

SUMMARY

In sum, the picture that emerges from these findings is that the Australian civil society sector most closely resembles the liberal pattern found in the other English-speaking countries covered by this study. This pattern is characterized by a fairly large civil society sector, relatively low levels of volunteer participation, and a dominance of service activities—all of these characteristics shared by the Australian civil society sector. Further, the other two characteristics of the liberal pattern are also clearly evident in Australia: a relatively low share of government support, at least by developed country standards, and high shares of fee income and private philanthropy in CSS revenue, though the latter was less pronounced in Australia than in the liberal cluster countries as a whole. This set of characteristics has remained relatively stable, moreover, over the 11-year period between 1995 and 2007 on which data are available, even though the civil society sector grew considerably faster than the economy as a whole during this time period.

Explaining Australia's Pattern of Civil Society Development

At first blush, the liberal outcome portrayed above seems to lend credence to the sentiment theory of nonprofit development about which we raised serious reservations in chapter 3. After all, the settlers who occupied Australia were refugees from Great Britain who could be expected to have brought with them the same Protestant sentiments of thrift, hard work, and private charity that created the liberal pattern in the United Kingdom. A closer look at the Australian developments suggests, however, that something more complicated than this simple cultural explanation was at work, though in ways that pose a paradox for the social origins theory. This paradox arises from the fact that the social origins theory links the emergence of a liberal pattern of civil society development to cases where urban commercial and industrial elements are in the ascendance. Yet in Australia, it was the labor elements that were in the ascendance through much of the formative period of the Australian civil society sector, a situation that the social origins theory links to the emergence of a social democratic pattern of civil society development.

How can we unravel this paradox, and to what extent can the social origins theory itself contribute to this understanding? The answer is that the social origins theory recognizes that the existence of an economic class does not automatically ensure that the class will recognize its interests and prove capable of acting on them. Rather, there are intervening factors, including particularly the institutions through which class interests are articulated and promoted, which we have termed power amplifiers. The agenda-setting role of these institutions is affected by the degree of unity within the social groupings that support them, the particular power balance that exists among any factions that emerge, and the environmental challenges these organizations face. From the evidence at hand, it appears that this set of dynamics explains the liberal outcome in Australia. Let us look briefly at this evidence.

THE BRITISH COLONIAL PERIOD: EARLY LIBERAL STIRRINGS

Like the other English-speaking countries, modern Australia was born out of colonization of the New World lands by the British. As a British penal colony, Australia initially developed a labor-repressive agricultural economy based on large sheep estates and convict labor. However, landed oligarchs never gained control of political institutions due to the strong presence of lower-class elements (small landholders, ex-convicts, and urban working and middle classes) and the British Crown's control of the colonial state.[5] As a consequence, the landed elite was not a serious countervailing force to the growth of a robust labor movement and a significant urban middle class.

In the mid-19th century, Britain granted Australians limited self-governance (mostly elected legislative councils) but retained control of the colonial government and of land administration. The colonial government reproduced British political institutions favoring protection of private property and democratic governance, which increased the political power of the commercial and industrial middle classes and small farmers.

This limited self-governance produced intense competition among various interest groups for influence in the colonial government, with the British colonial authorities acting as mediator. This in turn solidified the influence of moderate liberal elements and created a favorable climate for the formation of private associations and self-help groups to provide social services and insurance against illness or catastrophic events, and to organize recreational and athletic activities.

THE RISE OF ORGANIZED LABOR

A strong labor movement emerged in Australia in the 1880s. Following the British tradition, the early labor movement in Australia developed a network of self-help associations (the so-called friendly societies, building societies, and credit associations) to provide their members with support and social assistance in case of sickness or unemployment. After the formation of the Commonwealth of Australia in 1901, the push to organize labor led to substantial gains in union membership. In response, the government passed the Conciliation and Arbitration Act of 1904, which mandated union registration and arbitration of labor disputes. This act, which regulated labor relations in Australia until the 1990s, gave a clear advantage to smaller shop- and trade-specific unions pursuing limited demands over larger industrial unions that espoused more radical political goals.

The labor movement also turned to direct political activity, and in 1910, the Labour Party secured its first electoral victory. This Labour government promptly implemented a wide range of pro-labor policy measures, including social security, old-age and disability pensions, improved working conditions including a maternity allowance and workers compensation, the initiation of large public works (e.g., construction of the Trans-Australian Railway), the creation of the government-owned Commonwealth Bank of Australia, breaking up land monopolies, regulation of working hours and conditions, and labor legislation allowing a greater role for industrial unions in labor-management disputes.

However, the labour movement was internally divided between radical and conservative factions, with the radicals favoring strikes and other forms of direct industrial action and the conservative factions favoring more narrow bread-and-butter wage and hour negotiations. The onset of World War I provided the impetus for a split, as the radical elements sided with the rank and file workers in opposing conscription and Australian support for the British war effort, provoking the conservative faction to split from the Labour Party in 1916 and join forces with the liberal, anti-socialist, and nationalist elements in the Australian Liberal Party. This plus the limited success of direct industrial action marginalized the more radical unionists, while mainstream trade unions, which enjoyed a legal advantage under the Conciliation and Arbitration Act, never advanced beyond limited demands for wage increases. As a result, labor remained a relatively conservative force in Australia, the Labour Party was weakened, and nationalist or liberal parties controlled the national government throughout most of the 20th century, with only brief interludes of Labour control.

This contrasts sharply with the pattern that developed in the Scandinavian countries (e.g., Sweden) where the labor movement not only was more united internally but also formed a strong Socialist Party that forged a coalition with agrarian parties to pursue common political interests, especially implementation of wide-ranging social welfare measures. This explains why, despite having a relatively strong organized labor movement and relatively weak upper classes, Australia did not develop a social democratic pattern as did countries where labor was more united and able to form broader coalitions with organizations representing other socioeconomic classes.

THE INFLUENCE OF NEOLIBERALISM ON CIVIL SOCIETY IN AUSTRALIA

While the liberal pattern in Australia was never seriously challenged, Labour did succeed in forming majority governments on three occasions when significant events turned public opinion its way (1929–1932, 1941–1949, and 1972–1975). But the rise of neoliberalism in the 1980s and its push toward undermining the welfare state turned back much of whatever gains the Labour governments achieved, as both national and state governments in Australia adopted neoliberal policy orientations in an attempt to limit the influence of trade unions and redefine the delivery of social services. Thus, the Liberal/National Party coalition governments (1977–1983 and 1996–2007) introduced sweeping changes to employment laws that significantly reduced the capacity of workers to bargain collectively. In the area of social services, these governments moved toward replacing direct support to nonprofits with purchase-of-service contracts that required nonprofits to bid competitively for new contracts. This intensified competition from the for-profit sector, especially in the fields that depend to a significant degree on service fees (e.g., child care).

On the other hand, since its election in 1996, the conservative Liberal/National Party government, in contrast to its ideological principles favoring a free market, has adopted a policy of government-nonprofit partnership characteristic of the welfare partnership model. It encouraged the growth of nonprofit schools at the expense of government schools, which are fully funded and operated by state governments, and increased subsidies to nonprofit schools as a compromise to placate Labour's opposition to for-profit companies opening schools and obtaining government subsidies.

More generally, the neoliberal policy thrust has included encouragement of nonprofit-business partnerships in several service fields, the formation of a Prime Minister's Community Business Partnership encouraging business partnerships with social service nonprofits, and a number of small changes to laws and regulations to facilitate and encourage giving to nonprofits by high-income and high-wealth individuals. As a result, philanthropic donations to nonprofits, one of the signature characteristics of the liberal pattern, have been growing in this recent period.

Conclusion

Australia represents an interesting case for the social origins theory advanced in this book, because it developed a liberal pattern of CSS development even though the working class remained a significant economic and political force throughout most of the 20th century. But the power amplifying institutions that the social origins theory acknowledges must be in place to yield a social democratic pattern of civil society development were seriously fragmented along ideological and tactical grounds in Australia, significantly diminishing working-class power and influence. As a result, the Labour Party was unable to achieve the social democratic policy objectives that countries with more united labor movements implemented, advantaging more economically and politically conservative groupings and yielding a liberal pattern instead.

Notes

The 2007 data presented in this report come from the Non-Profit Institutions Satellite Account produced by the Australian Bureau of Statistics, available online at www .abs.gov.au/AusStats/ABS@.nsf/MF/5256.0. This chapter was prepared by S. Wojciech Sokolowski and Lester M. Salamon based on the input provided by Australian professor Mark Lyons before his untimely death.

1. Volunteer workers, part-time workers, and casual workers are transformed into "full-time equivalent workers" by estimating the average number of hours they work in a typical year and dividing this by the average number of hours worked by a full-time employee in Australia.

2. For the earlier data, see Salamon, Anheier, List, et al. 1999.

3. Unpublished JHU/CCSS data.

4. This revenue structure has not substantially changed since comparable data were reported for 1995. In 1995, government support accounted for about 31.1 percent of total civil society sector revenue in Australia, philanthropy for 6.4 percent, and fees for 62.5 percent (unpublished JHU/CCSS data). Some of the differences between the 2007 and 1995 revenue structure may be due to methodological differences in data assembly.

5. The narrative presented here draws from Stephens and Stephens 1992, 135–140; Green and Cromwell 1984; and McKinlay 1979.

CHAPTER TEN

The Netherlands

A Classic Welfare Partnership Model

S. WOJCIECH SOKOLOWSKI *and* LESTER M. SALAMON

THE NETHERLANDS BOASTS an enormous civil society sector. Employing over 1.3 million full-time equivalent staff (paid and volunteers), the Dutch civil society sector employs nearly 16 percent of the total economically active population, making it the largest among the 43 countries studied by the Johns Hopkins Comparative Nonprofit Sector Project.[1] Nearly two-thirds of that workforce performs service functions such as health care delivery, education, and social assistance. On the surface, this can seem puzzling given the fact that the Netherlands is an affluent country that provides a rather generous package of publicly funded social welfare services to its population. Why has the civil society sector in this country become such a major player in the economy, and, more specifically, in the delivery of social and educational services? Are Dutch people more altruistic than those in other countries?

The social origins theory, outlined in chapter 4, offers an alternative explanation that can help us put the key pieces of this puzzle together. This theory directs our attention to the intense religious rivalry between Catholics and Protestants dating back to the 17th century in the Netherlands. As we pointed out in chapter 4, this conflict and competition between two major organized religious groups had two profound consequences for the institutional layout of the social service delivery system. First, each of these religious denominations created a separate system of schools and social-support organizations exclusively serving their respective coreligionists. Second, this religious pillarization divided organized labor into two, often hostile, camps, thus preventing the formation of a strong and united labor movement, as emerged in Sweden, where organized religion was weaker. As a result, demands for radical institutional changes to improve the living conditions of the working class were muted and, in some cases, resisted. Most notably, when the government proposed to create a system of free public education funded through general taxation, the two religious communities were up in arms, leading to a near-permanent split of the country that was avoided only by what came to be known as the "pacification"—a pivotal deal that set the model for all future social welfare programs by establishing a program of vouchers that paid the cost of elementary and secondary education for all children but left it up to parents whether their children attended government schools or private, nonprofit, sectarian ones. The upshot was a welfare partnership pattern of civil society development.

In the following sections, this chapter will first outline the key dimensions of this pattern as evidenced by the Netherlands case and then review in a bit more detail the power relations that support the social origins theory explanation of how these dimensions came about. In the conclusion, we will discuss the implications of these findings for understanding the role of the civil society sector in a modern society like the Netherlands.

Dimensions of the Dutch Civil Society Sector

SIZE OF THE WORKFORCE

Perhaps the most striking feature of the civil society sector in the Netherlands is its enormous size. Civil society organizations (CSOs) employed over 840,000 full-time equivalent (FTE) paid workers as of 2002, accounting for about 10.7 percent of total paid employment in the country. In addition, these organizations engaged nearly 479,000 FTE volunteers, bringing the total workforce of Dutch civil society sector organizations to over 1.3 million full-time equivalent workers, or 15.9 percent of the country's economically active population (EAP). As shown in figure 10.1, this exceeds employment in four of the country's major industries: agriculture and fishing, manufacturing, construction, and transportation.

The enormity of CSO capacity in the Netherlands becomes fully apparent when compared to other countries. The Netherlands has the largest civil society sector among the 43 countries covered by this study. In fact, measured as a share of the EAP, the Dutch CSO sector exceeds the 41-country average of 5.7 percent by a factor of nearly 3:1 (for a comparison of all 41 countries, see figure 2.7).

The size of the Dutch civil society sector is large even in comparison to other countries in the same welfare partnership cluster. As shown in table 10.1, the CSO sector workforce in this cluster accounts, on average, for 11.2 percent of EAP, substantially above any other cluster identified in

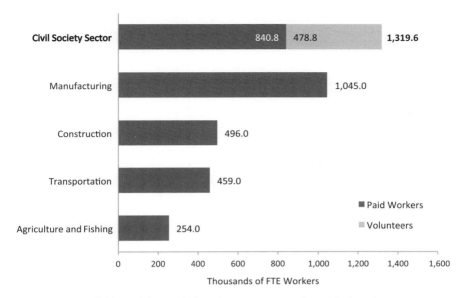

FIGURE 10.1. FTE workforce, civil society sector vs. selected industries, Netherlands, 2002.

TABLE 10.1   Civil society sector workforce as share of EAP, Netherlands vs. country clusters and 41-country average

Cluster	Workforce as a share of EAP (%)
The Netherlands	15.9
41 countries	5.7
Traditional	1.9
Liberal	9.6
Welfare partnership	11.2
Social democratic	8.2
Statist	2.3

the data. But the Netherlands' civil society sector, at 15.9 percent of EAP, is at the high end of even the welfare partnership cluster.

EXPRESSIVE AND SERVICE ACTIVITIES

As table 10.2 shows, most (64 percent) of the huge CSO workforce in the Netherlands is engaged in service activities, especially in the delivery of

TABLE 10.2   Distribution of the Dutch CSS workforce,
by field, 2002

Field	Share (%)
Service fields	64
Education and research	20
Social services	17
Health care	26
Economic development	1
Expressive fields	30
Culture, sports, and recreation	18
Religion	7
Advocacy	1
Professional associations and labor unions	2
Environmental protection	2
Other fields	6
Philanthropic intermediaries	4
International	2
N	1,319,587

health care (26 percent of the workforce), education (20 percent), and social services (17 percent). Expressive activities, in contrast, employ only 30 percent of the CSO workforce, of which culture, sports, and recreation account for more than half (18 percent).

This dominance of service-providing CSOs is characteristic of the welfare partnership pattern and is a direct consequence of the sector being charged with the delivery of state-mandated and state-financed services.

As table 10.3 shows, the Netherlands, with 64 percent of the CSO workforce in service-oriented fields, comes very close to the welfare partnership cluster average of 71 percent.

REVENUE SOURCES

Nearly two-thirds (63 percent) of all CSO revenue in the Netherlands (66 billion Euro, or US$56.8 billion) in 2002 came from government, as shown in table 10.4. The second-largest source was fees, which accounted for 32 percent, while private philanthropy provided just 5 percent of total income.

The share of government support was even higher in service fields that fall within the typical purview of government social policy, such as education (89 percent of total CSS revenue from government), social services

TABLE 10.3 Distribution of CSS workforce by type of function, Netherlands vs. country clusters and 41-country average

Cluster	Share of CSS workforce, by type of function* (%)		
	Service	Expressive	Other
The Netherlands	**64**	**30**	**6**
41 countries	59	37	4
Traditional	68	24	8
Liberal	55	36	9
Welfare partnership	71	25	4
Social democratic	39	59	2
Statist	50	47	4

*Figures may not add to 100% due to rounding.

TABLE 10.4   Sources of Dutch CSS revenue by field, 2002

Field	Government (%)	Philanthropy (%)	Fees (%)
All fields	63	5	32
Service fields	68	2	30
Health care	81	2	17
Education and research	89	3	8
Social services	83	1	16
Economic development	3	0	97
Expressive fields	28	22	51
Environmental protection	40	59	1
Culture, sports, and recreation	41	11	48
Religion	0	70	30
Professional associations and labor unions	0	0	100
Advocacy	5	46	49
Other fields	25	40	35
Philanthropic intermediaries	14	33	53
International	44	52	3

(83 percent), and heath care (81 percent). However, government support was considerably lower for the expressive fields (28 percent), with the exception of environmental protection (40 percent) and culture, sports, and recreation (41 percent).

The CSO revenue structure in the Netherlands resembles that found in other countries within the welfare partnership cluster. Thus, table 10.5 demonstrates that the 63 percent government share of CSO revenue in the

Cluster	Government (%)	Philanthropy (%)	Fees (%)
The Netherlands	63	5	32
41 countries	*35*	*14*	*50*
Traditional	11	24	65
Liberal	33	14	53
Welfare partnership	66	8	26
Social democratic	38	10	52
Statist	18	18	64

*Figures may not add to 100% due to rounding.

Netherlands is similar to the 66 percent average for the welfare partnership cluster, and while the 32 percent share of fee income in the Netherlands is slightly higher than the 26 percent welfare partnership average, it is still much lower than the average of any other cluster.

VOLUNTEER PARTICIPATION

As a consequence of being a government partner in social service delivery, the civil society sector in the Netherlands has developed certain characteristics that, while not defining attributes of the welfare partnership pattern, nonetheless illustrate the effects that that this pattern often has on CSO structure and operations. One of these consequential characteristics is the dominance of paid employees in the CSO workforce. Nearly two-thirds (64 percent) of CSO FTE workers are paid staffers. Because the overall size of this sector is so large in the Netherlands, however, the 36 percent of FTE CSO workers that volunteers represent in this country still constitutes quite an impressive force. Indeed, the total amount of volunteering is quite high in the Netherlands when measured as a share of the economically active population (EAP) as opposed to as a share of the CSO workforce—more than double the international average (5.8 vs. 2.2 percent of the EAP). Reflecting this, as table 10.6 shows, the volunteer share of the CSO workforce in the Netherlands, though smaller than the 41-country average (36 percent vs. 41 percent), is still larger than the welfare partnership average (29 percent).

The distribution of paid staff and volunteers also differs by field. While nearly the entire paid staff (89 percent) is concentrated in three major service

TABLE 10.6   Volunteer share of CSS workforce,
Netherlands vs. country clusters and 41-country
average

Cluster	Volunteers as a share of CSS workforce (%)
The Netherlands	36.3
41 countries	40.6
Traditional	53.1
Liberal	46.4
Welfare partnership	29.1
Social democratic	69.4
Statist	27.9

fields—education, health, and social services—slightly more than 60 percent of volunteer workers concentrate in the expressive fields—about 43 percent in culture, sports, and recreation, and an additional 17 percent in religion.

SUMMARY

The welfare partnership pattern is firmly established in the institutional framework of Netherlands and has remained relatively stable in recent times. Indeed, despite worldwide trends toward reductions in government social spending, the Dutch government share of CSO revenue actually increased from 58.5 to 62.6 percent between 1995 and 2002, while the share of fee income dropped from 38.4 to 32.4 percent. The revenue share of private philanthropy increased from 3.1 to 5.1 percent, which may have something to do with the significant growth of philanthropic organizational capacity in the country, as indicated by a sharp rise in the workforce in this field.

As a consequence of this continuing government support, the civil society sector workforce grew at a noticeably faster rate than did the economy as a whole (21 and 15 percent, respectively) in the same time period. On the other hand, the workforce share of service activities decreased from 72 to 64 percent. This is likely a result of rapid growth in nonservice fields, especially international activities, philanthropy, and religion, rather than a decline in the service fields, which also grew, but at a slower rate. Despite these differential growth rates, however, services remained by far the dominant activity of the Dutch civil society sector.

Explaining the Path of Civil Society Development in the Netherlands[2]

What are the historical origins of the welfare partnership pattern of civil society in the Netherlands? How do we explain the large size of the CSO workforce, the primacy of the service function, and the dominance of government payments in CSO revenue? According to the social origins theory, the development and entrenchment of this pattern can be credited to the interaction among major social forces in modern Dutch history. Three such forces in particular were especially important: first, a strong but internally divided labor movement posing continuous challenges to local powers-that-be; second, two powerful sets of religious institutions and communities further splitting the labor movement and exerting pressures on government to channel social welfare expenditures through religiously affiliated institutions rather than public institutions; and third, a generally accommodating government in the face of this religious and labor pressure, playing one off against the other to achieve an outcome that avoided the more radical governmental solutions pushed by the more extreme voices in the labor movement and instead channeled assistance through more moderate religiously affiliated channels. Let us look more closely at these three elements.

SOCIO-ECONOMIC CLASS INTERESTS

Industrialization brought with it growing working-class militancy in the Netherlands, especially in the urban industrial areas in the northern and western parts of the country. However, the labor movement was internally divided between more radical elements who formed the Social Democratic League (*Sociaal-Democratische Bond* or SDB) and the much larger moderate General Dutch Workingmans' Association (*Algemeen Nederlandsch Werklieden Verbond or* ANWV). The SDB itself was internally divided between socialists and anarchists, which led to an eventual split into two smaller groups—the more moderate Social Democratic Workers' Party (*Sociaal Democratische Arbeiders Partij*), the predecessor of modern Social Democrats, and radical anarcho-syndicalist factions, which sought to launch a proletarian revolution to replace the capitalist system and tended to resist participation in the "bourgeois" parliamentary process in favor of direct industrial action.

THE ROLE OF ORGANIZED RELIGION

These internal ideological divisions within the labor movement were further exacerbated by the sharp religious division within the country. The Netherlands came into existence as an independent state in the 16th century, during the religious wars unleashed by the Reformation. From the beginning, its population was split into a Protestant majority and a Catholic minority. In the absence of state provision of basic health, education, and related social services, both of these religious denominations created a separate system of schools and social support organizations exclusively serving either Catholic or Protestant populations, effectively using these organizations, as the supply-side theories of the nonprofit sector examined in chapter 3 above suggest, to retain the support of their adherents, a phenomenon known as "pillarization."

This religious conflict naturally spilled over into the labor movement and ultimately into the design of the social welfare measures promoted in response to labor militancy. Thus, the more militant wing of the labor movement was opposed by the moderate Protestant labor elements affiliated with the ANWV as well as by the Catholic Church, which maintained an especially strong foothold in the southern part of the country, where Spain once exercised control. Following directives of the encyclical *Rerum Novarum*, which called for providing more conservative alternatives to socialist labor organizations, the Catholic hierarchy explicitly prohibited Catholic workers from participating in Protestant or Socialist labor organizations.

MEDIATING ROLE OF GOVERNMENT

These internal divisions within the labor movement and the anti-institutional stance of its more radical elements, coupled with the strong opposition of both the Catholic and Calvinist religious authorities to state provision of social and educational services that church authorities preferred to deliver through their own religiously affiliated charitable institutions, profoundly affected the shape of social welfare provision in the Netherlands and effectively closed off the route pursued in Sweden or Norway.

This issue came to a dramatic head in the second decade of the 20th century in the so-called battle of the schools, when both Catholic and Protestant religious officials rallied their adherents to oppose a government initiative to establish a state-funded, but secular, public school system wholly financed through tax revenues.[3] The Dutch government, accustomed to playing a mediating role in resolving conflicting interests and demands even while making consistent efforts to curb labor militancy,[4] ultimately settled this crisis through a compromise that involved making payments for free, or nearly free, elementary and second education for all children regardless of whether they attended secular, public schools or sectarian religious or ideologically affiliated schools so long as the schools passed minimum qualification standards. As state support for social welfare services expanded in the wake of depression and war, this same pattern was extended to new fields of social welfare provision, creating separate faith-based pillars providing state-funded services ranging from pre-K through high school education, hospital care, nursing home care, higher education, and more through a combination of public bodies and private, nonprofit institutions.[5]

To be sure, the religious identity of social and educational service venues diminished after World War II, mainly as a result of political opposition by the social democratic and liberal elements to the pillarization system. However, the institutional pattern of private provision of publicly financed services remained firmly embedded in the Dutch institutional framework and expanded to other service fields, including health care, elderly care, and social services, creating the distinctive Dutch model of a publicly funded, privately delivered social welfare system.

In sum, the key factors that led to the welfare partnership pattern in the Netherlands were internal divisions in working-class institutions and movements intensified by deep-seated religious divisions and strong religious authorities that sought to keep the provision of key social welfare services channeled through their own faith-based institutional structures. This can be demonstrated by contrasting the Netherlands with Norway and Sweden, where labor was more unified and politically powerful and organized religion had been subdued by the state. This difference can explain the different outcomes in social welfare policies and the role of CSOs: while Sweden and Norway adopted a social democratic welfare model centered around state agencies, the Netherlands reached for a social compromise by creating a welfare partnership model in which the civil society sector delivers much of the publicly funded social assistance.

Conclusions

The civil society sector in the Netherlands thus exhibits in dramatic fashion the central characteristics of what we have identified as the welfare partnership model of civil society development characterized by the dominance of government payments in the sector's revenue, large organizational size, and a prevalence of service activities. In addition, the emergence of this pattern can be traced to a set of power relationships very close to those hypothesized in the social origins theory—a labor movement weakened by internal ideological divisions that were in turn intensified by deep-seated religious differences, a church hierarchy willing to block public benefits that might disadvantage their own faith-based institutions, and a government with a penchant for compromise and a willingness to buttress the position of moderate religious institutions in the face of more radical labor demands.

These findings suggest that, far from being politically neutral and benevolent, civil society organizations can also be important actors in the exercise of political power and a significant battleground in political disputes. They can solidify allegiances to special interest groups or divide groups sharing similar economic interests. By serving as a major venue of social service delivery, they can also help weld popular attachment to religious and political movements.

Perhaps the most important lesson from the Dutch case for the civil society sector today, however, is that it provides a powerful empirical refutation to the still-dominant market failure/government failure theory of the CSO development. As outlined more fully in chapter 3, this theory suggests a zero-sum image of the relationship between the CSO sector and government by positing that nonprofits arise where religious or other heterogeneity impedes government action, giving rise to nonprofit organizations to fill the resulting gaps. But here religious heterogeneity stimulated government involvement, which then substantially expanded the CSO sector's size and reach.

The mechanism that led to this outcome was not an alternative economic theory but an alternative political arrangement not acknowledged in the market failure/government failure theory but widely documented in the work of political scientist Arendt Lijhpart and found in many Western European countries. Lijhpart calls this "consensus democracy," an institutional arrangement fostering collaboration among diverse interest groups leading to compromise solutions to seemingly intractable issues.[6] In a sense, the Dutch government was a past master of consensus democracy and found an arrangement that may have violated certain bedrock beliefs of classical economics but pragmatically solved a potential breakdown of democratic norms, leading to a pattern that has both proved durable in the Netherlands and been copied in an increasingly widespread array of other countries as well.

Notes

The authors wish to thank Bob Khury of the Sociaal en Cultureel Planbureau of the Netherlands for providing quantitative data on the civil society sector in the Netherlands used in this chapter.

    1. Burger et al. 1997.

    2. The history of the civil society sector in the Netherlands is explored in greater detail in Veldheer and Burger 1999.

    3. Bakvis 1981; Cox 1993.

    4. For example, the government outlawed the militant SDB in 1893 and frequently suppressed attempts to organize direct industrial action (strikes, protests, etc.).

    5. Cox 1993; Berger and Broughton 1995, ch. 3.

    6. Lijphart 1999.

CHAPTER ELEVEN

Chile

A Latin Welfare Partnership Model

IGNACIO IRARRAZAVAL, S. WOJCIECH SOKOLOWSKI,
and LESTER M. SALAMON

THE CIVIL SOCIETY SECTOR in Chile is an exception among Latin American countries. Its workforce is considerably larger than that found in all other Latin American countries except Argentina. What is more, volunteers account for a much larger share of that workforce then elsewhere in Latin America. More importantly, government support accounts for a significant share of the civil society sector's revenue in Chile, more than double the share found in all other Latin American countries and even several Western European countries. At the same time, Chile is one of the two Latin American countries that does not meet the conditions defining any of the five patterns of civil society development identified in chapter 4 (the other exception is again Argentina). How can we explain this exceptionalism?

The social origins theory offers some crucial elements of such an explanation by focusing our attention on the array of social groupings and related institutions that emerged in Chile in the late 19th and early 20th century. Especially notable was the early development of the mining industry and its industrial offshoots in Chile, which attracted peasants to the resulting mining and industrial enclaves and cities, creating an incipient working class. Reacting to the unfavorable working and living conditions to which they were subjected, these workers began to organize and press for improved social welfare protections. These demands were supported by elements of the Catholic Church following the dicta of the 1891 papal encyclical calling on Church leaders to support improved conditions for workers and worker self-organization; they were supported as well by urban commercial and professional groups who also felt aggrieved by the policies of the landed elites in power. A brief civil war between forces representing the congress and the president ended in a victory of the congressional forces, opening a window of opportunity for parties representing the working class to enter national politics. As a result, an unusual social compromise emerged among these potentially conflicting class interests of landowners, middle-class commercial and professional groups, and the working classes. Brokered by a set of newly emerged political parties and supported by the Church, this compromise established a relative peaceful period of political stability by creating a redistributive mechanism that channeled public funds to civil society organizations affiliated with the main political parties and the Church to carry out service activities on behalf of the state. This quasi–welfare partnership arrangement persisted in Chile throughout most of the 20th century and resulted in a substantial expansion of the sector's capacity, although it had to endure a setback during a disruptive, nearly 20-year period of military control in the 1970s and 1980s before being substantially strengthened in the period since then.

To pursue these themes, the discussion here proceeds in three steps. First, we examine the major dimensions of the Chilean civil society sector as they emerge from the empirical work we have undertaken. Then we look into the social and economic dynamics of Chilean development to search for explanations of the pattern that emerges. Finally, we offer some conclusions about the broader implications of the Chilean case.

Dimensions of the Chilean Civil Society Sector

SIZE OF THE WORKFORCE

The data gathered for this project show that civil society organizations employ a considerable component of the Chilean workforce and contribute substantially to the country's economy. As of 2004, the latest year for which data are available, employment in Chilean civil society organizations accounted for over 165,000 full-time equivalent (FTE) jobs, or approximately 2.6 percent of the country's economically active population (EAP). In addition, these organizations engaged the equivalent of another 157,000 full-time volunteers, bringing the total workforce of the Chilean civil society sector to over 323,000 full-time equivalent workers, or about 5 percent of the country's EAP. As figure 11.1 shows, the total civil society workforce is comparable to, albeit slightly lower than, employment in two key Chilean industries, transportation and construction. It is also equivalent to more than a third of all manufacturing employment and nearly half of agricultural employment.

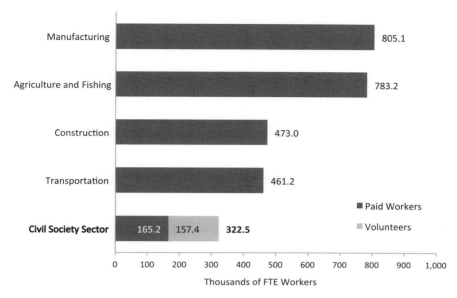

FIGURE 11.1. FTE workforce, civil society sector vs. selected industries, Chile, 2004.

The size of the civil society sector in Chile is in the middle range in relation to other countries. Measured as a share of the economically active population, the workforce of the Chilean civil society sector as of 2004, at 5.0 percent, ranked slightly below the 41-country average for which such data are available (5.7 percent of EAP), as table 2.1 demonstrates.

Although this puts Chile below most of the high-income countries of Europe and North America, it also places it second in Latin America, after Argentina, and above several Western European countries (e.g., Spain, Italy, and Portugal) as well as all of the developing countries covered in this book. Although the size of the civil society sector in Chile falls somewhat below the range defining the welfare partnership pattern (6.8 of the EAP or more), it also falls significantly above the averages of the statist and traditional pattern countries, which are found mainly among developing countries (table 11.1). This indicates that Chile is a borderline case of a pattern found in the developed countries.

As will be explained in more detail later in this chapter, the size of the civil society sector in Chile would have been significantly larger if it had not suffered a major setback under military rule between 1973 and 1989. This offers further argument for treating Chile as a borderline case of one of the patterns found among the developed countries.

TABLE 11.1 Civil society sector workforce as share of EAP, Chile vs. country clusters and 41-country average

Cluster	Workforce as a share of EAP (%)
Chile	**5.0**
41 countries	5.7
Traditional	1.9
Liberal	9.6
Welfare partnership	11.2
Social democratic	8.2
Statist	2.3

VOLUNTEER PARTICIPATION

About 7 percent of the adult population in Chile contributed part of their time to volunteer work in 2004. Over the course of a year, each volunteer worked, on average, about one-fourth of a full workday for a civil society sector organization. This translates into 157,000 full-time jobs generated by the sector, equivalent to 2.4 percent of the economically active population of Chile, a level comparable to that in neighboring Argentina (2.7 percent) and in Ireland (2.3 percent), Switzerland (2.6 percent), and Australia (2.9 percent). Nearly half (49 percent) of the entire civil society workforce is composed of full-time equivalent volunteer workers.

This share of volunteer input in Chile's civil society sector (CSS) workforce, at nearly 49 percent, is quite high by international standards and exceeds the 41-country average of 41 percent. This also places Chile significantly above the statist pattern average (28 percent) found in most other Latin American countries (table 11.2).

Such a high share of volunteers in the civil society workforce offers further evidence that Chile is an exception among Latin American countries.

SERVICE AND EXPRESSIVE ACTIVITIES

Service activities engage most (about 56 percent) of Chile's civil society sector workforce (paid and volunteer), as shown in table 11.3.

Education and research organizations engage an especially high percentage of the CSS workforce in Chile (29 percent), which is a rather typical

TABLE 11.2   Volunteer share of CSS workforce,
Chile vs. country clusters and 41-country average

Cluster	Volunteers as a share of CSS workforce (%)
Chile	**48.8**
41 countries	*40.6*
Traditional	53.1
Liberal	46.4
Welfare partnership	29.1
Social democratic	69.4
Statist	27.9

TABLE 11.3   Distribution of Chile's CSS workforce, by field,
2004

Field	Share (%)
Service fields	56
Education and research	29
Social services	16
Health care	2
Economic development	9
Expressive fields	42
Culture, sports, and recreation	15
Religion	6
Advocacy	3
Professional associations and labor unions	18
Environmental protection	1
Other fields	3
Philanthropic intermediaries	1
International	0
Not elsewhere classified	2
N	322,521

feature of the civil society sector in Latin American countries. It is also
noteworthy that the share of CSS activities linked to professional and labor
interests is unusually large in Chile by international standards (18 vs.
5.3 percent average). This demonstrates the relative significance of professional and labor interest groups in Chile.

This relatively high share of CSS workers involved in service functions
places Chile within the parameters defining both the welfare partnership and
the traditional patterns (service share exceeding the expressive share) even

TABLE 11.4   Distribution of CSS workforce by type of function, Chile vs. country clusters and 41-country average

	Share of CSS workforce, by type of function* (%)		
Cluster	Service	Expressive	Other
Chile	56	42	3
41 countries	59	37	4
Traditional	68	24	8
Liberal	55	36	9
Welfare partnership	71	25	4
Social democratic	39	59	2
Statist	50	47	4

*Figures may not add to 100% due to rounding.

though it falls below the averages of both patterns (71 and 68 percent, respectively), as shown in table 11.4.

REVENUE SOURCES

Government grants, contracts, and reimbursements are the main sources of civil society sector revenue in Chile, accounting for 45 percent of the total income (table 11.5). The second-largest source is service fees, which accounted for 35 percent, while private philanthropy provides 19 percent of the total income of the sector.

The dominance of government funding of the civil society sector is particularly salient in the service fields, especially in the areas of economic development (75 percent of total revenue), education (61 percent), and social services (43 percent).

As table 11.6 demonstrates, the government share of the civil society sector revenue in Chile markedly exceeds the averages of all country clusters except the welfare partnership one. It is also close to the defining range of that pattern (50 percent or more) even though it falls somewhat below it.

On the other hand, the share of philanthropy in Chile, at 19 percent of revenue, is higher than the 41-country average and falls within the range defining the liberal pattern (9 percent of revenue or more).

TABLE 11.5   Sources of Chile's CSS revenue by field, 2004

Field	Government (%)	Philanthropy (%)	Fees (%)
All fields	45	19	35
Service fields	58	19	22
Health care	18	71	11
Education and research	61	15	25
Social services	43	28	29
Economic development	75	18	7
Expressive fields	16	17	68
Environmental protection	15	77	8
Culture, sports, and recreation	24	12	64
Religion	0	77	23
Professional associations and labor unions	7	9	84
Advocacy	55	29	16
Other fields	26	46	29
Philanthropic intermediaries	16	30	54
International	92	0	8
Not elsewhere classified	26	46	29

TABLE 11.6   Shares of CSS revenue by source, Chile vs. country clusters and 41-country average*

Cluster	Government (%)	Philanthropy (%)	Fees (%)
Chile	**45**	**19**	**35**
41 countries	*35*	*14*	*50*
Traditional	11	24	65
Liberal	33	14	53
Welfare partnership	66	8	26
Social democratic	38	10	52
Statist	18	18	64

*Figures may not add to 100% due to rounding.

SUMMARY: A BORDERLINE WELFARE PARTNERSHIP CASE?

As the data presented in this chapter show, the civil society sector in Chile does not neatly fit any of the five patterns of civil society development identified in chapter 4. Still, it comes close to patterns found among the developed countries in terms of the size of its workforce, the volunteer share of that workforce, the dominance of service activities in its focus, and the government share of its revenues, especially in the service fields. This offers a persuasive reason for treating Chile as a borderline case of one of the patterns found among the developed countries covered by this study. The question is: which?

Among the three possible candidates, liberal, welfare partnership, and social democratic, the latter is the least likely candidate because Chile falls significantly short of meeting its two defining attributes, the dominance of expressive over service activities and volunteers over paid staff. On the other hand, Chile meets or falls close to the ranges defining two other patterns: liberal and welfare partnership. The strongest argument for placing Chile under the liberal rubric is the high share of philanthropy in the funding base of its CSS; the strongest argument for placing it in the welfare partnership cluster is the dominance of service activities of its workforce and the relatively high share of government support in its funding base.

To judge the relative weight of these arguments we need to place them in a geopolitical context. High shares of philanthropy in the funding of civil society are common in Latin America and, for that matter, in medium- and low-income countries, so they are not necessarily indicative of liberal influences limiting government welfare spending. More likely, this reflects a tendency for the nonprofit sector in such countries to be oriented toward high-end educational and other services geared to upper-income residents. By the same token, government support to civil service organizations (CSOs) is rather low in these countries (about 22 percent of total CSO revenue on average). The fact that the government share of revenue in Chile is more than double that average indicates a very substantial level of government support for the civil society sector in this country compared to medium- and low- income country standards.

Due to this unusually high level of government support, Chile falls closer to the welfare partnership than the liberal pattern and can be considered a borderline case of this pattern. The size of its workforce, the dominance of service activities, and the dominance of government-based revenues fall close to the levels defining that pattern. This represents a rather unusual development among Latin American countries, where the statist pattern seems to be the most commonly found pattern of civil society development.

Explaining Chile's Pattern of Civil Society Development[1]

How can we explain this unusual pattern of civil society development in Chile? Clearly, sentiment and preference theories cannot carry us very far, since Chile had the same Roman Catholic colonial origins as other Latin American countries and therefore the same posture towards altruism and charity. So, too, Chile did not have a particularly different combination of native and colonial residents creating a significantly different set of demands for collective goods, the factor emphasized in the government failure/market failure line of theory. To what extent, therefore, can the social origins theory help us explain this unusual Latin American outcome? To answer this question, we need to look briefly at the peculiar historical development of Chile.

COLONIAL LEGACY

The development of the civil society sector in Chile was shaped initially by Spanish colonization and the social forces it triggered. The colonizers transplanted from Spain a variety of social, economic, and political structures, including a hierarchical governance system directly linked to the Spanish monarchy, a rural gentry to which the Crown bequeathed landed estates, and the Catholic Church. Large landowner interests, wealthy merchants, and foreign capitalists, buttressed by the army, maintained control of the government throughout most of the 19th century, staving off pressures from liberal upper classes.

Landowner power eventually came under pressure in the latter 1800s, when the expansion of mining industries spurred economic growth, industrialization, and a massive migration of peasants to mining and industrial enclaves and to the cities, producing a great agglomeration of the popular classes in the cities and giving rise as well to a professional and commercial middle class. Because of the unfavorable living and working conditions and total absence of public services, workers' organizations and movements along with mutualist associations for health care, education, cultural development, and other purposes emerged. The turning point was a civil war that broke out in 1891 pitting the country's president, backed by the Chilean army, against the Chilean congress, backed by the Chilean navy and the professional classes. This conflict ended with the victory of the congressional side, which led to an opening of political life reflected in the establishment of a parliamentary system and the rise of political parties representing various socioeconomic classes and interest groups. These latter included the center-right Conservative Party, backed by the Roman Catholic Church and elements of the landed and industrial oligarchy, and the Liberal Alliance, composed of the Liberal Party, the Liberal Democratic Party, and the Radical Party and supported mainly by middle-class professionals and labor interests. Further industrialization in the early 20th century led to the rapid growth of urban middle and working classes and to a fuller elaboration of the party structure. By the end of the 1910s a Socialist Workers Party, associated with the labor movement, had formed and was gaining importance; a decade later, in 1922, the Communist Party of Chile was established.

CONFLICTING SOCIOECONOMIC GROUP INTERESTS
AND POLITICAL COMPROMISE

These growing urban professional and labor groupings threw their political support behind reformist elements in the government, demanding public services to meet the most basic of human needs. Unfavorable living and working conditions also spurred the further growth of mutual help and housing associations. These organizations were perceived as mechanisms for moderating labor militancy and received support from political parties and the Catholic Church, which, following the issuance of the encyclical *Rerum Novarum,* adopted a more supportive, reformist stance on social and labor issues while still opposing Communism and other radicalisms.[2] The relationship between these associations and the state was mainly one of cooperation, providing the embryonic architecture for what would ultimately emerge as the welfare partnership pattern of civil society development. An important step in this direction came with the adoption of the 1925 constitution establishing new public social assistance systems and the enactment of laws providing for assistance to victims of work-related accidents and legalizing labor unions and professional associations.

Not surprisingly, these developments were met with resistance on the part of conservatives, leading to political instability, a series of military coups, and massacres of striking workers. Constitutional rule was finally restored in 1932, with the Radical Party representing middle-class interests becoming the leading force in subsequent coalition governments. Indeed, the coalition led by the Radical Party was instrumental in providing political stability over a 20-year period stretching between 1932 and 1952 by brokering political compromises among conflicting class interests but also dispensing patronage and social protection in exchange for political support.

The post-1932 political compromise represented a significant sociopolitical change in Chile. It introduced public education, health care, housing, and social services and led to the democratization of the electoral system and the definitive incorporation of the urban professional and working classes into the country's sociopolitical organizations. The patronage system also created favorable conditions for the development of civil society organizations, which political parties used as vehicles for expanding their social power base, mainly among the urban classes and organized labor. With the state assuming at least partial responsibility for social assistance and protection matters formerly under the sole charge of private organizations or the Catholic Church, the first tangible manifestations of a welfare partnership system linking the state and private groups took shape, with the private groups serving in an auxiliary role to the state.

The 1960s witnessed an institutional consolidation of civil society organizations as well as an extension of social services by the state. A great number of organizations were legalized, such as neighbors' associations, mothers' centers, sports clubs, and, most importantly, peasants' unions, which were legalized in 1967. Thus, legal existence was granted to organizations that had been operating for decades without it. Important to these developments was the overwhelming victory of the Christian Democratic Party in the 1964 election, with a program of structural reforms called "Revolution in Liberty." This reformist political project was an outcome prompted in important part by fears on the part of both domestic actors—mainly the political right and important Chilean Catholic sectors—and international ones—including particularly the United States—about the growing influence of the leftist forces in Chile and the potential of a Castro-type revolution in Chile.[3]

This Christian Democratic government also implemented a wide range of social and economic reforms, particularly in education, housing, and unionization of rural agricultural workers. These developments further extended the embryonic welfare partnership pattern by expanding the role of the civil society sector in the delivery of these services and gave legal recognition to a great number of community organizations, neighborhood associations, and, most importantly, farm workers' unions. However, these reforms encountered opposition both from the conservatives, who viewed them as excessive, and from leftists, who considered them inadequate. In the end, the reforms could not stop growing pressure from the left, which culminated in the electoral victory of the Popular Unity alliance of Salvador Allende in 1970.[4] Although conflicts among socioeconomic groups intensified under the Allende government and the government faced constant opposition and pressure from the US government,[5] most of the political party establishment and the judiciary insisted on maintaining the parliamentary system and democratic governance in Chile.

GENERAL PINOCHET AND MILITARY RULE: STALLED CIVIL SOCIETY DEVELOPMENT

The polarization of Chilean society, Allende's inability to govern and control the political situation, the economic failure of his administration, and pressures from both domestic and international forces, mainly the US government, led ultimately to a military coup on September 11, 1973, by the armed forces led by General Augusto Pinochet.[6] The result effectively ended the era of political party–brokered compromise and corporatist policies that characterized Chilean democracy for most of the 20th century. The military government not only cracked down on organized labor and the civil society organizations linked to it but also embarked on radical neoliberal reforms that drastically reduced public welfare programs and privatized many government functions.

The crackdown led to a substantial reduction of civil society sector activity—the number of grassroots organizations was reduced by approximately 30 percent, and most community organizations, labor unions, and guild associations lost their autonomy altogether. The organizations least affected by the crackdown were those affiliated with the Catholic Church. Consequently, many human rights organizations or organizations providing assistance to the victims of the military regime reconstituted themselves under the auspices of the Church.

A RETURN TO DEMOCRACY AND A RESTART FOR CIVIL SOCIETY

Between 1983 and 1986, high unemployment and social discontent caused a wave of protests that led Pinochet to acquiesce to a constitutionally mandated referendum in 1988 that ultimately ended in his political defeat. This opened the way for the election of a new democratic government in 1989 and the introduction of considerable changes to Chile's civil society sector.

Perhaps the most important was the adoption of policies aiming to repair the relationship between government and civil society organizations, which had been severely strained under the Pinochet regime. The new government took steps to strengthen civil society as part of the process of consolidating democracy, assigning priority to social issues, increasing social expenditure, and expanding the provision of social programs. A dialogue between government officials and civil society representatives was established, leading to the development of national public policies aimed at strengthening the civil society sector.

These developments created conditions for the emergence of new civil society organizations linked to the urban professional classes, reflecting their interest in human and civil rights, gender equality, environmental protection, rights of the indigenous peoples, and the promotion of redemocratization. In contrast to the pre-1970 pattern, however, these new organizations distanced themselves from political parties, maintaining their independence and concentrating on service provision.

Government financial support for service activities increased during the democratization period, though it was concentrated on service activities, such as education and social assistance. As a result, unlike in other Latin American countries, government payments are today the main source of civil society sector support in Chile, giving rise to the characterization of Chile's nonprofit sector as reflecting the welfare partnership pattern. Most government support to the civil society sector in Chile is provided in the form of reimbursements for services provided by CSOs, mainly in the educational sector. Some direct payments are also allocated to poverty reduction and support for persons with disabilities. Other support is provided in the form of service contracts, tax exemptions for CSOs, and tax credits for private donors to these organizations.

Summary and Conclusion

The Chilean civil society sector was shaped by the balance of power that emerged from the struggle among conservative landed and industrial elites and more liberal commercial, professional, and working-class elements after the country gained independence from Spain. In Chile this power struggle was relatively constrained and eventually resulted in an outcome that opened a window for urban professional and working classes to gain power while the landed and industrial elites and the Catholic Church managed to preserve their power as well. This, in turn, resulted in a compromise between these conflicting socioeconomic interests brokered through a reinvigorated parliamentary system and the support of the Catholic Church, leading to state assumption of responsibility for financing—if not necessarily delivering— social welfare protections. This set of compromises ultimately led to the development of a welfare partnership model in Chile, with state support channeled to an assortment of secular and religiously affiliated nonprofit or mutual associations. Although this pattern was interrupted by the military dictatorship between 1973 and 1990, it was subsequently restored and expanded. This outcome contrasts sharply with the pattern that emerged in Mexico, where, as chapter 15 will show, the struggle among social classes was far more protracted and intense, weakening not only landed and industrial elites but also commercial and professional middle class elements, the working class, and the Church, opening the way for a far different outcome.

In addition to highlighting the importance of social groupings, the Chilean story also illustrates the role that power amplifiers can play in civil society development, as the social origins theory acknowledges. In Chile, the role of power amplifiers was played by political parties representing, but simultaneously mediating, the conflicting interests of landed and industrial elites, professional urban classes, and organized labor. This led to relative social peace for an extended period of time and a social compromise that featured the dispensation of patronage through civil society organizations, which gave rise to the development of a welfare partnership between public institutions and political parties, on the one hand, and the civil society sector on the other. This compromise persisted for nearly 50 years and was broken only by the military coup d'etat of 1973. The Pinochet regime reversed the welfare partnership relations of the pre-1970 era and embarked on neoliberal policies that led to the privatization of many government functions and significantly reduced government support to the civil society sector. In addition, the regime engaged in authoritarian repression of civil society activities. The result of these policies was a significant reduction of the sector's organizational capacity and an undermining of its relationship with government. However, the return to democratic rule in 1990 reestablished cooperation between public institutions and the civil society sector with a focus on service-providing organizations, which is a characteristic feature of the welfare partnership pattern.

The Chilean story also illustrates another causal element specified by the social origins theory: the role of foreign powers in shaping civil society development. In Chile, two distinct waves of such outside influence powerfully affected the nation. The first was Spanish colonial rule, which created a landed aristocracy in the countryside and a powerful Catholic Church and related church-affiliated civil society organizations. The former constituted the backbone of Chile's conservative political parties, and the latter provided the framework for a welfare partnership pattern.

In more recent years, the outside actor was the United States. Ever fearful of the expansion of Communist influence in the Americas following the Castro takeover in Cuba, the United States threw its support behind forces perceived to provide a countervailing influence to the growing radicalization of Chile's urban and rural masses. This initially took the form of support to the reformist elements in the Christian Democratic Party. But when that failed, the United States gave a green light to a military coup d'état that ousted the democratically elected regime of Salvador Allende. This is not to say that the United States was solely, or even chiefly, responsible for the current shape of Chilean civil society. But its involvement had significant political and economic influence that helped to shape the result, first by enhancing the role of civil society in Chile in the 1960s and second by weakening it under Pinochet's regime.

In sum, the social origins theory makes it possible to account for Chile's welfare partnership pattern of civil society development, unusual for Latin America, by going beyond cultural traits or consumer preferences and examining specific power relations among social classes as mediated through political institutions over an extended historical period.

Notes

This chapter reports the results of a comprehensive empirical study of the civil society sector's organizational capacity in Chile as part of the Johns Hopkins Comparative Nonprofit Sector Project. The results of this study, which represent the first comprehensive assessment of Chile's nonprofit sector institutions, were first reported in Irarrázaval et al. 2006.

1. This section draws on the following sources: Bauer 1975; Drake 1996; Irarrazaval et al. 2006; Rueschemeyer, Stephens, and Stephens 1992; Stepan 1985; Wright 1982; and Wright 2007.

2. The encyclical *Rerum Novarum*, issued by Pope Leo XIII on May 15, 1891, addressed the need for amelioration of harsh working conditions during industrial-

ization. It supported the rights of labor to form unions and affirmed the right to private property. It also denounced radical ideologies, including Communism and laissez-faire capitalism.

3. United States Senate 1975.

4. Popular Unity was a political alliance that brought together leftist parties, mainly the Socialist and Communist Parties, under the candidacy of Salvador Allende in the 1970 presidential election.

5. Kornbluh 2004.

6. See Valenzuela 1978; Loveman 2001, 257–260.

CHAPTER TWELVE

Austria

A Dualistic Pattern of Civil Society Development

MICHAELA NEUMAYR, ULRIKE SCHNEIDER, MICHAEL MEYER,
ASTRID PENNERSTORFER, S. WOJCIECH SOKOLOWSKI,
and LESTER M. SALAMON

AUSTRIA AND GERMANY SHARE a common language and cultural identity, and there was a strong movement to unify these two countries in the first half of the 20th century. Given this cultural affinity, one may expect the Austrian civil society sector to follow the welfare partnership pattern found in Germany. Yet the data show otherwise. Instead, the sector in Austria squarely meets all three defining criteria of the social democratic pattern of civil society development, making it more similar to that found in the Scandinavian countries than to its counterpart in Germany. In particular, the sector is relatively large, has a very high rate of volunteer participation, and engages a larger share of the workforce in expressive activities than service ones. On the other hand, it enjoys a higher level of government financial support than is common for the civil society sectors in the other countries exhibiting the social democratic pattern, though not as high as the civil society sectors in the welfare partnership countries.

How do we explain this surprising divergence? After documenting the dimensions of the civil society sector in Austria, this chapter seeks to explain this apparent puzzle by analyzing whether the power relations that the social origins theory links to the emergence of the social democratic pattern were present in Austria. What we find is that many of these features were in evidence in Austria. These include a weakened landed elite, a fairly strong labor movement with an effective political arm in the form of an effective Socialist Party, and post–World War II nationalization of key industries, which limited the strength of the commercial and professional middle classes. At the same time, however, labor was not strong enough to counter a strong conservative current from a heavily Catholic small farmer population in the countryside. The upshot was a bifurcated country, with a social democratic pattern in the cities and vestiges of a welfare partnership one in the countryside. This bifurcation was sustained by a power-sharing agreement worked out by the urban-oriented Socialist Party and the rural-based Christian Democrats.

Dimensions of the Austrian Civil Society Sector

SIZE OF THE WORKFORCE

The civil society sector is a considerable component of the Austrian economy. As of 2001,[1] Austrian civil society organizations employed about 116,400 full- and part-time paid workers.[2] This translates into nearly 86,000 full-time equivalent (FTE) jobs, or approximately 2.2 percent of the country's economically active population (EAP). In addition, these organizations engaged the equivalent of another 222,000 full-time equivalent volunteer employees, bringing the total workforce of the Austrian civil society sector to nearly 308,000 FTE workers, or 7.8 percent of the country's EAP.[3]

As shown in figure 12.1, the Austrian civil society FTE workforce is comparable to employment in the country's construction industry, is consider-

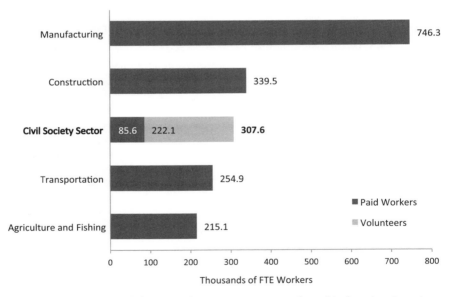

FIGURE 12.1. FTE workforce, civil society sector vs. selected industries, Austria, 2001.

TABLE 12.1   Civil society sector workforce
as share of EAP, Austria vs. country clusters
and 41-country average

Cluster	Workforce as a share of EAP (%)
Austria	7.8
41 countries	5.7
Traditional	1.9
Liberal	9.6
Welfare partnership	11.2
Social democratic	8.2
Statist	2.3

ably larger than employment in transportation (255,000 workers) and agriculture and fishing (215,000), and is a little over 40 percent as large as that employed in all branches of manufacturing.

The civil society sector in Austria is quite sizable in relation to other countries as well. Measured as a share of the EAP, the workforce of the Austrian civil society sector in 2001 ranked substantially above the 41-country average for which such data are available (7.8 vs. 5.7 percent of EAP, respectively), as figure 2.7 demonstrates.

This puts Austria above several of the high-income countries of Europe and North America, most notably its northern neighbor, Germany (6.8 percent of EAP) and its western neighbor, Switzerland (6.9 percent). The size of the civil society sector in Austria easily meets the defining range of the social democratic pattern (6.8 percent of EAP or more) and is on a par with the average of the social democratic country cluster (table 12.1).

VOLUNTEER PARTICIPATION

A high level of volunteer participation is one of the defining attributes of the social democratic pattern of civil society sector development, and this feature is certainly in evidence in Austria. Over 55 percent of males and 47 percent of females 15 years of age or older engage in some form of volunteering in Austria.[4] During the year 2000, volunteers contributed over 370 million hours to civil society organizations. This translates into more than 222,000 FTE jobs, which represents 2.4 percent of the EAP and accounts for nearly three-fourths (72 percent) of the entire civil society workforce.

Austria: A Dualistic Pattern of Civil Society Development   199

TABLE 12.2 Volunteer share of CSS workforce, Austria vs. country clusters and 41-country average

Cluster	Volunteers as a share of CSS workforce (%)
Austria	72.2
41 countries	40.6
Traditional	53.1
Liberal	46.4
Welfare partnership	29.1
Social democratic	69.4
Statist	27.9

This share of volunteer input in Austria is quite high by international standards and falls well within the range defining the social democratic pattern (56 percent of the workforce or more). It even exceeds the 69 percent average for countries exhibiting the social democratic pattern, as shown in table 12.2.

SERVICE AND EXPRESSIVE ACTIVITIES

The third defining characteristic of the social democratic pattern of civil society development is a high proportion of civil society sector (CSS) workers engaged in expressive activities, and this feature is also present in Austria. As shown in table 12.3, 50 percent of Austria's civil society sector workforce (paid and volunteer) is concentrated in expressive activities, especially culture, sports, and recreation (23 percent).

The high share of workers engaged in expressive, as opposed to service, activities places Austria close to the social democratic pattern average (table 12.4). The social origins theory claims that the dominance of expressive activities in the social democratic pattern is a result of the public provision of services. As the state assumes the responsibility for social welfare, civil society is freed to deploy its resources to expressive activities. While Austria technically meets this defining criterion of the social democratic pattern, however, the share of the workforce engaged in expressive activities is only slightly larger than that engaged in service activities (50 and 49 percent, respectively), suggesting elements of the welfare partnership model operating in current-day Austria.

TABLE 12.3 Distribution of Austria's CSS workforce, by field, 2001

Field	Share (%)
Service fields	49
Education and research	11
Social services	25
Health care	13
Economic development	0
Expressive fields	50
Culture, sports, and recreation	23
Religion	12
Advocacy	3
Professional associations and labor unions	8
Environmental protection	4
Other fields	1
Philanthropic intermediaries	0
Not elsewhere classified	1
N	307,632

TABLE 12.4 Distribution of CSS workforce by type of function, Austria vs. country clusters and 41-country average

Cluster	Share of CSS workforce, by type of function* (%)		
	Service	Expressive	Other
Austria	**49**	**50**	**1**
41 countries	59	37	4
Traditional	68	24	8
Liberal	55	36	9
Welfare partnership	71	25	4
Social democratic	39	59	2
Statist	50	47	4

*Figures may not add to 100% due to rounding.

REVENUE SOURCES

The total revenue of the civil society sector in Austria was over 4 billion Euros (US$5 billion) in 2005. Half of that amount was derived from government grants, contracts, and reimbursements, as table 12.5 shows. The second-largest source of income to the sector was service fees, which accounted for 37 percent of income, while private philanthropy provided 13 percent.[5]

TABLE 12.5   Sources of Austria's CSS revenue by field, 2001

Field	Government (%)	Philanthropy (%)	Fees (%)
All fields	50	13	37
Service fields	56	7	36
Health care	49	3	48
Education and research	59	6	36
Social services	60	10	31
Expressive fields	35	22	43
Environmental protection	48	16	37
Culture, sports, and recreation	16	30	54
Religion	65	5	29
Professional associations and labor unions	32	2	66
Advocacy	38	23	40
Other fields	25	58	17
International	25	75	0
Not elsewhere classified	25	4	72

Service fields received higher levels of government support than expressive fields (56 vs. 35 percent, respectively), a pattern found in most other countries on which data are available. The most common instruments of public funding are government grants (lump-sum subsidies) and performance-related contracts, which have begun to replace lump-sum subsidies in Austria, especially in the field of social services. These contracts, which in 2005 accounted for nearly 31 percent of total civil society sector revenue,[6] specify the type, amount, and quality of services the organization is to deliver.

Private philanthropy is of relatively minor importance in the service fields, but it is a significant revenue source in expressive fields, especially international activities (75 percent of income), culture, sports, and recreation (30 percent), and advocacy (23 percent). The religion field derives 65 percent of its income from government payments. This underlines the close relationship between the state and the Roman Catholic Church in Austria. There is still a compulsory church tax for Catholics, initially introduced by the Nazis after the annexation (*Anschluss*) of Austria by Hitler in 1938 but retained after World War II to maintain a political compromise with the conservatives.

As shown in table 12.6, this distribution of income sources places Austria above the social democratic country average for government support (38 percent) and reflects the presence of the welfare partnership model ele-

TABLE 12.6   Shares of CSS revenue by source, Austria vs. country clusters and 41-country average*

Cluster	Government (%)	Philanthropy (%)	Fees (%)
Austria	50	13	37
41 countries	35	14	50
Traditional	11	24	65
Liberal	33	14	53
Welfare partnership	66	8	26
Social democratic	38	10	52
Statist	18	18	64

*Figures may not add to 100% due to rounding.

ments in Austria suggested by the previously cited data on the relatively high share of the CSS workforce engaged in service activities, very likely subsidized by the state. But at 50 percent, the government share of CSS income in Austria remains well below the welfare partnership cluster average of 66 percent.

SUMMING UP: A SOCIAL DEMOCRATIC PATTERN WITH A TWIST

In sum, the civil society sector in Austria meets the defining features of the social democratic pattern of civil society development. It has a sizeable workforce, a high rate of volunteer participation, and expressive functions engaging at least a slightly larger share of the workforce than service functions. The level of government support is higher than that found in other social democratic countries but markedly below the level observed in welfare partnership countries.

This sets Austria apart from her northern neighbor, Germany, whose CSS falls squarely into the welfare partnership pattern. To what extent can the social origins theory help us understand this surprising finding? It is to this question that we now turn.

Explaining Austria's Pattern of Civil Society Development

Austria's civil society sector developed differently from her neighbor's because of a different configuration of power relations that emerged in the 20th century. Of central importance was the unusually strong position of the country's working class and the Socialist Party with which it was closely allied. This outcome was facilitated by the weakening of both potential opponents of labor influence: first, the pre-existing landed elites, which were effectively banished along with the emperor in the aftermath of World War I; and second, the embryonic commercial and industrial elites, which were weakened by the German invasion during World War II and then by the postwar nationalization of much of the country's industry to forestall a Soviet takeover. To understand the emergence of this unusual social democratic pattern of civil society development in Austria, it is thus necessary to look briefly into Austrian history and the impact on this country of the 20th century's two world wars.

THE AUSTRO-HUNGARIAN EMPIRE

Austria's history is closely tied to the rise, and subsequent dissolution, of the Habsburg dynasty, the Germanic nobility who, throughout the 17th and 18th centuries, expanded their control of southern and eastern Europe by subjugating various Slavic, Romanian, and Hungarian groups, occupying these areas and establishing Germanic barons in control of the rural countryside. The multinational character of the resulting Habsburg empire, coupled with growing nationalist sentiments of the subjugated populations, posed obvious challenges to effective governance of the empire, however. The Habsburg administration met this challenge by taking a relatively light-handed approach, resulting in the so-called Austro-Hungarian Compromise of 1867, which created a dual sovereignty of the Austrian Empire and the Kingdom of Hungary. This led to the development of a large centralized bureaucracy, which Austria inherited after the breakup of the empire.

The modern civil society sector emerged in the aftermath of the Austro-Hungarian Compromise with the passage of a law on registered associations in 1867.[7] This law spurred the rapid growth of civic associations ranging from charitable societies and savings clubs to cultural and sports clubs as well as political organizations.

WORLD WAR I AND THE RISE OF THE SOCIALIST PARTY

While these various civic and political associations gave vent to some of the tensions inherent in this multicultural melting pot, ultimately the deepening social divisions along ethnic, class, ideological, and urban vs. rural lines contributed to World War I and the ultimate breakup of the empire into several independent states after the defeat of the Austro-German axis in this war. For our purposes here, the most important outcome of the war was not that Austria was forced to cede much of its territory to a set of newly created or reconstituted Slavic states (Czechoslovakia, Poland, and Yugoslavia) but that the Austrian nobility was forced to flee along with the Habsburg emperor, leaving behind a rural landscape of small freeholders and merchants, and that the war significantly emboldened the country's embryonic working class, on whom the war had inflicted heavy burdens. While some elements of the working class pushed a radical agenda, looking to an outright Communist revolution, others fell behind the relatively young Socialist Party, which became a leading force pushing for peace as well as social reforms. After a postwar flirtation with the idea of unifying Austria with Germany in the hope of strengthening the prospects for a socialist outcome in Austria through a union with the stronger German Social Democratic Party, the Austrian Socialist Party got to work proclaiming a democratic republic and pushing for a program of "cradle to grave" social reforms benefiting the workers.[8] Included here were measures establishing an eight-hour workday, workers' councils, and a republican constitution that included provisions for federalism and a resulting decentralization of power.

The Socialist Party's reform agenda was not universally embraced, however. The departure of the Habsburg nobility still left behind a rural population heavily influenced by conservative Catholic social doctrine and suspicious of left-wing socialist ideology. A sharp urban-rural divide thus came to dominate Austrian political life, with the right-leaning Christian Social Party representing the rural population and the left-leaning Socialist Party dominating the urban areas. Under the postwar constitution, which established a parliamentary system and a federal administrative system, this ideological division found reflection in a regionally bifurcated social welfare structure. Forced to compromise, Socialists and Christian Social Party advocates divided the country into geographic spheres of influence and enacted different social welfare regimes in their respective spheres—extensive state social welfare provision in the urban areas and something closer to a welfare partnership pattern engaging long-standing Catholic Church–affiliated service organizations in the rural areas.[9]

THE FALL OF PARLIAMENTARY DEMOCRACY
AND ANNEXATION BY HITLER

The rural-urban split papered over by means of a compromise between Austria's two leading political parties was not the only division within the country, however. Both of these political groupings had moderate and radical factions. The Socialists, favoring a more liberal democracy and expansion of the welfare state, faced a challenge from a more radical Austromarxist faction that pushed for an out-and-out Communist revolution. The right, too, was internally split between more moderate supporters of the Christian Social Party and a strident proto-fascist faction. These splits led to growing political instability, which in turn spurred increased militancy within the political parties and led to increased political violence.[10]

These developments created fertile ground for fascist agitation, in which Austria's civil society organizations, especially sports associations, played an active role.[11] Political assassinations and riots solidified conservative opposition to the standing government and led to the suspension of parliamentary rule and the establishment of an authoritarian Austrofascist regime under the leadership of the Fatherland Front (*Vaterländische Front*) formed by the Christian Social leader Engelbert Dollfuss and right-wing paramilitary groups. This Austrofascist regime outlawed the Socialist Party in 1933 and instituted a series of social and economic reforms modeled after similar developments in Italy, including the corporatist model of labor-employer relations.[12] However, the infighting among conservative factions continued, leading to the total collapse of the government and the annexation of Austria by Hitler in 1938.

German annexation had a devastating effect on Austria's civil society sector, as many organizations were disbanded by the Nazis. The remaining registered associations were either aligned with the nationalistic policies of the fascist state or eliminated altogether. The former, especially mass sports clubs, were co-opted by the fascist regime and contributed significantly to the diffusion of Nazi culture and politics.[13]

POSTWAR COMPLETION OF THE AUSTRIAN WELFARE STATE

The defeat of the Nazis by the Red Army in 1945 opened the door to the resumption of parliamentary government and completion of the Austrian welfare state. This was facilitated by a number of crucial postwar developments. In the first place, although parts of Austria came under the Soviet sphere of influence, the Western powers—Great Britain, France, and the United States—maintained a stronger role in Austria than they did in the more eastern portions of the new Soviet sphere, restraining the Soviet impact to insisting on Austrian neutrality and extracting war reparations. Second, the coalition government that came to power in the first postwar election in 1945 moved quickly to nationalize a number of Austrian industries in order to forestall Soviet takeover.[14] This had the effect of limiting the emergence of a robust commercial and industrial elite that might stand in the way of further state-sponsored social welfare protections. Finally, the postwar period witnessed extensive rural-urban migration, thus reducing the drag of rural opposition to labor's social democratic reform agenda.

In political terms, the first postwar democratic election fundamentally restored the pre-Austrofascist interlude arrangement, as the Socialists (renamed the Social Democratic Party) reached out to the Christian Social Party (reconstituted as the Christian Austrian People's Party) to form a "grand coalition" operating on a principle known as *proporz*, which involved the appointment of government officers by each of the grand coalition parties "in proportion" to their respective political power, which in practice, at least initially, translated into each party appointing equal numbers of officials.[15] Because the right-wing parties were somewhat discredited due to the support some of their factions gave to the fascist regime and the urbanization trends sapping these parties of rural voters, the Social Democrats enjoyed an upper hand in this coalition and were able to complete the development of the social democratic pattern of welfare provision that they had inaugurated in the urban areas beginning two decades earlier. Significantly expanded social welfare protections were not only financed but also delivered by Austria's well-developed public administration. The fact that Austria's imposed postwar neutrality freed up resources that had formerly gone into military spending doubtless facilitated this expanded social welfare spending.

As a result, the public sector delivers most of public welfare services in Austria today. It accounts for 84 percent of total employment in education and 52 percent of total employment in the health field, extending a development established by the Socialists in Austrian urban areas beginning in the 1920s. However, vestiges of the welfare partnership pattern favored by the old Christian Social Party also survived, though only in the field of social services, where the civil society sector outdistances government employment 55 percent to 25 percent.

With social protections provided largely by the public welfare system, the civil society sector has taken more of an expressive role in Austrian society, bridging the gap between the left and the right by mobilizing popular support for both political parties. As a result, many civil society organizations receive support from either the Social Democrats or the People's Party, following the *proporz* principle. Due to their close affiliation with political parties and labor unions, civil society organizations gained considerable political influence and access to public funding.[16]

At the same time, the civil society sector in Austria became rather politicized and divided into "red" wing groups affiliated with the Social Democrats and "black" wing groups affiliated with the People's Party.[17] This also created an entry barrier for organizations not affiliated with the major political parties and spurred a rivalry between "old" and "new" organizations that played out especially dramatically in the 1970s environmental and human rights movements.

Another development that has significantly impacted the civil society sector in Austria—especially with regard to volunteer participation—was the implementation of civilian public service in lieu of mandatory military service in 1975. In 2004 about 1,020 organizations offered a total of 12,538 places for citizens to carry out their social work obligation.[18] And this has encouraged general volunteer participation beyond the civil service requirements.

Conclusion

Austria has a sizeable civil society sector staffed predominantly by volunteers and engaged half in expressive and half in service activities. These characteristics place it in the social democratic pattern of civil society development. However, the share of expressive activities is considerably lower than the social democratic pattern average, while the level of government support and the share of service activities are noticeably larger than those in other countries following this pattern and close to those in countries exhibiting the welfare partnership pattern. This indicates that the Austrian CSS is more of a hybrid case, combining elements of the social democratic and welfare partnership patterns.

In both respects, the social origins theory, with its emphasis on power relations among social groupings and political institutions, offers important clues to why this pattern emerged. First, despite its strong affinity to German culture and political institutions, Austria did not simply copy the welfare partnership model that prevailed in Germany but rather developed its own path, which reflected the divergent political interests of the urban working class and the rural small farmers and merchants strongly influenced by the Catholic Church. Contributing to this outcome, and particularly to its unusual social democratic characteristics, was the relative influence of the Austrian working class, which was facilitated by the elimination of the country's landed elites following World War I and the impediments to the power of commercial and industrial elites created first by the Nazi takeover and then by the post–World War II nationalization of much of the Austrian economy.

But labor was not strong enough to govern on its own and therefore found it necessary to reach a *modus vivendi* with a Christian Social Party supported by rural freeholders. The result was a virtual partition of the country into alternative welfare regimes, with a social democratic pattern established in the urban areas, especially Vienna, and more of a welfare partnership one established in the countryside. Although this duality was suppressed during the Nazi interlude, it re-emerged after World War II as the prewar power relations were restored, though with the labor-oriented Social Democratic Party holding the upper hand. The resulting hybrid system evident in our data reflects these power relations all too clearly, with a dominant social democratic pattern of civil society development of the sort favored by urban workers coexisting with marked elements of the welfare partnership one favored by more conservative rural and Catholic-oriented elements.

Notes

This study was possible thanks to the effort of a broad group of researchers under the direction of Ulrike Schneider at the Research Institute for Non-Profit Organisations at WU Vienna University of Economics and Business.

1. The data on the size and composition of the civil society sector in Austria were gathered for the first time in 1995 and reported in the first volume of this series: Salamon, Anheier, List, et al. 1999. However, the 1995 data are not comparable to those reported here because of substantial differences in methodologies used to compile these two data sets. For more recent data on employment in the Austrian

CSS, see Pennerstorfer, Schneider, and Badelt 2013; Schneider and Haider 2009; and Haider et al. 2008.

2. Contract workers are not included in this figure, because data on this type of work are not available in the 2001 workplace and business census. See Schneider and Hagleitner 2005, on which employment figures presented here are based.

3. Volunteering data reported here are for the year 2000.

4. Excluding unpaid work in lieu of compulsory military service.

5. Neumayr et al. 2007, 7.

6. *Ibid.*, 8.

7. Simsa, Schober, and Schober 2006, 10.

8. Beller 2007.

9. Brook-Shepherd 1996.

10. *Ibid.*

11. Simsa, Schober, and Schober 2006, 28.

12. Fascist corporatism favors management of sectors of the economy by government or privately controlled corporations representing occupational concerns of both employers and workers. In theory, this arrangement was supposed to reduce class conflict and promote harmony among socioeconomic classes, but in reality this was a mechanism for reducing opposition and rewarding political loyalty.

13. Heitzmann and Simsa 2004, 715; Wachter 1983, 69.

14. Katzenstein 1985.

15. Brook-Shepherd 1996.

16. Pennerstorfer, Schneider, and Badelt 2013, 57.

17. Katzenstein 1985.

18. Zivildienstverwaltung 2006.

CHAPTER THIRTEEN

Denmark

A Social Democratic Pattern with a Twist

THOMAS P. BOJE, BJARNE IBSEN, TORBEN FRIDBERG,
ULLA HABERMANN, S. WOJCIECH SOKOLOWSKI,
and LESTER M. SALAMON

DENMARK HAS ONE of the most generous welfare states in the world, allocating 28.7 percent of its GDP to social safety net programs.[1] It also has a fairly robust civil society sector. This coexistence of a generous welfare state and a robust civil society may look like a paradox to those who assume that government welfare "crowds out" private initiative. Yet this apparent paradox is not confined to Denmark but is also found in other European countries following the social democratic pattern of civil society development.

With a large workforce, relatively high share of volunteers, about equal distribution of service and expressive activities, and a sizeable level of government support, Denmark's civil society sector can best be categorized as a borderline case between the social democratic and welfare partnership patterns of civil society development. How did this pattern come about? The social origins theory points our attention to a shift in the agrarian economy that began in the 18th century, leading to the replacement of large landed estates with small, owner-operated farms and facilitating the formation of a rather unusual alliance among three influential socioeconomic classes—commercially oriented small farmers, industrial workers, and middle-class merchants and professionals. Over the next two centuries, this coalition managed to put in place a robust program of government social protections and subsidies for commercial businesses, particularly in the agricultural sector.

The balance of this chapter explores how this alliance came about and demonstrates, in the process, how factors identified by the social origins theory can help explain the civil society pattern that resulted. First, however, it is necessary to document this pattern more precisely.

Dimensions of the Danish Civil Society Sector

SIZE OF THE WORKFORCE

The civil society sector represents a considerable component of the Danish economy. As of 2004, Danish civil society organizations (CSOs) employed over 140,000 full-time equivalent (FTE) paid workers, which represents nearly 5 percent of the country's economically active population (EAP). In addition, these civil society organizations engaged nearly 1.5 million volunteers, or over 27 percent of the total population and 35 percent of the adult population. The input of these volunteers to civil society organizations translates into another 110,000 FTE jobs, bringing the total workforce of the Danish CSO sector to nearly 251,000 FTE workers, or 8.8 percent of the country's EAP.

As figure 13.1 shows, the size of the CSO workforce is second only to manufacturing (435,000 employees) and exceeds employment in transportation (186,000), construction (185,000), and agriculture and fishing (81,000).

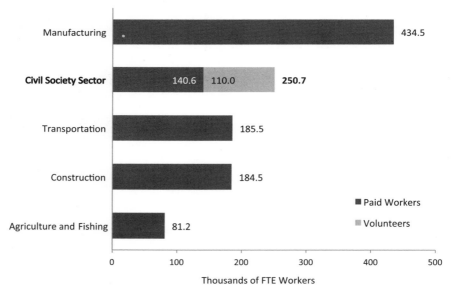

FIGURE 13.1. FTE workforce, civil society sector vs. selected industries, Denmark, 2004.

TABLE 13.1   Civil society sector workforce
as share of EAP, Denmark vs. country
clusters and 41-country average

Cluster	Workforce as a share of EAP (%)
Denmark	8.8
41 countries	5.7
Traditional	1.9
Liberal	9.6
Welfare partnership	11.2
Social democratic	8.2
Statist	2.3

The CSO sector in Denmark is also quite sizable in relation to other countries. Measured as a share of the economically active population, the workforce of the Danish CSO sector as of 2004, at 8.8 percent, ranked substantially above the 5.7 percent average for the 41 countries on which such data are available, as figure 2.7 demonstrates.

This places Denmark's civil society sector above several high-income countries in Europe and North America, most notably its neighbors Germany (6.8 percent of EAP) and Norway (7.3 percent), but below that in Sweden (9.6 percent), Belgium (13.1 percent), and the Netherlands (15.9 percent). As table 13.1 shows, the Danish CSO sector is slightly larger than the average of the social democratic country cluster, of which Denmark is a borderline member.

VOLUNTEER PARTICIPATION

High levels of volunteer participation are one of the defining characteristics of the social democratic pattern. Over 27 percent of the Danish population engaged in some form of volunteering in 2004. As noted, this translates into the equivalent of more than 110,000 full-time jobs and accounts for 44 percent of the entire civil society workforce.

This share of volunteer input in Denmark, while slightly above the 41-country average (40 percent), falls short of the social democratic country cluster average (69 percent), as table 13.2 demonstrates. The relatively low proportion of volunteers in the Danish CSO workforce can be explained by

TABLE 13.2 Volunteer share of CSS workforce, Denmark vs. country clusters and 41-country average

Cluster	Volunteers as a share of CSS workforce (%)
Denmark	**43.9**
41 countries	*40.6*
Traditional	53.1
Liberal	46.4
Welfare partnership	29.1
Social democratic	69.4
Statist	27.9

the relatively large proportion of civil society organizations operating in the social services field in Denmark, as will be noted more fully below. In addition, however, this figure underestimates the actual level of volunteering because it encompasses only volunteering channeled through civil society organizations as defined in this book. A significant amount of volunteering also occurs in borderline entities that were not covered by this study, notably, the Home Guard (volunteer territorial self-defense) and a variety of self-help groups. Including this volunteer effort in our estimates would bring Denmark closer to the social-democratic cluster average.

SERVICE AND EXPRESSIVE ACTIVITIES

Another defining feature of the social democratic country cluster is the dominance of expressive functions in civil society sector activities. However, only 43 percent of the workforce in Denmark is engaged in expressive activities, with the field of culture, sports, and recreation accounting for 25 percent of the workforce alone (table 13.3). On the other hand, about 50 percent of the CSO workforce (paid and volunteer) in Denmark is engaged in service activities, primarily in education and research (22 percent) and social services (19 percent).

Although the relative share of the CSO workforce engaged in expressive activities in Denmark falls a bit short of meeting the definitional benchmark of the social democratic model, it is nevertheless well above the 41-country average, as shown in table 13.4. And this does not take account of the sub-

TABLE 13.3　Distribution of Denmark's CSS workforce, by field, 2004

Field	Share (%)
Service fields	50
Education and research	22
Social services	19
Health care	3
Economic development	6
Expressive fields	43
Culture, sports, and recreation	25
Religion	3
Advocacy	3
Professional associations and labor unions	11
Environmental protection	1
Other fields	7
Philanthropic intermediaries	0
International	2
Not elsewhere classified	4
N	250,661

TABLE 13.4　Distribution of CSS workforce by type of function, Denmark vs. country clusters and 41-country average

Cluster	Share of CSS workforce, by type of function* (%)		
	Service	Expressive	Other
Denmark	50	43	7
41 countries	59	37	4
Traditional	68	24	8
Liberal	55	36	9
Welfare partnership	71	25	4
Social democratic	39	59	2
Statist	50	47	4

*Figures may not add to 100% due to rounding.

stantial volume of volunteer work in self-help organizations and the Home Guard.

REVENUE SOURCES

The Danish civil society sector resembles other social democratic cases far more closely in its revenue pattern. In Denmark, government support

TABLE 13.5   Sources of Denmark's CSS revenue by field, 2004

Field	Government (%)	Philanthropy (%)	Fees (%)
All fields	40	7	53
Service fields	65	3	32
Health care	13	41	46
Education and research	76	0	24
Social services	75	4	21
Economic development	7	1	92
Expressive fields	9	11	80
Environmental protection	7	44	49
Culture, sports, and recreation	25	20	55
Religion	15	35	50
Professional associations and labor unions	1	6	93
Advocacy	27	12	60
Other fields	39	13	49
Philanthropic intermediaries	39	0	61
International	50	27	22
Not elsewhere classified	23	3	74

accounted for 40 percent (105 billion Danish Krone, or US$19.2 billion) of the total revenue of the sector in 2004, as shown in table 13.5. More than half (53 percent) came from fees and market sales, while private philanthropy provided the remaining 7 percent.

As table 13.6 reveals, this funding structure bears close relationship to the average for countries exhibiting a social democratic pattern of civil society development. Compared to the 40 percent government share of CSO income in Denmark, the average for all the social-democratic cluster countries is 38 percent. And the 53 percent and 7 percent of CSO revenue coming from fees and philanthropy, respectively, in Denmark compare closely to the 52 percent and 10 percent averages for all the social democratic countries.

In some fields, however, such as social services and education and research, the CSO revenue structure in Denmark looks more like the welfare partnership pattern than the social democratic one. As table 13.5 shows, in these fields government support accounts for 75 percent or more of CSO revenue, a pattern quite characteristic of countries utilizing a welfare partnership structure that relies heavily on government financing of civil society organizations to carry out social welfare functions.

TABLE 13.6 Shares of CSS revenue by source, Denmark vs. country clusters and 41-country average*

Cluster	Government (%)	Philanthropy (%)	Fees (%)
Denmark	40	7	53
41 countries	*35*	*14*	*50*
Traditional	11	24	65
Liberal	33	14	53
Welfare partnership	66	8	26
Social democratic	38	10	52
Statist	18	18	64

*Figures may not add to 100% due to rounding.

SUMMARY

In sum, Denmark is one of only a handful of countries on which we have data that do not fit neatly into one of the five patterns of civil society identified in chapter 4. While it shows significant resemblance to the social democratic pattern in its general contours (size, volunteer participation, and share of expressive activities), it also shows some features of the welfare partnership model (high level of service activities and extensive government funding), at least in selected key welfare service fields. To what extent can the social origins theory of civil society development explain this particular outcome?

Explaining Denmark's Pattern of Civil Society Development[2]

The social origins explanation of the hybrid pattern of civil society development in Denmark links this development to a rather unique balance of power among three dominant socioeconomic classes: small farmers, industrial workers, and the professional and commercial middle classes. This pattern started to emerge in the 18th century, as population growth increased pressures on agricultural production and highlighted the inefficiencies of the existing feudal landholding system, with peasants operating small portions of the landlord's estate in return for an obligation to supply a certain amount of labor to the landlord. Unable to eke out a sufficient income from this system, and therefore unable to keep their progeny engaged in agriculture and away from the more lucrative opportunities emerging in trade, landlords began selling portions of their estates to their former tenants. These transactions were encouraged by the Crown, itself a large landowner eager to find ways to modernize the agricultural sector and reap more in taxes. By the latter 19th century, two-thirds of all Danish farmers had become became owner-occupiers, and 75 percent of all agricultural land was farmed by owners of midsized farms.[3]

To remain economically viable, these smallholders organized agrarian cooperatives to pool their landholdings or to process and market their products. The cooperative organization of agricultural production allowed the midsized and small farmers to benefit from economies of scale and significantly increased agricultural productivity, allowing the farmers to take advantage of new opportunities to export their wheat and other agricultural products.[4] This, in turn, empowered the farmer and merchant classes and increased their demands for a greater role in government than the monarchy yet provided.

These pressures, coupled with the antifeudal and antimonarchic uprisings that erupted throughout Europe in 1848, provided the spark to convince Danish King Frederick VII to accept the idea of a constitutional monarchy, which was embodied in a new Danish constitution enacted in 1849. This constitution made provision for a stronger parliament and guaranteed the inviolability of private property rights and of contracts. The resulting liberalization further stimulated the growth of the Danish export economy and opened new organizing opportunities for wide segments of Danish society, creating fertile ground for a robust growth of the civil society sector.

In the second half of the 19th century, belated industrialization triggered mass migration to the cities, which in turn spurred the growth of popular movements addressing the social problems it brought about, from poverty to the breakdown of traditional communities and the breach of social order. The concept of a division between the deserving and undeserving poor, which provided a clear, morally founded, ideological dividing line between public and private responsibility, was gradually dissolved from 1890 on, and with it the ideological resistance to universal public-welfare assistance.[5] Central actors in this development were associations of landowning farmers and urban labor movements that together pressured government for public social reforms to improve the social conditions for both rural and urban workers.[6] The arguably most important development came in 1891 with the introduction of a universal, tax-financed pension scheme that eventually replaced the old, means-tested system of poor relief.[7] Another important development was the restructuring of "pioneer" philanthropy associations into self-organized associations that successfully advocated for a more efficient public social service delivery system.[8]

The growing Danish working class found powerful institutional representation in the Social Democratic Party founded in 1871 by three socialist labor leaders—Louis Pio, Harald Brix, and Paul Geleff. Following World War I, the Social Democratic Party became a leading political force in Denmark, and in 1924 it formed the government that laid the foundations for the welfare state based on a close collaboration between labor unions and the government. Another push came from the agricultural sector and professional middle-class elements striving to establish a more efficient and professional social service delivery system. These developments ultimately led to the passage of the Social Reform Act of 1933, which placed major social service institutions within the purview of the state and local authorities. This arrangement formed the basis of the welfare state that is the quintessential characteristic of the social democratic model of civil society development.

Although the government assumed a major role in funding and providing social welfare services, civil society nonetheless maintained a significant role in service delivery. The freedom of association guaranteed by the Constitutional Act of 1849 created ample opportunities for self-organization of the working classes. Thus, the labor movement set up a wide variety of institutions, such as sick benefit associations, burial funds, strike funds, and saving banks. The co-operative movement founded co-operatives, and sports clubs were organized as part of the "popular Enlightenment" movement. The movement to strengthen the defense of the nation created the Danish Rifle Association, which also promoted sports activities for the country's youth. As a result of these two latter sets of organizations, a substantial proportion of the CSO sector still consists of organized sports, and about one-third of the adult Danish population and two-thirds of the school-aged children are members of a sports club. Other examples of the robust civil society development in Denmark were housing associations, housing cooperatives,[9] voluntary unemployment funds,[10] the Grundtvigian movement, which aimed to establish "free education and the promotion of 'sports for all,'"[11] free schools of many types (frequently subsidized by the state), and even a Home Guard (a popular movement set up after World War II to provide territorial self-defense).

Interestingly, the popular movements were not dominated by individual socioeconomic classes but rather represented a wide variety of interests addressing a wide range of social and political problems. These movements included members of the working classes, farmers, and those tied to the professional and commercial middle classes, and they pursued a balanced set of political, economic, and social-welfare reforms that provided something for every interest in the coalition. In fact, one of the most characteristic features of Danish developments was their peaceful character and the relative absence of radical factions within the various constituencies, which significantly reduced social conflicts and facilitated the smooth passage of significant social and political reforms. One possible explanation of this was the fact that no powerful landed elite had to be overcome through violent revolutionary action earlier in Danish history: in a sense, the landlords solved this problem themselves by selling out their properties. This ultimately paved the way to a peaceful transition to a liberal constitutional monarchy, which in turn established a template for working out social problems through political cooperation, or what Arendt Lijphart calls "consensus democracy" (discussed in chapter 5 of this volume). As a result, farmers, workers, and professionals, as well as industrialists, could agree on a hybrid type of welfare regime that benefited their respective class interests.

The development of the welfare state in Denmark accelerated after World War II, as the state, under pressure from voluntary interest organizations, assumed increased responsibility for providing health and social services.[12] Although the salience of private voluntary organizations in service delivery substantially diminished, the level of public sector support and cooperation, and in some cases fusion, between government agencies and private associations solidified during this period and was codified in law.

The expansion of the welfare state in Denmark peaked with the passage of the Local Government Reform Act of 1970 and the Danish Social Assistance Act of 1976, which significantly reduced the role of voluntary organizations as social service providers. At the same time, the public sector increased its support to associations and organizations for culture, leisure, and sport. This happened primarily through increased capture of lottery and other betting proceeds for national organizations and direct and indirect economic subsidies from the local government (municipality) to local sports, culture, and leisure associations. Under the Danish Act on Popular Education and the Leisure-Time Activities, sports and leisure activities for children and youth are eligible for funding if organized under voluntary auspices. It is characteristic of public-sector funding for cultural and leisure activities that relatively few, not very specific strings are attached, and the sphere has enjoyed a tradition of wide-ranging autonomy.

The trend of increased state involvement in social welfare increased further during the 1980s with the global ascendance of neoliberalism, which deemphasized the welfare state in favor of voluntary assistance. Advocates of the neoliberal ideology extolled the virtues of private philanthropy and self-help and challenged the foundations of the Danish welfare state—social insurance, universal benefits, equality, and preventive social programs—sparking an intense political debate.[13]

These influences resulted in a policy shift toward increased recourse to civil society organizations in service delivery and the promotion of private philanthropy in addressing social needs. The Danish Social Service Act of 1998 affirmed this shift by directing local authorities to delegate the provision of certain government services to private voluntary associations. This not only gave the civil society sector greater visibility and legitimacy but also resulted in an increase in public financial support and the appearance of features commonly associated with the welfare partnership, rather than the social democratic, pattern of civil society development, precisely as our empirical data revealed.

Conclusions

The civil society sector is a significant economic force in Denmark, but its structure has elements of both the social democratic and welfare partnership patterns. This outcome is a product of a unique balance of interests among three influential socioeconomic classes that surfaced in Denmark in the 19th century and shaped the institutional landscape of the country that is evident today. Included in this working coalition were the sizable group of yeoman farmers who secured ownership of land from previously dominant landed elites during the 18th and early 19th centuries; middle-class merchants and professionals who gained prominence in the commercial thrust of Denmark that followed this rural transformation; and urban industrial workers whose numbers swelled as industry belatedly took off in the mid-19th and early 20th centuries. Working in tandem through a robust Social Democratic Party, this set of interests was able to secure the democratic reforms, peaceful transition from absolute monarchy, and strong guarantees of private property wanted by the merchants and professionals, along with the favorable economic incentives and generous social protections wanted by the farmers and laborers.

Although these elements were able to put in place a full battery of welfare state protections, the liberal reforms in the mid-19th century and the need of the owner-farmers for cooperative institutions to facilitate their engagement in the lucrative grain trade encouraged the growth as well of a lively civil society sector. In some fields, such as education and sports, these organizations were later made the beneficiaries of state support, giving the Danish civil society sector some of the characteristics of the welfare partnership pattern. This facet of the sector's structure subsequently gained additional support from the ascent among certain conservative elements of the neoliberal ideology with its emphasis on shrinking the welfare state and placing more reliance on philanthropy and the nonprofit sector. By focusing on the power relationships among different social groups as mediated by various political and other institutions, the social origins theory thus helps us to understand how the civil society sector of Denmark has taken the shape that it has.

Notes

This study was possible thanks to the effort of a broad group of researchers at the Danish National Centre for Social Research, the University of Southern Denmark, and Roskilde University, Department of Society and Globalization, led by Inger Koch-Nielsen, Torben Fridberg, Bjarne Ibsen, and Thomas P. Boje.

1. Source: www.oecd.org/social/socialpoliciesanddata/socialexpendituredatabasesocx.htm.

2. The balance of this chapter draws heavily from Ibsen and Haberman 2005.

3. Henriksen 2003.

4. Henriksen 1999, 2006.

5. Henriksen and Bundesen 2004.

6. Petersen 2004.

7. *Ibid.*

8. Jørgensen, Bundesen, and Henriksen 2001.

9. Neville 1998.

10. See Bender, Jansen, and Johansen 1977.

11. Habermann and Ibsen 1997; Lorentzen 1993; Klausen 1995; Klausen and Selle 1995b.

12. Wollebæk and Selle 2000; Svedberg and Grassman 2001; Andersen, Andersen, and Torpe 2000.

13. Villadsen 2004; Habermann 2001.

CHAPTER FOURTEEN

Russia

A Classic Statist Model

IRINA MERSIANOVA, OLGA KONONYKHINA,
S. WOJCIECH SOKOLOWSKI, *and* LESTER M. SALAMON

M OST RUSSIANS ARE GENEROUS and eager to engage in community work, self-help activities, and other forms of assistance for their friends and neighbors, and, according to one study, they believe that everyone else in their community should do so also.[1] At the same time, however, the civil society sector in Russia is quite small: It engages only about 1 percent of the country's economically active population (EAP).

This seeming paradox between the willingness of Russian citizens to help neighbors and friends, and the small size and low legitimacy of Russia's civil society institutions, suggests that the scale and shape of the civil society sector in the country is not simply a product of popular sentiments and preferences. Rather, the Russian experience seems to confirm a central feature of the social origins theory of civil society development outlined in chapter 4: namely, that the shape and character of the civil society sector in a country is a product of deeper sociopolitical forces that either foster or impede its development, and that the constellation of these forces results in different emergent patterns of civil society development. We find that the development of the civil society sector in the specific case of Russia follows what we have termed the statist pattern of civil society development and argue that this outcome flows from the kind of factors outlined in the social origins theory of civil society.

To see this, the chapter reviews what is known about the size, composition, and financing of the civil society sector in Russia, drawing on the first systematic, empirical study of the Russian civil society sector ever undertaken. It then puts the resulting findings into context in terms of the five patterns of civil society development outlined in chapter 4. Finally, the chapter assesses the extent to which the factors identified in the social origins theory account for the pattern of civil society development evident in these data. Fundamentally, the central conclusion that emerges is that Russia exhibits a pattern of civil society development that closely resembles the statist pattern, and that the sociopolitical factors that the social origins theory associates with this pattern are fully evident in the Russian experience.

Dimensions of the Russian Civil Society Sector

SIZE OF THE WORKFORCE

As of 2008, Russian civil society organizations employed 554,000 paid full-time-equivalent (FTE) workers, or 0.7 percent of the EAP.[2] What is more, these organizations engaged nearly 2 million volunteers, which translate into an additional 316,000 FTE jobs, bringing the total workforce of the Russian civil society organizations to 870,000 FTE workers, or 1.2 percent of the country's EAP. In absolute terms, this is a large number of people working in the civil society sector, larger than the number of such workers in all but five European countries on which data are available.[3] However, Russia is also a big country, and when this number is scaled to the size of Russia's economy, a different story emerges.

Figure 14.1 compares the size of the civil society sector's workforce against a number of key of industries: agriculture and fishing, manufacturing, construction, and transportation. In Russia, the size of the civil society workforce, even with volunteers included, is much smaller than that of any of these industries.

The size of the civil society sector in Russia is also small in relation to that of other countries, at least as measured in relative terms. Thus, measured as a share of the economically active population, the workforce of the Russian civil society sector as of 2008, at 1.2 percent, ranked substantially below the 5.7 percent average for the 41 countries for which such data are available, as figure 2.7 demonstrates. The size of the civil society workforce in Russia falls within the range defining the statist pattern (4.5 percent of the EAP or less) as described in chapter 4, but it falls below the average of all countries that exhibit this pattern (2.3 percent), as table 14.1 shows.

Although the size of the civil sector in Russia is markedly below all Western European countries, it is greater than that in Poland, Slovakia and Romania, which were part of the Soviet bloc prior to 1989. However, it is somewhat smaller than those in the two other former Soviet bloc countries on which we have data, the Czech Republic (1.7 percent) and Hungary (2.0 percent).

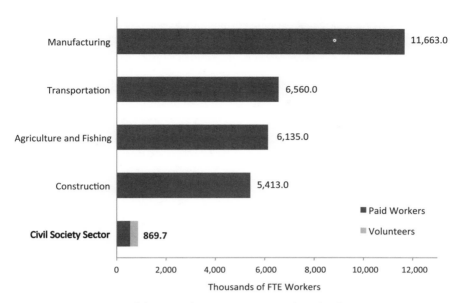

FIGURE 14.1. FTE workforce, civil society sector vs. selected industries, Russia, 2008.

TABLE 14.1 Civil society sector workforce as share of EAP, Russia vs. country clusters and 41-country average

Cluster	Workforce as a share of EAP (%)
Russia	**1.2**
41 countries	5.7
Traditional	1.9
Liberal	9.6
Welfare partnership	11.2
Social democratic	8.2
Statist	2.3

VOLUNTEER PARTICIPATION

A second key feature of the Russian civil society sector relates to its level of volunteer support. As noted above, about 2 million people (1.4 percent of the population) volunteered in Russia in 2008. This level of volunteer participation is rather low by international standards, especially in industrialized

TABLE 14.2   Volunteer share of CSS workforce,
Russia vs. country clusters and 41-country average

Cluster	Volunteers as a share of CSS workforce (%)
Russia	36.3
41 countries	*40.6*
Traditional	53.1
Liberal	46.4
Welfare partnership	29.1
Social democratic	69.4
Statist	27.9

Western countries, where more than 20 percent of the population engage in volunteer activities of some kind. Similarly, as noted above, the time contributed by these 2 million volunteers amounts to the equivalent of 316,000 FTE jobs, which constitutes 36 percent of the total civil society workforce, falling somewhat below the international average of 41 percent.

A low level of volunteer participation is a defining characteristic of the statist pattern of civil society development, as discussed in chapter 4. While the volunteer share of the workforce in Russia, at 36 percent, is higher than the 28 percent average of countries that exhibit the statist pattern, as table 14.2 shows, it nonetheless falls within the range defining that pattern (less than 38 percent).

SERVICE AND EXPRESSIVE ACTIVITIES

Most (about 57 percent) of the civil society sector workforce (paid and volunteer) in Russia is engaged in expressive activities, especially advocacy (18 percent), culture, sports, and recreation (16 percent), and labor unions (14 percent). Service activities employ only 34 percent of the workforce, of which social services account for 21 percent (table 14.3).

The dominance of expressive activities, while not a defining feature of the statist model, is nonetheless a characteristic legacy of the Soviet-style policies that shaped the civil society sector in Eastern Europe. This peculiarity brings Russia closer to the social democratic model, which is characterized, in part, by the dominance of such expressive activities since the state in such settings delivers the bulk of social welfare assistance directly (table 14.4).

TABLE 14.3   Distribution of Russia's CSS workforce,
by field, 2008

Field	Share (%)
Service fields	34
Education and research	3
Social services	21
Health care	3
Economic development	7
Expressive fields	57
Culture, sports, and recreation	16
Religion	8
Advocacy	18
Professional associations and labor unions	14
Environmental protection	1
Other fields	9
Philanthropic intermediaries	4
International	0
Not elsewhere classified	5
N	869,690

TABLE 14.4   Distribution of CSS workforce by type of function, Russia vs.
country clusters and 41-country average

Cluster	Share of CSS workforce, by type of function* (%)		
	Service	Expressive	Other
Russia	34	57	9
41 countries	59	37	4
Traditional	68	24	8
Liberal	55	36	9
Welfare partnership	71	25	4
Social democratic	39	59	2
Statist	50	47	4

*Figures may not add to 100% due to rounding.

This resemblance is not coincidental. As will be discussed in more detail later in this chapter, the Soviet Union implemented a policy of providing educational, health, and social assistance through state agencies and effectively ousted private providers from these arenas. The civil society sector's activities were restricted to expressive areas, especially recreation, political mobilization, professional associations, and trade unionism.

TABLE 14.5 Sources of Russia's CSS revenue by field, 2008

Field	Government (%)	Philanthropy (%)	Fees (%)
All fields	15	33	51
Service fields	25	43	32
Health care	40	60	1
Education and research	41	5	54
Social services	24	63	12
Economic development	13	0	87
Expressive fields	13	31	57
Environmental protection	10	57	32
Culture, sports, and recreation	12	8	80
Religion	0	82	18
Professional associations and labor unions	13	6	81
Advocacy	15	62	23
Other fields	7	26	67
Philanthropic intermediaries	10	39	52
International	5	75	20
Not elsewhere classified	2	0	97

REVENUE SOURCES

The total revenue of the civil society sector in Russia was 314.3 billion rubles (US$12.3 billion) in 2008. More than half of that amount (51 percent) came from fees, as table 14.5 shows. The second-largest source is philanthropy, especially business philanthropy, which accounted for 33 percent, while government payments provided the remaining 15 percent of the total.

The unusually high share of philanthropy is a result of very high levels of business philanthropy in the fields of health care (60 percent) and social services (63 percent), though this must be seen in the context of the limited overall scale of Russian civil society. The level of government support of the civil society sector is rather low by international standards, especially in the context of Europe, but it meets the defining criteria of the statist model (below 36 percent of total revenue). As table 14.6 shows, the level of government support of the sector in Russia is close to the average of 18 percent of total revenue for countries following the statist pattern.

TABLE 14.6   Shares of CSS revenue by source, Russia vs. country clusters and 41-country average*

Cluster	Government (%)	Philanthropy (%)	Fees (%)
Russia	15	33	51
41 countries	35	14	50
Traditional	11	24	65
Liberal	33	14	53
Welfare partnership	66	8	26
Social democratic	38	10	52
Statist	18	18	64

*Figures may not add to 100% due to rounding.

Explaining the Pattern of Civil Society Development in Russia

As the data in the previous section show, the civil society sector in Russia squarely fits the statist model of civil society development, characterized by limited size, relatively low levels of volunteer participation, and a low level of government financial support. According to the social origins theory, this pattern emerges in agrarian societies where reform-minded forces seize government power and use it to pursue rapid industrialization. Such policies foster economic development at the expense of the quality of everyday life and entail a fair amount of political repression to curb popular dissent. Only those institutional forms that are instrumental to economic development policies receive government support, while other forms are either neglected or altogether banned. Consequently, citizen initiative independent of government tutelage is restricted mainly to the informal sphere. To what extent do these developmental features apply to the Russian case? From the evidence at hand, the answer to this question is: quite well.

Russia entered the 20th century still a heavily agrarian society. After abolishing the *ancien regime* following the 1917 revolution, the Bolshevik revolutionaries turned their attention to instituting a wide range of industrialization policies in which the state was the central, and for the most part the only, actor.[4] These policies thoroughly redefined the entire shape of Russian society. The role of the state, which was already strong prior to the 1917 revolution, became even more dominant and overbearing over most aspects of Russia's social, political, and economic life, including its civil society sector.

PREREVOLUTIONARY PERIOD: THE FIRST ASSOCIATIONS

Civil society organizations were present in Russia prior to this revolutionary upheaval, though in relatively muted form. Due to the dominance of large-scale landowners, Russia remained a heavily rural country with relatively few and sparse urban centers at the dawn of the 20th century. The urban classes, such as merchants, artisans, or professionals, which in Western Europe were a major social force behind civil society development throughout the 18th and 19th centuries, remained relatively weak in Russia. Consequently, the growth of the civil society sector in Russia was much slower than in Western Europe during this time period.[5]

This, of course, does not imply the total absence of civil society in prerevolutionary Russia, as some observers have suggested.[6] The first public charitable associations emerged in the 18th century and were influenced by Western European ideas of counterbalancing the power of state institutions.[7] Initially these associations were linked to the Russian nobility, but as the professional class (the so-called intelligentsia) started gaining prominence, it became the main force behind the creation of scientific, technical, medical, and cultural societies.

The liberal reforms introduced in the 1860s by Tsar Alexander II (the chief of which was the abolition of serfdom) spurred the social, economic, and political transformation of the country. Russian municipalities gained greater autonomy, which led to improvement and extension of local government services and a greater role for nongovernmental institutions (*zemstva*, or district councils) in providing some of these services.[8] Numerous new associations, mainly scientific, technical, medical, pedagogical, and cultural societies, were created in the aftermath of the reform. However, the state never fully relinquished its control and passed legislation subjecting the establishment of new societies to the authority of the Ministry of Internal Affairs.[9]

By the early 20th century a sizeable network of public associations existed in Russia, especially in the spheres of culture, education, and social protection. However, these associations were concentrated mainly in major urban centers, especially Moscow and St. Petersburg; they were far less numerous in the vast rural areas where most of Russia's population lived.[10]

THE SOVIET PERIOD: ACCELERATED INDUSTRIALIZATION AND GOVERNMENT CONTROL OF CIVIL SOCIETY

The relative backwardness of the Russian economy, coupled with the series of military defeats it suffered at the hands of more industrialized powers prior to the revolution,[11] led to massive social unrest, which culminated in two revolutions in 1917. The February 1917 Revolution deposed the tsar and established a government that was largely controlled by social democrats (the so-called Kerensky government). However, Russia's continuation of the unpopular war effort led to further social unrest and the eventual toppling of the Kerensky government by the Bolshevik faction of the Communist movement.

After consolidating its power, the victorious Communist government nationalized the economy and initiated redistribution of the land, which dramatically changed Russia's socioeconomic class structure. At the same time, it initiated an ambitious program of massive industrialization in which the central government was the dominant actor. These policies drew huge numbers of peasantry to industrial projects, which in turn necessitated the provision of a large, if rudimentary, social safety net, again arranged by the state.[12] Here, in short, were the classic features of a modernizing "revolution from above" hypothesized to yield a statist pattern of civil society development.

In the early years of the new regime, however, a different dynamic surfaced. The dramatic social changes initially provided a new impetus for the growth of civil society organizations. With newly adopted legislation that reaffirmed the freedom of association to all citizens, new organizations started to emerge to deal with a variety of issues, ranging from the allotment of accommodations, food, fuel, and clothing to building schools and playgrounds and providing a wide array of cultural and educational activities.[13] Notwithstanding the increasing bureaucratic obstacles erected by the Soviet authorities, a great number of cultural, literary, artistic, and scientific associations emerged in the 1920s, raising hopes for a rapid development of civil society.[14]

However, internal strife among different political factions, which intensified after Lenin's death in 1924, hampered these initial developments. Joseph Stalin, who emerged victorious from that strife, unleashed a reign of terror to undermine opposition and solidify his dictatorial rule while pursuing increasingly unpopular economic development policies.[15] As a consequence, most voluntary associations were either dissolved or subjected to tight government control. Legislation adopted in 1932, which remained in effect until the 1980s, established rigid ideological control of all aspects of social life and created hierarchical bureaucratic structures for organizing and controlling all grassroots associations.[16]

At the same time, however, the government established and sponsored mass membership organizations, whose aim was the mobilization of political support for government policies (mainly among the youth). These organizations were almost exclusively engaged in expressive activities, such as representation of occupational interests, cultural and political events, or hobbies and leisure pursuits. Service functions (such as the provision of education, health care, social assistance, or housing) were performed by state agencies. Thus, despite their massive membership, these organizations had rather small paid staffs and consumed relatively little financial resources. As a consequence, the overall level of government financial support for civil society organizations remained rather low.[17]

A political thaw in the aftermath of Stalin's death in 1952 spurred a brief revival of civic activism, especially among the intelligentsia, giving birth to new associations in the area of science, culture, and education, which were considered "leisure activities" and were thus permitted some degree of independence from government control.[18] In addition, new organizational forms, called "citizen initiative bodies," started to emerge. These bodies came in a wide range of forms—rural, street, district and housing committees, parents' committees, women's councils, councils of medical and cultural-educational institutions, and voluntary people's guards for the protection of public order. These mainly volunteer-run organizations, whose numbers reached the hundreds of thousands by 1985, were the nascent form of citizens' self-governance at the community level that started taking hold in Russia only in the 1990s and made headway starting from the mid-2000s.[19] Although they were still subjected to the ideological control of the Communist Party and shared the excessive formalism and bureaucratization characterizing most state institutions of that time, these organizations nonetheless formed the foundation for the rebirth of civic activism after the dissolution of the Soviet system.

POST-SOVIET DEVELOPMENTS: STRAINED
GOVERNMENT-CIVIL SOCIETY RELATIONS

The far-reaching political reforms (*perestroika*) initiated by Mikhail Gorbachev in the late 1980s removed the Communist Party's control of associational life and created a favorable climate for the growth of the civil society sector. Hundreds of new organizations, from ecological clubs to youth organizations and charitable societies, began to appear.[20] Apart from political liberalization, the growth of citizen initiatives was stimulated by socioeconomic factors, especially a decline in the standards of living, and dramatically reduced government support for culture, the arts, education and science. Although many organizations initially formed in that period were influenced by Western European and American models, the indigenous forms, grounded in local traditions of self-governance and supported by domestic resources (such as business philanthropy) became the core of the "new" Russian civil society sector.[21]

Despite political liberalization, however, the singularly most critical issue facing the civil society sector in Russia today is its relationship with the government. The state has been the central player in the Russian economy and society throughout modern history, and its relationship to the civil society sector remains tenuous. Following democratic reforms, state financial support to the sector, already low in the Soviet era, was further reduced, mainly resulting from the mutual distrust between government officials and civil society leaders. As evidenced by the data presented in this chapter, government financial support for the sector in Russia is among the lowest of the 41 countries on which data are available, and the policies that guide government–civil society relations have not been well defined.

This tenuous relationship between the government and the civil society sector began to improve with the establishment of the Public Chamber of the Russian Federation in 2005, a state institution with consultative powers designed to facilitate interaction between government agencies and the citizenry. Since the creation of the Public Chamber, government policy toward the civil society sector has moved toward constructive cooperation. Government agencies increasingly see CSOs as valuable resources for addressing social problems in Russia. This new attitude resulted in greater public sector support, mainly in the form of competitive grants awarded to CSOs working in areas of social importance (such as youth services, health, environment, education, culture, and public diplomacy), and simplified registration requirements.

Although these policy initiatives represent important steps in improving government–civil society relations in Russia, the overall level of cooperation remains relatively low, and negative or distrustful views of the government's role in civil society development persist. This distrust was aggravated with the passage in 2012 of a law that requires Russian nonprofits receiving foreign support to register as "foreign agents," to report to authorities regularly on their sources of funding and activities, and to endure limits on their participation in political activities. A subsequent 2015 law placing additional burdens and penalties on "undesirable" organizations only added further to what one group of analysts termed the "dual realities" facing Russian nonprofits as they navigate a political environment that simultaneously exhibits contradictory signs of restriction and support.[22]

Whether a more constructive government–civil society relationship can be fostered in such a climate remains open to question. One way to change the unfavorable perception on both sides, however, may be the dissemination of factual knowledge about the civil society sector and its relationship to other social and political institutions, both domestically and internationally.

Conclusions

The civil society sector in Russia remains a rather fragile organism. Its relative size is considerably smaller than that found in most industrialized countries, and it also enjoys far less generous levels of public sector support. Volunteer participation is also low by international standards. These are the characteristic features of the statist model of civil society development. The social origins theory links that model to the emergence of a strong developmental state pursing rapid economic development. In Russia, this was the outcome of the 1917 Revolution, which pushed for rapid modernization and solidified the role of the state as the primary, and for the most part only, agent of modernization. This hegemonic position of the state, and the suspicion on the part of autocratic leaders toward any form of independent civic action, stifled the development of the civil society sector throughout most of the Soviet period. As a consequence, the only organizations that could legally operate were mass membership organizations aligned with the Communist Party; most other social solidarity and self-help activities were displaced to the informal sphere, including neighbors, circles of friends, and extended family networks.

While democratic reforms in the aftermath of Soviet rule opened up new opportunities for civil society development, they were insufficient to spur a rapid growth of the civil society sector. Although new organizations started to emerge, they are relatively few in number and viewed with suspicion by a large segment of the Russian society that still looks to the state for social assistance.

Although economically small, the Russian civil society sector nonetheless provides an important lesson for our understanding of civil society sector development. It demonstrates that popular sentiments, preferences, and charitable impulses alone are not a sufficient condition for the development of civil society institutions. Far more important is the configuration of socioeconomic group relations and the relative power of various social and political institutions. The dominance of labor-repressive agricultural policies in prerevolutionary Russia stifled the growth of urban professional and working classes that elsewhere were the main forces behind the growth of civil society. The economic backwardness resulting from these policies led to social unrest and eventually a revolution. The revolutionary government launched a massive modernization program, but political in-fighting and unpopularity of certain development policies led to the suppression of civic activism, which was seen as a subversive force by government officials. These developments substantially weakened organized civil society in Russia and pushed spontaneous self-help activities into the informal sphere. This explains the paradox between the well-known willingness of Russian citizens to help neighbors and friends and the continued small size and tenuous legitimacy of civil society institutions in Russia today.

Notes

This study was made possible thanks to the effort of the Center for Studies of Civil Society and the Nonprofit Sector at the National Research University Higher School of Economics in Moscow under the leadership of Lev Jakobson and Irina Mersianova with support from the Basic Research Program of the National Research University Higher School of Economics.

1. Mersianova and Yakobson 2010.

2. Nearly 680,000 workers are employed by Russian civil society organizations, but a number of these work part-time.

3. The United Kingdom, Germany, France, the Netherlands, and Italy.

4. For more detail see Moore 1966; Gerschenkron 1992.

5. Although the Russian Orthodox Church began to establish charities in the 16th century, its power was soon restricted by the state, and the role of its charities in providing a social safety net vanished; see Khlystova 1998, 13.

6. Trotsky 1906.

7. Chernykh 1993.

8. Bradley 1994.

9. Общественное и частное призрение в России. СПб., 1907. С. 61. (*Social and Private Care in Russia*. St. Petersburg, 1907, 61).

10. Anufriev 1917, 39; Tumanova 2008, 7.

11. The most noteworthy is Russia's 1905 defeat by the newly modernized Meiji-restoration Japan and a series of defeats by German forces during World War I.

12. Gerschenkron 1992.

13. Zhukova et al. 1988, 9.

14. Avakyan 1996, 36.

15. Chief among them was collectivization of agriculture in 1929 and 1930, which reversed earlier Bolshevik policies of land redistribution to peasantry. The aim of collectivization was modernization of agriculture through consolidation of peasant land into large state-owned farms.

16. Zhukova et al. 1988; Gromov and Kuzin 1990, 14; Belyaeva 1994, 105.

17. The actual amount is impossible to gauge due to the lack of reliable statistics.

18. Borzenkov 1998, 272.

19. Shchiglik 1988, 9–12; Statistics Collection 1986, 51.

20. Zhukova et al. 1988, 97.

21. Yakobson 2007, 43–58.

22. Salamon, Benevolenski, and Jakobson 2015. For further information on these recent restrictions, see Bourjaily 2006; Maxwell 2006; ICA, INP 2007; Ljubownikow, Crotty, and Rodgers 2013; BBC 2015.

CHAPTER FIFTEEN

Mexico

A Persistent Statist Pattern

JORGE VILLALOBOS, LORENA CORTÉS VÁZQUEZ,
CYNTHIA MARTÍNEZ, S. WOJCIECH SOKOLOWSKI,
MEGAN A. HADDOCK, *and* LESTER M. SALAMON

MEXICO AND RUSSIA (chapter 14) lie a world apart, with different histories, different cultures, and different geopolitical conditions. Despite this gulf, however, the civil society sectors in these two countries share remarkable similarities. Both sectors are relatively small in size, receive low levels of government support, and count volunteers as a relatively small share of their respective workforces. These similarities place both countries in the statist pattern of civil society development. Is it a coincidence that these disparate countries would end up with civil society sectors that share these characteristics? This chapter shows that, far from being coincidental, these similarities resulted from similar arrangements of power relations among social groupings and institutions leading to significant constraints on civil society.

More specifically, prolonged power struggles among the modernizing and conservative factions of the Mexican elites after gaining independence from Spain, and growing economic inequality between landowners and the peasantry, culminated in a revolutionary outbreak in 1910 that pitted different elite factions, the working class, and the peasantry against each other. This factional power struggle stretched over 10 years and substantially weakened not only the elites but the lower classes and the Catholic Church as well, creating a power vacuum exploited by military-backed leaders who consolidated their power and established a one-party rule on the promise of restoring stability and promoting economic development. Their control of the government and the military enabled them to crush opposition from both conservative and radical elements and coopt political parties and other representative institutions—"power amplifiers," in social origins theory terms—representing the military, industrial interests, labor, the peasantry, and other segments of society into a single party structure, thus creating a statist pattern of civil society development.

To explore these points, the discussion in this chapter proceeds in three steps. First, we examine the major dimensions of the Mexican civil society sector as they emerge from the 2008 satellite account on nonprofit institutions (NPIs) produced by Mexico's National Institute of Statistics and Geography (INEGI) in cooperation with the Mexican Center for Philanthropy, and from supplementary estimates we have undertaken to fill certain gaps in the official satellite account data.[1] Then we examine the social and economic patterns of historical development in Mexico to assess whether there is evidence supporting the hypothesized causal connections between the power relations among key social groupings and the statist pattern of civil society development in Mexico. Finally, we offer some conclusions about the broader implications of the Mexican case for the social origins theory outlined in this book.

Dimensions of the Mexican Civil Society Sector

SIZE OF THE WORKFORCE

In 2008, Mexico's civil society organizations employed 1,005,170 full-time equivalent (FTE) paid employees and 323,791 FTE volunteers, excluding volunteering for religious and political organizations.[2] Assuming that religious and political organizations employ about a third of the total number of FTE volunteers, or about 160,000,[3] this brings the estimated total number of volunteers to about 484,000 and the total civil society workforce to nearly 1.5 million FTE workers, which represents 3.1 percent of the economically active population (EAP) in Mexico.

Figure 15.1 compares these estimates of the size of the civil society sector's workforce to that of a set of four major Mexican industries: agriculture and fishing, manufacturing, construction, and transportation. As this figure shows, the current size of the civil society sector (CSS) workforce in Mexico is much smaller than the workforce in any of these industries, even including the estimated employment of NPIs controlled by government and volunteers engaged in religious and political organizations.

The size of the civil society sector in Mexico is also on the small side in relation to other countries. At 3.1 percent of the EAP, it ranks 27th among the countries for which such data are available, substantially below the 41-country average of 5.7 percent of EAP, as figure 2.1 demonstrates.

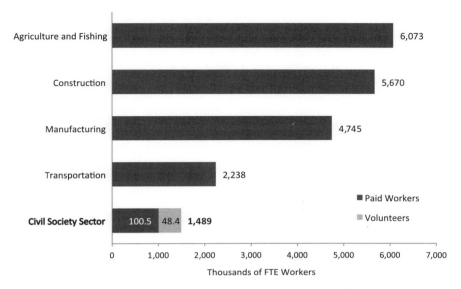

FIGURE 15.1. FTE workforce, civil society sector vs. selected industries, Mexico, 2008.

This estimate still falls within the range defining the statist pattern (4.5 percent of the EAP or less) but puts Mexico above that cluster's average of 2.3 percent, as shown in table 15.1. As discussed later in this chapter, the relatively small size of the civil society sector is a legacy of statist policies under the Institutional Revolutionary Party (PRI), which ruled the country for most of the 20th century. However, the fact that this figure is above the statist pattern's average may reflect the growth that the sector has undergone with reformist policies in the post-PRI era.[4]

VOLUNTEER PARTICIPATION

Volunteer participation is one of the defining characteristics of the statist pattern of civil society sector development. In the Mexican case, assessing the exact scale of volunteer participation is difficult due to the limitations of the available data, as discussed previously. The NPI satellite account report identifies 323,791 FTE volunteers engaged in civil society organizations, and we estimate that in addition to this about 160,000 FTE volunteers are engaged in religious and political organizations. This brings the total number

TABLE 15.1   Civil society sector workforce as share of EAP, Mexico vs. country clusters and 41-country average

Cluster	Workforce as a share of EAP (%)
Mexico	**3.1**
41 countries	*5.7*
Traditional	1.9
Liberal	9.6
Welfare partnership	11.2
Social democratic	8.2
Statist	2.3

TABLE 15.2   Volunteer share of CSS workforce, Mexico vs. country clusters and 41-country average

Cluster	Volunteers as a share of CSS workforce (%)
Mexico	**33.0**
41 countries	*40.6*
Traditional	53.1
Liberal	46.4
Welfare partnership	29.1
Social democratic	69.4
Statist	27.9

of FTE volunteers in Mexico to about 484,000, which constitutes about 33 percent of the entire civil society organization (CSO) workforce.

This estimated volunteer share of the civil society workforce in Mexico is lower than the international average of 41 percent and falls within the range defining the statist model (below 38 percent of the workforce). However, this share is somewhat above the statist average, as shown in table 15.2.

EXPRESSIVE AND SERVICE ACTIVITIES

The picture that emerges from the 2008 NPI satellite account shows that service functions, consisting primarily of education, health, and social assistance, employ about 59 percent of the Mexican CSO workforce, while expressive activities account for only about 35 percent (table 15.3).[5] The actual share of expressive activities is likely higher because the satellite account data do not cover volunteering for religious or political organizations, but it is impossible to estimate this precisely at this time due to data limitations.[6]

This distribution of service and expressive activities is not a defining feature of the statist pattern, as many patterns share similar distributions of these activities (table 15.4). Nevertheless, the distribution of these activities in Mexico (59 and 35 percent, respectively) is close to the 41-country averages (59 and 37 percent, respectively) and would likely be virtually identical to the statist pattern if the estimated volunteering for religious and political organizations were more precisely known and added to these estimates.

TABLE 15.3   Distribution of Mexico's CSS workforce, by field, 2003

Field	Share (%)
Service fields	59
Real estate	2
Accommodation services	1
Professional services	2
Education	32
Health and social assistance	22
Expressive fields	35
Arts and recreation	5
Civic organizations	30
Other fields	6

TABLE 15.4   Distribution of CSS workforce by type of function, Mexico vs. country clusters and 41-country average

Cluster	Share of CSS workforce, by type of function* (%)		
	Service	Expressive	Other
Mexico	59	35	6
41 countries	59	37	4
Traditional	68	24	8
Liberal	55	36	9
Welfare partnership	71	25	4
Social democratic	39	59	2
Statist	50	47	4

*Figures may not add to 100 due to rounding.

A low level of government financial support for civil society activities is another defining feature of the statist pattern, which the social origins theory attributes to the historically adverse relationship between these two sectors in statist countries. Unfortunately, the NPI satellite account data on the civil society sector in Mexico compiled by INEGI do not cover financial flows, so estimates of revenue sources for the sector had to be derived separately. According to the 2003 estimates compiled for the Johns Hopkins Comparative Nonprofit Sector project, the total revenue of the civil society sector in Mexico was nearly 29 billion pesos (US$2.7 billion) in 2003. More than three-quarters of that amount (78 percent) came from fees charged for goods and services provided, as table 15.5 shows. Government funding and philanthropic donations accounted for 11 percent each.

This low share of government income places Mexico well within the range defining the statist model (below 36 percent of revenue) and falls close to the statist pattern average of 18 percent (table 15.6), likely reflecting the fact that public policy toward the sector in Mexico was still underdeveloped as of 2003. Despite enabling legislation such as the 2004 Federal Law for the Encouragement of CSO Activities, Mexico still lacks a robust CSO promotion policy to encourage government support for civil society.[7] What is more, the legal framework regulating the tax status of charitable donations to civil society organizations is far from fully supportive.[8]

TABLE 15.5   Sources of Mexico's CSS revenue by field, 2008

Field	Government (%)	Philanthropy (%)	Fees (%)
All fields	11	11	78
Service fields	15	6	79
Health care	28	7	64
Education and research	6	6	89
Expressive fields	9	13	78
Culture, sports, and recreation	7	1	92
Professional associations and labor unions	2	9	89
Advocacy	22	33	45

TABLE 15.6 Shares of CSS revenue by source, Mexico vs. country clusters and 41-country average*

Cluster	Government (%)	Philanthropy (%)	Fees (%)
Mexico	**11**	**11**	**78**
41 countries	*35*	*14*	*50*
Traditional	11	24	65
Liberal	33	14	53
Welfare partnership	66	8	26
Social democratic	38	10	52
Statist	18	18	64

*Figures may not add to 100% due to rounding.

SUMMARY

In sum, the data presented in this chapter indicate that the civil society sector has become a much larger economic force in Mexico since we first reported our findings from 1995. Some of this growth represents actual increase of civic activity in Mexico during the past decade, and some is the result of the inclusion in the current data of some quasigovernmental institutions that were not included earlier.[9] It is clear, however, that even if the size of the civil society sector in Mexico is slightly overestimated in the satellite account data presented in this chapter, it still falls within the bounds of the statist pattern of civil society development, that is, a rather small civil society sector with low levels of government financial support and a relatively low share of volunteers in the civil society workforce.

How can we account for this statist pattern of civil society development in Mexico, and to what extent does the social origins theory provide useful clues? It is to these questions that we turn next.

Explaining Mexico's Pattern of Civil Society Development

The social origins theory attributes the emergence of the statist pattern to a power structure that emerges as a result of a "revolution from above," or the assumption of state power by a group of military leaders, modernizing bureaucrats, or other actors with the objective of breaking the power of socioeconomic classes that stand in the way of modernization and economic growth. In the process, civil society is subjected to government suppression to neutralize any potential opposition to the new rule. This is precisely the situation that emerged in Mexico when the military-dominated National Revolutionary Party (PNR), later renamed the Institutional Revolutionary Party, or PRI, seized power in 1926 following a prolonged period of political instability and internal strife.

A CENTURY OF ATTEMPTED REFORMS
AND CONSERVATIVE REACTION

Like most other Latin American countries, Mexico was a Spanish colony and inherited the Spanish feudal system in which the nobility and Catholic clergy played prominent roles. The prolonged struggle for national independence in the first decade of the 19th century weakened the colonial aristocracy and increased the power of republican forces, represented chiefly by high-ranking military officers and government officials, leading to the establishment of a Federal Republic of the United Mexican States in 1824. However, political instability continued, fueled by successive economic reform attempts that were opposed by conservative elements and disrupted by occasional international interventions. Thus, the *La Reforma* era following Mexico's loss in the 1846 war with the United States, during which reform elements sought to limit the power of the Catholic Church, still the largest landowner at that time, was ended by conservative reaction and French intervention. The extensive modernization project launched by President Porfirio Diaz from 1876 to 1911 delivered most of its benefits to wealthy industrialists and landowners and ultimately sparked a rebellion of peasants, farm workers, miners, and urban workers led by such popular leaders as Pancho Villa and Emiliano Zapata. However, factional and regional splits prevented the consolidation of power by any of these revolutionary elements, eventually leading to a civil war and the emergence of a counter-revolutionary regime that crushed both the conservative opposition as well as the Catholic Church elements that initially supported it. Indeed, in-fighting was evident on all sides, weakening not only the working class and peasantry but also key elements of the elites and the Catholic Church, the latter of which was attacked by both the revolutionaries and the counter-revolutionaries.[10]

Into the resulting vacuum in 1929 came a group of military leaders who promised to provide stability by expanding the powers of the state through a system of one-party rule manifested in what was initially called the National Revolutionary Party (PNR). This move co-opted various revolutionary factions by taking aim at big industrialists and the Catholic Church, nationalizing key industries such as petroleum and railroads, confiscating Church property, limiting the civil rights of the Catholic clergy, and neutralizing in the process the radical challenge from the Communist-controlled labor unions.[11]

The strategy that PNR deployed to cement its political position and forestall opposition from below involved cooptation of the peasant and working classes into the structure of the party while suppressing any challenge from both the conservative right (the Catholic Church and landowners) and the Communist left. The effect of this strategy was to prevent the independent articulation of class interests. To do so, the PNR established centralized party structures intended to exclusively represent the major sectors of the economy and society, the military, labor, the peasantry, and the population at large. By so doing the PNR, by then called PRI, effectively monopolized the political representation of a diverse array of social actors and effectively muscled out independent voices from the public arena. This served the purpose of neutralizing popular discontent with the economic policies it pursued in partnership with the wealthy industrialists—a pattern that one team of observers described as "sustained economic growth at the cost of increasing inequality and economic dependence."[12]

In the process, however, little room was left for a vibrant nonprofit sector in a position to pursue independent activity. Rather, despite constitutional guarantees of civil rights, the PRI regime was quite authoritarian in practice, recognizing rights and providing benefits only to those organizations and individuals that were affiliated with the governing party.[13] As a result of these constraints, Mexico ended up with a smaller civil society sector than might be expected given its level of economic development.

Despite these restrictions, a few organizations managed to remain independent of state influence because they did not seek to influence public policy. This included higher education institutions, a tamed Catholic Church, and religious organizations providing social assistance.[14] Together, these organizations formed the nucleus of a small private civil society sector during the PRI governing period.

THE EROSION OF GOVERNMENT CONTROL

Three developments contributed to the erosion of the PRI-controlled institutional structure and opened up space for the development of new civil society institutions, but these developments did not really begin to materialize until the 1960s. The hegemony of the PRI-controlled state was initially challenged in the 1960s by a social protest movement involving students, workers, and urban middle-class elements. The brutal suppression of these protests in 1968 by the use of military force undermined the legitimacy of the PRI government in wide segments of Mexican society.[15]

At the same time, the growing Liberation Theology movement within the Roman Catholic Church provided the impetus for the growth of new grass-roots civil society organizations. Church officials began to deepen their ties with the working and professional classes and became involved in creating savings institutions and self-help organizations aiming to improve living conditions of the poor.[16] As a result, by 1964 more than a million cooperatives were founded that subsequently became independent of the Church.

Finally, the massive migration from the rural areas to the metropolitan zone of Mexico City generated an increasing demand for services that the state was not ready to provide. Shortages in public service delivery became particularly evident in the aftermath of the 1985 earthquake that devastated the Mexico City area. This unmet demand for public services was addressed by the emergence of new CSOs, some of which became increasingly involved in the political arena, including promotion of human rights, gender equity, and environmental protection. This created a new type of social actor in Mexico—urban movements—which became increasingly popular with the middle class by voicing concerns about political corruption and electoral fraud.[17] Increasingly, these organizations became a voice of public opposition to government corruption and authoritarianism[18] and were later involved in monitoring local and federal elections in the 1990s.[19]

The popular protest movement that broke out in January 1994 in the Chiapas region of the rural south, known as the Zapatista Army for National Liberation (EZLN), ushered in a period of growth for indigenous initiatives seeking to encourage more inclusive and respectful state policies.[20] Several CSOs in the Chiapas region formed the umbrella group Chiapas

NGOs Coordination for Peace (CONPAZ) to monitor the humanitarian work in the Chiapas region and the accuracy of the information being provided about the movement. The situation in Chiapas also brought a new international presence to Mexico, including UN observers, the United Nations Population Fund, the UN Food and Agriculture Organization, the International Labor Organization, and the International Committee of the Red Cross. The participation of these international organizations was essential in the peaceful resolution of the conflict and in influencing other indigenous organizations.[21]

These growing social movements, coupled with economic liberalization furthered by the North America Free Trade Agreement (NAFTA), undermined the PRI, causing it to lose its majority status in the election of 1997. The political liberalization that followed led to policy shifts supportive of the civil society sector and helped spur the growth of the Mexican civil society sector.[22] Despite these recent political changes, however, the inconsistent legal framework for philanthropy and civil society operations inherited from the past continues to pose significant obstacles to the sector's development.[23] This helps to explain why, despite significant growth and development of the civil society sector during the last decade, the vestiges of the statist pattern are still visible in the civil society sector dimensions in Mexico today.

Conclusions

The picture that emerges from the 2008 NPI satellite account data clearly indicates that despite its recent growth, the civil society sector in Mexico still belongs to the statist cluster, characterized by its relatively small size, low level of government support, and moderate levels of volunteer participation. The social origins theory attributes the emergence of this pattern to the rise to power of reformist elements in the military, government service, or other arenas that use state power to implement modernizing reforms from above but in the process subjugate the civil society sector to neutralize any potential opposition to this program. In Mexico, this role was played by reform-minded military leaders who created the Institutional Revolutionary Party, which established a system of single-party rule throughout most of the 20th century and stifled the growth of independent civil society institutions.

The crucial role of power relationships among various social and economic groupings in civil society development can be further demonstrated by comparing Mexico to two other countries discussed in this book: Russia (chapter 14) and Chile (chapter 11). Mexico shares a common culture and Spanish colonial heritage with Chile. What is more, the array of social actors competing for control of political and economic space was quite similar—landed and industrial elites, a generally conservative Catholic Church, urban commercial and professional middle-class elements, and an increasingly restive labor movement that had begun to flirt with communist sentiments.

What differentiated these two countries appears to have been the successful survival of these competing interests into the industrial era in Chile and the emergence in that country of political institutions in the form of political parties—"power amplifiers" in the terminology introduced here—that, after an initial period of violence and political instability early in the twentieth century, were able, apparently with the encouragement of the Catholic Church, to work out a *modus vivendi* in the form of progressive social welfare and economic policies sufficient to satisfy the demands of the competing groups, leading to cooperative relations between the government and civil society organizations as well. As a consequence, the political parties and the Catholic Church mediated conflicting class interests for most of the 20th century (except for the 1973 military coup), creating a balance of power conducive to the emergence of a quasi–welfare partnership pattern of civil society development.

By contrast, Mexico experienced prolonged, frequently violent, internal conflicts that culminated in the 1910–1920 Mexican revolution. The factional power struggle during this revolutionary outbreak weakened the power of all socioeconomic classes and the Catholic Church, and it created a power vacuum that allowed a group of reform-minded revolutionary leaders to take control of the Mexican state, establish single-party (PRI) rule, and eliminate or co-opt all potential opposition, resulting in a statist pattern of civil society development.

Equally revealing is the relationship between Mexico and Russia. Clearly, these two countries have very little in common culturally. But they shared common sociopolitical histories characterized by powerful landed and religious elites that endured periods of considerable violence—World War I in the case of Russia and the 1911 revolutionary era in Mexico—that weakened and, in the case of Russia, discredited prevailing elites, opening the way for reformist cliques to seize power, establish one-party rule, suppress independent civil society activity, and push through forced-march programs of rapid economic change. In both cases, the result was a statist pattern of civil society development. The fact that key features of Mexico's civil society sector resemble those in Russia to a greater degree than those in Chile testifies to the relatively limited ability of common cultural and religious norms as compared to the common power relationships emphasized in the social origins theory to explain how common patterns of civil society development emerge, even in widely divergent parts of the world.

Notes

1. Instituto Nacional de Estadística y Geografía 2011. This satellite account followed the methodology defined by the Johns Hopkins Comparative Nonprofit Sector Project to a significant degree. On the supplementary sources needed to fill certain gaps in the INEGI satellite account data, see note 2.

2. The NPI employment figure is derived from two different data elements reported in the Mexican NPI satellite account. First, employment in NPIs assigned to the NPISH or corporations sectors in the national accounts was derived directly from the satellite account data tables. This portion of the NPI sector employed just under 500,000 workers. Second, employment in the NPIs assigned to the government sector in the national accounts, which we refer to as "publicly funded NPIs," was estimated by dividing the total employee compensation reported for these NPIs in the satellite account tables by the average wage of public administration workers in Mexico. This yielded an estimate of an additional 500,000 workers. In using the term "publicly funded NPIs" to depict the NPIs allocated to the government sector in national accounts we do not mean to suggest that other NPIs do not receive government funding, but rather that these NPIs are predominantly government funded, which is a major reason they have presumably been allocated to the government sector under then-existing SNA sectoring guidelines.

We believe this provides a high-end estimate of the NPI paid workforce, however, due to the fact that some of the NPIs covered in the INEGI NPI satellite account (for example, the national statistics agency and the national bank) are actually government entities, would not meet SNA conventions about what can be considered an NPI, and have not been covered in the other countries covered in this book. Excluding these individual organizations from the aggregate employee compensation data reported in the NPI satellite account was not possible at this time. However, even this high-end estimate of the size of the NPI workforce still falls within the boundaries defining the statist pattern of civil society development. For further details on this point, see Salamon, Villalobos, et al. 2012.

Another limitation of the INEGI NPI satellite account is the absence of data on financial flows, making it impossible to assess the revenue structure of the sector. To mitigate this shortcoming, this chapter reports the revenue data assembled in 2003 by Gustavo Verduzco, professor and researcher at El Colegio de Mexico, as part of the Johns Hopkins Comparative Nonprofit Sector Project.

3. This estimate is based on the assumption that religious and political volunteering in Mexico is similar to that observed in Argentina (about 33 percent). The main reason for including this estimate is to prevent incomplete data on volunteering from incorrect assignment of Mexico to the appropriate country cluster, since the volunteer share of the workforce is a defining attribute of three civil society patterns.

4. Also at work, however, is very likely the fact, mentioned in note 2, that the satellite account data in Mexico included a number of government-controlled entities such as the country's statistical agency, national bank, and national university not included in the data on the other countries.

5. The 2008 data only show employment in NPIs that receive little or no public support, and classify them by the North American Industry Classification System (NAICS) rather than the International Classification of Nonprofit Organizations (ICNPO) used in other chapters of this book. It was, however, possible to group NAICS industries into service and expressive functions that roughly correspond to those based on ICNPO.

6. As mentioned earlier, to correct for the 2008 NPI satellite account data gaps, we estimated the missing data at the total level to avoid the misclassification of Mexico to a wrong country cluster, but we are unable to distribute these totals by the type of activity. As a result, the exact shares of NPI workforce in service and expressive activities cannot be estimated with any precision beyond what has been reported in this section. If we were to include the estimated 160,000 volunteers in political and religious organizations, which are types of expressive activities, this would boost the share of expressive activities to about 46 percent, and the share of service activities would fall to about 49 percent, virtually identical to the statist pattern averages.

7. Favela Gavia 2004, 124.

8. Tapia Álvarez and Robles Aguilar 2006.

9. See note 2 for further detail.

10. Coatsworth 1978; Haber 1992; Meyer 1991.

11. Buchenau 2007; Meyer 1991.

12. Rueschemeyer, Stephens, and Stephens 1992.

13. Olvera 2004.

14. Cadena Roa 2004, 160; Reygadas 1998.

15. Cadena Roa 2004, 171.

16. Reygadas 1998.

17. Loaeza 1998.

18. Favela Gavia 2004, 131; Butcher and Serna 2006, 392.

19. Monroy 1993.

20. Reygadas 1998, 421.

21. Reygadas 1998, 580.

22. One example of these policy changes was the adoption of the 2004 Federal Law for the Encouragement of CSO Activities, which encouraged the extension of welfare partnership forms of cooperation between government and the nonprofit sector.

23. Favela Gavia 2004, 124; Tapia Álvarez and Robles Aguilar 2006.

CHAPTER SIXTEEN

Portugal

In Transition from Statist to Welfare Partnership

RAQUEL CAMPOS FRANCO, S. WOJCIECH SOKOLOWSKI,
and LESTER M. SALAMON

PORTUGAL DOES NOT MEET the defining criteria of any pattern of civil society development identified in chapter 4. However, it comes close to two such patterns, welfare partnership and statist. This is a somewhat surprising finding for a country in Western Europe, where the welfare partnership or social democratic models are far more common. This apparent puzzle is solved, however, when we examine the power relations in Portugal prior to the European Union (EU) accession, which greatly shaped the current characteristics of the country's civil society sector.

As this chapter will demonstrate, the dictatorial regime that emerged in 1926, in the aftermath of a modernizing revolution that toppled the monarchy, severely circumscribed the civil society sector to quell labor militancy and left far-reaching imprints on the civil society sector. That regime was ousted only in 1974 by the "Carnation Revolution" staged by left-wing groups aligned with the Portuguese military. This revolution pushed the country in two different directions, one that created space for the civil society sector and one that transferred nonprofit health services from Catholic Church–affiliated *Misericórdias* to the public sphere. While the process of strengthening the civil society sector in Portugal started after the 1974 revolution, Portugal's EU accession in 1986 accelerated the process by fostering closer partnerships between the Portuguese government and the civil society sector to deliver public services, setting the country on a course toward a welfare partnership model. It is thus possible to interpret Portugal's civil society sector as in transition from a statist past toward a welfare partnership future.

Dimensions of the Portuguese Civil Society Sector

SIZE OF THE WORKFORCE

As of 2006, the latest year for which data are available, Portuguese civil society organizations employed 184,660 full-time equivalent (FTE) paid workers.[1] In addition, these organizations engaged the equivalent of another 67,000 FTE volunteer employees,[2] bringing the total workforce of Portuguese civil society organizations to about 252,000 FTE workers, or about 4.5 percent of the country's economically active population (EAP).

As figure 16.1 shows, even without counting the FTE volunteers, the size of the civil society workforce in Portugal exceeds that in the country's agriculture and transportation industries, which stood at 98,000 and 169,000, respectively. However, even with FTE volunteers included, the civil society workforce is considerably smaller than employment in the manufacturing and construction industries, which had 820,000 and 494,000 workers, respectively.

The size of the civil society sector in Portugal falls in the mid-range in relation to other countries. Measured as a share of the EAP, the workforce of the Portuguese civil society sector, at 4.5 percent of EAP, ranked below the

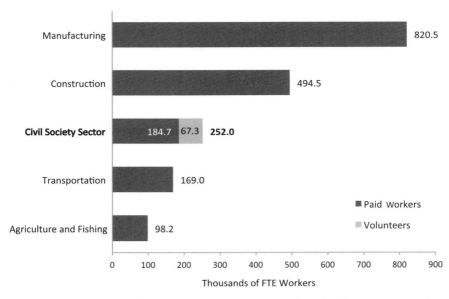

FIGURE 16.1. FTE workforce, civil society sector vs. selected industries, Portugal, 2006.

TABLE 16.1   Civil society sector workforce as share of EAP, Portugal vs. country clusters and 41-country average

Cluster	Workforce as a share of EAP (%)
Portugal	**4.5**
41 countries	5.7
Traditional	1.9
Liberal	9.6
Welfare partnership	11.2
Social democratic	8.2
Statist	2.3

41-country average of 5.7 percent, as figure 2.1 demonstrates. This places Portugal below most of the high-income countries of Europe and North America but on a par with Europe's Mediterranean countries, at least those on which data are available, Spain and Italy (both at 4.3 percent). The size of the Portuguese civil society sector workforce falls below the range defining the social democratic pattern (6.8 percent of the EAP or higher) and well below the average of the welfare partnership cluster (11.2 percent). But, as table 16.1 shows, the size of Portugal's civil society sector stands significantly above the statist average of 2.3 percent.

VOLUNTEER PARTICIPATION

About 25 percent of the adult population did some kind of volunteering in Portugal in 2002. However, most of that volunteering (about 60 percent) was informal in nature (i.e., involved individuals helping other people directly), and only about 10 percent of the population volunteered for an organization. This latter translates into approximately 67,000 FTE jobs and accounted for about 27 percent of the entire civil society workforce in 2006.[3]

This 27 percent volunteer share of the CSS workforce in Portugal falls well below the 41-country average of about 41 percent and close to the 28 percent average for countries that fall into the statist cluster, as table 16.2 demonstrates. However, Portugal's share also falls close to the welfare partnership average of 29 percent.

TABLE 16.2 Volunteer share of CSS
workforce, Portugal vs. country clusters
and 41-country average

Cluster	Volunteers as a share of CSS workforce (%)
Portugal	**26.7**
41 countries	*40.6*
Traditional	53.1
Liberal	46.4
Welfare partnership	29.1
Social democratic	69.4
Statist	27.9

TABLE 16.3 Distribution of Portugal's CSS
workforce, by field, 2002

Field	Share (%)
Service fields	63
Social services	48
Education and research	9
Health care	6
Expressive and other fields	37
N	252,002

SERVICE AND EXPRESSIVE ACTIVITIES

As shown in table 16.3, most (about 63 percent) of Portugal's civil society sector activity is concentrated in service provision, particularly social services, which accounts for nearly half (48 percent) of the sector's entire workforce.[4] Education and health care account for a much smaller 9 and 6 percent, respectively. Expressive and other activities account for 37 percent.[5]

This heavy dominance of service delivery over expressive activities in the civil society sector is a defining characteristic of the welfare partnership pattern, and Portugal meets that criterion. As table 16.4 shows, the service share of the civil society workforce in Portugal, while somewhat below the average for welfare partnership countries, is larger than the averages of the other developed country clusters.

TABLE 16.4 Distribution of CSS workforce by type of function, Portugal vs. country clusters and 41-country average

Cluster	Share of CSS workforce, by type of function* (%)		
	Service	Expressive	Other
Portugal	**63**	**37**	**n/a**
41 countries	*59*	*37*	*4*
Traditional	68	24	8
Liberal	55	36	9
Welfare partnership	71	25	4
Social democratic	39	59	2
Statist	50	47	4

*Figures may not add to 100 due to rounding.

TABLE 16.5 Shares of CSS revenue by source, Portugal vs. country clusters and 41-country average*

Cluster	Government (%)	Philanthropy (%)	Fees (%)
Portugal	**40**	**11**	**49**
41 countries	*35*	*14*	*50*
Traditional	11	24	65
Liberal	33	14	53
Welfare partnership	66	8	26
Social democratic	38	10	52
Statist	18	18	64

*Figures may not add to 100% due to rounding.

REVENUE SOURCES

Portuguese civil society organizations generated nearly €5.9 billion (about $7.7 billion) in revenue in 2006. Based on 2002 estimates,[6] fees constitute the main source of civil society sector revenue in Portugal, accounting for about 49 percent of total income to the sector. The second-largest source of income, accounting for 40 percent of the total, is government grants and contracts. Finally, private philanthropy accounts for about 11 percent of the total revenue.

This revenue structure differs markedly from both the statist and the welfare partnership patterns, suggesting the hybrid character of the Portugal civil society sector. At 40 percent of income, the government share of nonprofit revenue is well above the statist percentage but well below the welfare partnership share (table 16.5). Similarly, the fee component is well below

TABLE 16.6   Sources of Portugal's CSS revenue by field, 2002

Field	Government (%)	Philanthropy (%)	Fees (%)
All fields	40	11	49
Service fields	48	4	48
Health care	82	3	16
Education and research	66	0	34
Social services	26	7	66
Economic development	40	0	60
Expressive fields	13	20	67
Culture, sports, and recreation	16	29	55
Advocacy	12	15	73
Other fields	5	67	29
Not elsewhere classified	5	67	29

the statist cluster average but well above that for the welfare partnership cluster.[7]

The fact that government support is particularly evident in the fields of health care and education in Portugal, as shown in table 16.6, lends credence to the view that significant elements of the Portuguese nonprofit sector were already taking on the appearance of a welfare partnership pattern as of 2002.

SUMMARY: A PARTIALLY DEVELOPED WELFARE PARTNERSHIP PATTERN

As the data discussed above show, Portugal's civil society sector seems a hybrid case that meets some of the criteria of both the statist and welfare partnership patterns. We believe, however, that it falls closer to the welfare partnership pattern because of the rather large share of service activities and the considerable level of government support that it receives. In a sense, it may therefore be possible to view Portugal's nonprofit sector as in transition from a statist to a welfare partnership pattern. To what extent can this finding be explained in terms of our social origins theory?

Explaining Portugal's Pattern of Civil Society Development[8]

The answer to this question lies in two broad sets of developments: first, the socioeconomic and political power struggle that engulfed Portugal throughout most of the 19th and 20th centuries and eventually brought the country under a dictatorial regime that stifled the civil society sector in an attempt to undermine the growing power of organized labor; and second, the democratic opening that occurred in the mid-1980s, and the subsequent accession of Portugal to the European Union. Given the power of path dependence, the residue of the years of constraint is still very much present as the Portuguese civil society sector undertakes a transition toward what appears to be a welfare partnership future. To understand the current hybrid character of the Portuguese nonprofit sector, it is therefore necessary to look briefly at both of these historical developments.

EARLY ORIGINS: A BIFURCATED REGIME

Portugal entered the modern world as a bifurcated nation—a feudal countryside dominated by a landed aristocracy beholden to a hereditary monarch, and a go-go urban merchant-explorer maritime operation that came to dominate the major trade routes between Europe, Asia, Africa, and South America and built a sprawling colonial empire that delivered substantial profits to the Crown and to the commercial middle class from its trade in spices, sugar, gold, and slaves. Holding these disparate components together was not only the monarchy but a powerful Catholic Church, which offered doctrinal blessing both to landed aristocrats and seafaring colonizers and which captured a portion of the colonial plunder to provide modest social protections to those on the bottom of the social pyramid, including the many women and children left behind by the colonial adventurers, through a network of charitable organizations that included, most prominently, the Holy Houses of Mercy, or *Misericórdias*. In this way, social peace was maintained in the countryside, merchants were allowed to amass fortunes and stretch the borders of the known universe, and the Crown was rewarded for its protections and left free to handle matters of state. At the same time, under the banner of solidarity preached by the Church, various professions were free to establish a variety of guilds and self-help organizations to protect the interests of the professions and offer charitable assistance to members and nonmembers alike, a model that was ultimately taken over by the laboring classes once industrialization started in earnest.

COLONIAL DECLINE AND A PUSH TOWARD INDUSTRIALIZATION

This equilibrium of social forces held so long as the colonial and trade operations kept the skids greased. But in the middle of the 18th century, a decline set in as a result of pressure from foreign powers. On top of this, in 1755 a major earthquake destroyed much of the country's capital, Lisbon, causing further economic and political instability. The economic decline was further accelerated after Portugal lost its main colonial possession, Brazil. Economic decline and resulting political instability made the country vulnerable to foreign interference from more economically advanced neighbors, especially France. Between 1807 and 1811 French forces led by Napoleon invaded Portugal three times.

In response to this decline and foreign threats, the liberal elements in the military and the professional class launched the Liberal Revolution of 1820, which established a constitutional monarchy and initiated reforms aiming to break the power of the aristocracy and the Church, expropriate the Church's substantial landholdings, and promote industrialization. This industrialization, in turn, changed the class structure of Portuguese society, giving birth to an industrial bourgeoisie and a working class while hastening the decline of the landed aristocracy.[9]

This period also saw the formation of many mutual associations providing a social safety net and organizing cultural activities for the urban working class, small farmers, and agrarian workers. The urban middle classes, especially state officers, liberal professionals, and merchants, formed their own mutual associations as well. At the same time, business owners established business associations to represent their interests before the government, with some of the most influential connected to the production and export of wine and other products.

REPUBLICAN REVOLUTION

While trade surged, however, industrialization lagged. Well into the 19th century, Portugal remained prone to economic crises and vulnerable to foreign interference, this time from Great Britain. In 1890 the British issued an ultimatum demanding a change in the Portuguese intention to occupy the vast territory between its colonies, Angola and Mozambique, as portrayed on the so-called Rose-Colored Map.[10] This loss was perceived as a humiliation by large segments of the population at home and resulted in prolonged political turmoil.

This growing political instability, coupled with the extravagant expenses of the royal court, provoked wide public dissent culminating in the October 1910 Republican Revolution. The political forces behind this "revolution from above" were liberal elements of the industrial bourgeoisie, the professional class, and the nationalist, centrist, and left-leaning elements united under the Portuguese Republican Party. A central objective of this 1910 revolution was the eradication of Portugal's feudal past and the displacement of the Catholic Church that continued to help prop it up. The new Republican government expelled religious orders, confiscated their property, and imposed numerous restrictions on the Church's public activities.

However, this first Republican government in Portugal found itself under severe pressure from both conservative and socialist forces. Its strong anticlerical stance quickly provoked a backlash from monarchist rural groups, while working class and liberal movements demanded further political reforms. This situation resulted in growing political instability and escalating political violence.[11]

THE EMERGENCE OF THE AUTHORITARIAN STATE

As attempts to form a stable government repeatedly failed, the military, aligned with the conservative elements of the republican coalition, staged a coup in 1926. Authoritarian rule was established, led by António de Oliveira Salazar, whose "New State" regime implemented a series of policies aiming to both suppress socialist and liberal influences in the labor movement and retain the remaining Portuguese colonies. Political parties were abolished, and independent civil society organizations, especially mutual associations linked to peasant and working-class interests, faced severe restrictions. To pacify working-class dissent, the New State regime installed a corporatist system under which different occupations and industrial sectors were represented by syndicates controlled by the state. Freedom of association was seen as contrary to the national interest and thus forbidden and persecuted. As a result, civil society sector capacity decreased. Hit particularly hard was the mutualist movement, whose leaders and activists were imprisoned and whose service functions were transferred to state institutions.

THE CARNATION REVOLUTION, DEMOCRATIC REFORMS, AND EU ACCESSION

Authoritarian rule in Portugal persisted until 1974, when it was ended by a military coup, the "Carnation Revolution" staged by left-wing military elements dissatisfied with the increasing burden of colonial wars. The new democratic government installed by this coup launched broad reforms and created an environment conducive to the development of the civil society sector. In particular, it restored freedom of association, unleashing a substantial revival and strengthening of civil society organizations. Unlike its predecessor, this new government perceived the civil society sector as an important resource in the delivery of community services. New social movements concerned with every aspect of social life started to emerge, such as resident associations, employment development organizations, organizations focused on the improvement of working conditions, parent associations, and organizations designed to offer services to children.[12]

However, this new democratic period was not without its setbacks for civil society sector development. In the push for the development of a national health care system, the Holy Houses of Mercy (*Misericórdias*), the major network of health providers linked to the Catholic Church, saw some of its health services taken over by the public health care system, resulting in a reduction of the civil society sector's capacity.[13] State policy toward the civil society sector gradually started to improve only in the 1980s as a result of the country's preparation for accession to the European Union. New legislation strengthening private welfare associations, enacted in 1979 and further expanded in 1983, initiated the provision of publicly financed welfare services through the so-called Private Institutions of Social Solidarity (*Instituições Particulares de Solidariedade Social*).

Portugal's accession to the European Union in 1986 further strengthened the civil society sector as a result of the structural funds provided by the European Union to bolster the economies of lagging regions and the general principle of subsidiarity established in the 1992 Treaty of Maastricht, which, though applicable principally to relations between the European Union and the member states, particularly in the area of social policy, also carried over into relations between member states and their civil society sectors. As a consequence, Portuguese civil society organizations gained access to these structural funds to expand their own services, boosting the share of their revenues coming from government and laying the groundwork for a possible welfare partnership future.

Conclusions

The picture of the Portuguese civil society sector evident in our data suggests a hybrid character, with some features characteristic of a statist pattern and others of a welfare partnership pattern. Our analysis suggests that this pattern reflects the power of path dependence to retain elements of a prior period even as new developments bring forth new characteristics.

More specifically, the social origins theory points us to a typical scenario of constrained economic development triggering a revolution from above and a statist pattern of civil society development. As the loss of colonial possessions and foreign trade routes caused economic decline and political instability, the reformist elements in the military, industrial bourgeoisie, and the professional class launched a series of revolutions from above to remove obstacles to modernization and promote industrial development. However, those revolutionary changes, which spanned nearly a century, did not initially suppress the freedoms of association and expression. The upside of these changes was that charities and mutualist associations could thrive, but the downside was the continuation of political instability. In response, the military launched a coup in 1926 and established an authoritarian government that suppressed civil society development for nearly 50 years.

This statist pattern of development ended only in 1974 with the Carnation Revolution that toppled the authoritarian regime and restored democracy, creating a more favorable climate for the growth of the civil society sector. Portugal's ensuing EU accession set the country on the path of welfare partnership development, built on the institutional base of charitable organizations affiliated with the Catholic Church and the mutualist associations with origins dating back to the colonial era.

An interesting aspect of the Portuguese case for the social origins theory is the role that the military played in civil society development. The reformist elements of the military were a major force behind several of the revolutionary changes that transformed the institutional landscape of the country in the 19th and 20th centuries. The 1926 military coup imposed the authoritarian rule that resulted in a heavily statist model of civil society development. The subsequent 1974 Carnation Revolution launched by left-wing elements in the military, by contrast, reestablished democracy and set the country's civil society sector on the path toward a welfare partnership model.

The case of Portugal also demonstrates the dynamic nature of some of the patterns of civil society development identified in chapter 4. Indeed, the lasting impacts of authoritarianism in Portugal remain visible in the data today. The Salazar regime's suppression of civil society organizations that it perceived as antagonistic to its policy objectives reduced the civil society sector's capacity in the long run and caused lasting strain on government–civil society relations.

This legacy of the past is gradually changing, however, and Portugal's civil society sector appears to be in transition from a statist past to a welfare partnership future. Indeed, the sector can be viewed as a bellwether marking both the pace and the direction of this change. While that pace may be slower than some observers would like, the direction is unmistakable.

Notes

This chapter presents updated data first published in Franco et al. 2006. The updated data were produced by Portugal's *Instituto Nacional de Estatística* (National Institute for Statistics) and published in Salamon, Sokolowski, Haddock, and Tice 2012. Our research in Portugal was supported by the Calouste Gulbenkian Foundation, the Luso-American Foundation, the Ilídio Pinho Foundation, and the Aga Kahn Foundation.

1. This represents a 15 percent increase over the number of such jobs reported for 2002 (Franco et al. 2006). However, at least some of this change is due to differences in data coverage. The 2006 data include 6,643 jobs in nonprofit institutions (NPIs) that under the System of National Accounts guidelines then in effect were assigned to the public sector in official statistics on grounds that they were "controlled by government." These organizations were not covered in the 2002 data, and there remains some question about whether they would have been included in an NPI satellite account under the refined criteria for determining "control by government" adopted in the 2008 revision of the System of National Accounts. We have included them here, but their inclusion does not significantly alter the overall picture of the scope or structure of the Portuguese civil society sector. However, these organizations meet the defining criteria of NPIs as adopted in this study.

2. Volunteering data for 2006 are not available. Data on volunteers are only available as of 2002.

3. The volunteer data used here was estimated as of 2002, rather than 2006, which is the year on which our employment data is estimated. Using 2002 employment data, instead of the 2006 data used here, the volunteer share of the civil society workforce

would be slightly higher at about 30 percent. The difference is due in large part to differences in data coverage (see note 2).

4. This field includes the Holy Houses of Mercy *(Misericórdias)*, a network of Catholic social assistance and health care providers. Separation of health care and social assistance functions of these institutions was not possible due to data limitations.

5. It was not possible to separate these two groups in the data.

6. Franco et al. 2006. In these estimates, fees represented the residual category after the shares of government and private philanthropy have been estimated. A more recent 2006 satellite account estimate found a similar 40 percent of income coming from government and 10 percent from philanthropy but identified only 19 percent coming from fees. However, this estimate left 19 percent of the revenue unaccounted for. We therefore use the 2002 estimate here.

7. The most significant part of government support to the civil society sector comes in the form of reimbursements for services to households. These reimbursements are treated as service fees in macroeconomic data and are difficult to distinguish from private service fees. It is therefore likely that the fee income shown in this chapter contains nontrivial amounts of government reimbursements that cannot be identified as such due to data limitations.

8. This section draws heavily on Franco 2005 and Franco et al. 2006.

9. Solsten 1993; Payne, n.d.

10. Clarence-Smith 1985.

11. Sardica 2011; Solsten 1993.

12. Linz and Stepan 1996, 116–129.

13. The *Misericórdias* survived as institutions performing related social service functions and subsequently regained certain health functions as well.

The Johns Hopkins Comparative Nonprofit Sector Project
Objectives, Conceptualization, and Approach

The work presented in this book is the product of a unique international collaboration engaging some 200 researchers and statisticians in countries throughout the world. Begun in 1991, this project initially focused on 13 countries—eight developed and five developing—and has since been extended to more than 40 countries. However, only 41 countries produced data that are suitable for the analysis performed in this book.

Objectives

From the outset, this project has sought to accomplish five principal objectives:

- First, to *document* the scope, structure, financing, and role of the civil society sector for the first time in solid empirical terms in a significant number of countries representing different geographic regions, cultural and historical traditions, and levels of development;
- Second, to *explain* why this sector varies in size, composition, character, and role from place to place and identify the factors that seem to encourage or retard its development, including differences in history, legal arrangements, religious backgrounds, cultures, socioeconomic structures, and patterns of government policy;
- Third, to *evaluate* the impact these organizations are having and the contributions they make, as well as the drawbacks they entail;
- Fourth, to *improve awareness* of this set of institutions by disseminating the results of the work; and
- Fifth, to *build local capacity* to carry on the work in the future.

Approach

To pursue these objectives, we formulated an approach that is:

- *Comparative*, covering countries at different levels of development and with a wide assortment of religious, cultural, and political traditions. This comparative approach was a central feature of the project's methodology. Far from obscuring differences, systematic comparison is the only way to identify what the differences among various countries actually are. As one analyst has put it: "Thinking without comparison is unthinkable. And, in the absence of comparison, so is all scientific thought and scientific research."[1] When carefully and sensitively done, comparison is not simply a technique for understanding others; it is also a necessary step toward understanding oneself.

- *Systematic,* utilizing a common definition of the entities to be included and a common classification system for differentiating among them. Comparison is only possible if reasonable care is taken in specifying what is to be compared. Given the conceptual ambiguity, lack of knowledge, and ideological overtones that exist in this field, this task naturally had to be approached with care. As outlined more fully below, our approach was to proceed in a bottom-up fashion, building up our definition and classification from the actual experiences of the project countries. The goal throughout was to formulate a definition that was sufficiently broad to encompass the diverse array of entities embraced within this sector in the varied countries we were covering yet sharp enough to differentiate these entities from those that constitute the market and the state, the two other major sectors into which social life has traditionally been divided.

- *Collaborative,* relying extensively on local analysts to root our definitions and analysis in the solid ground of local knowledge and to build the indigenous capability to ensure such work would be carried forward in the future. Accordingly, we recruited a principal Local Associate in each country to assist us in all phases of project work. This included not only data collection and data analysis but also the formulation of the project's basic conceptual equipment—its working definition, treatment of borderline organizations, classification system, and data-collection strategies. Local Associates met regularly throughout the life of the project to formulate research strategies, review progress, and fine-tune the approach. These individuals in turn recruited colleagues to assist in the effort. The result was a project team that has engaged at least 150 local researchers around the world in the development and execution of the project's basic tasks.

- *Consultative,* involving the active participation of local civil society activists, government leaders, the press, and the business community in order to further ensure that the work in each country was responsive to the particular conditions of the country and that the results could be understood and disseminated locally. To achieve this, we organized advisory committees in each project country and at the international level. These committees reviewed all aspects of the project approach, assisted in the interpretation of the results, and helped publicize the findings and think through their implications. Altogether, more than 600 nonprofit, philanthropic, government, and business leaders have taken part in the project through these advisory committees.

- *Empirical,* moving wherever possible beyond subjective impressions to develop a body of empirical data on this set of organizations. Obviously, not all facets of the civil society sector can be captured in empirical terms, and some components of the project, such as the legal analysis, the historical analysis, and the impact analysis, consequently used more qualitative techniques, including case studies, focus groups, and literature review. Nevertheless, given the general confusion about the real scope and structure of this sector, we felt it important to develop a set of empirical measures of the overall level of effort that civil society organizations mobilize in each country; the distribution of this effort among various activities, including both service activities and more expressive activities (e.g., policy advocacy, environmental protection, and arts and culture); and the sources of support for this activity. This required the formulation of a set of research protocols defining the data items being sought and suggesting ways to secure the needed data. It also required the tailoring of these protocols to the realities of the individual countries, a process that was accomplished in collaboration with our Local Associates, as noted more fully below.

Conceptualization
The Challenge

One of the main challenges facing the project was the diversity of institutional forms and actions considered in scope of the civil society in various countries of the world and the ongoing debate whether they can be treated as a coherent sector. Indeed, the very definition of the third sector is ardently contested. Some observers insist on very broad definitions that include various types of organizations, unorganized collective and individual actions, and the social value systems enabling these actions. Others prefer more narrow definitions that delineate sets of institutions performing certain social or economic functions, such as serving "public purpose" or producing "public goods," or possessing certain formal characteristics.

As a result of this bewildering diversity, the first step in developing a definition of the civil society sector suitable for international comparisons was answering the question of whether such definition is even possible. Some observers question that possibility, quoting high level of disagreement among scholars, policy makers, and stakeholders of what is in scope of the third sector. However, the task of defining the civil society is not as daunting as it appears. The civil society sector is not the only societal sector that has faced the challenge of dealing with diversity in finding a suitable conceptualization of itself. Certainly the business sector has every bit as much diversity as civil society, with multiple legal structures, organizational forms, radically different lines of activity, gross variations in scale, complex interactions with government funding and regulatory regimes, and widely divergent tax treatments. Yet scholars, policy-makers, and statisticians have found reasonable ways to conceptualize this complex array of institutions and distinguish it from other societal components. It is therefore reasonable to assume that similar conceptualizations are possible for civil society.

To meet this challenge, we adopted a bottom-up, inductive approach to defining the civil society sector, building up our definition from the actual experiences of the broad range of countries embraced within our project. In particular, we first solicited from our Local Associates a roadmap of the kinds of entities that would reasonably be included in the third or civil society sector in their respective countries. We then lined these roadmaps up against each other to see where they overlapped and identified the basic characteristics of the entities that fell into this overlapping area. Finally, we made note of the "gray areas" that existed on the fringes of this core concept and created a process, in cooperation with our Local Associates, for determining how to treat entities that occupied these gray areas.

The Structural-Operational Definition

Out of this process emerged a consensus on five structural-operational features that defined the entities at the center of our concern. For the purpose of this project, therefore, we defined the civil society sector as composed of entities that are:

- *Organized:* They have some structure and regularity to their operations, whether or not they are formally constituted or legally registered. This means that our definition embraces informal, nonregistered groups as well as formally registered ones. What is important is not whether the group is legally or formally recognized but that it have some organizational permanence and regularity as reflected in regular meetings, a membership, and some structure of procedures for making decisions that participants recognize as legitimate.
- *Private:* They are not part of the apparatus of the state, even though they may receive support from governmental sources. This feature differentiates our approach from the economic definitions noted above that exclude

organizations from the civil society sector if they receive significant public sector support.

- *Not profit-distributing:* They are not primarily commercial in purpose and do not distribute profits to a set of directors, stockholders, or managers. Civil society organizations can generate surpluses in the course of their operations, but any such surpluses must be reinvested in the objectives of the organization. This criterion serves as a proxy for the "public purpose" criterion used in some definitions of civil society, but it does so without having to specify in advance and for all countries what valid public purposes are. Rather, it leaves these decisions to the people involved on the theory that if there are people in a country who voluntarily support an organization without hope of receiving a share of any profit the organization generates, this is strong evidence that they must see some public purpose to the organization. This criterion also usefully differentiates civil society organizations from for-profit businesses.
- *Self-governing:* They have their own mechanisms for internal governance, are able to cease operations on their own authority, and are fundamentally in control of their own affairs.
- *Voluntary:* Membership or participation in them is not legally required or otherwise compulsory. As noted above, this criterion also helped relate our definition to the concept of public purpose, but in a way that allows each country's citizens to define for themselves what they consider to be a valid public purpose by virtue of their decisions to take part in the organizations affected.

Obviously, like any definition, this one cannot eliminate all gray areas or borderline cases. As these were identified, efforts were made to interpret them in the context of the basic thrust of the definition, and clarifications were issued as appropriate. Thus, for example, the "not profit-distributing" criterion was included to differentiate civil society organizations from private business firms as well as from the large-scale cooperative and mutual enterprises that dominate the banking and insurance industries in many European countries. But when it became clear that this criterion inadvertently threatened to exclude as well an important class of community-based cooperatives serving essentially anti-poverty purposes in Latin America and elsewhere in the developing world, language was added to make clear that the latter institutions could be included.

Our structural-operational definition has been tested in every country included in the project. The definition has proved to be sufficiently broad to encompass the great variety of entities commonly considered to be part of the third or civil society sector in both developed and developing countries, yet sufficiently sharp to distinguish these institutions from those in the other two major sectors—business and government. The result is a definition that encompasses *informal* as well as *formal* organizations; *religious* as well as *secular* organizations;[2] organizations with paid staff and those staffed entirely by volunteers; and organizations performing essentially *expressive* functions—such as advocacy, cultural expression, community organizing, environmental protection, human rights, religion, representation of interests, and political expression—as well as those performing essentially *service* functions, such as the provision of health, education, or welfare services. While the definition does not embrace individual forms of citizen action, such as voting and writing to legislators, it nevertheless embraces most organized forms, including social movements and community-based cooperative activities serving fundamentally solidarity objectives, such as the *stokvels*, or revolving credit associations, in Africa. Intentionally excluded, however, are government agencies, private businesses, and commercial cooperatives and mutuals.[3]

Classification

While the formulation of a common definition was necessary to identify the full range of entities in-scope of the "sector" we were examining and to differentiate them from other societal institutions, such as governments, and for-profit businesses, it was only one part of the conceptual equipment that had to be created to carry out this project. Side by side with their significant commonalities, nonprofit or civil society organizations also have many differences, and these also had to be distinguished. For this purpose, a classification structure was needed.

Fortunately, a sophisticated International Standard Industrial Classification (ISIC) system was available in the international statistical community for identifying the primary activity of different economic units globally. Unfortunately, however, this system was not sufficiently detailed to differentiate adequately the diverse activities of nonprofit organizations.

Accordingly, to provide a way to classify civil society organizations in different countries, we developed the International Classification of Nonprofit Organizations (ICNPO). This classification system emerged through a collaborative process involving local associates from many different regions.

The ICNPO is a classification scheme that groups civil society organizations among 12 major fields, including a "not elsewhere classified" category, based on their primary activity (see table A.1). The primary activity is the activity that engages the greatest share (in most cases, more than half) of an organization's resources (financial or human).

To ensure some consistency with existing economic classification systems, the ICNPO adheres closely to the service sector classification of the International

Group 1	Culture and recreation	Group 5	Environment
1 100	Culture and arts	5 100	Environment
1 200	Sports	5 200	Animal protection
1 300	Other recreation and social clubs	Group 6	Development and housing
Group 2	Education and research	6 100	Economic, social, and community development
2 100	Primary and secondary education	6 200	Housing
2 200	Higher education	6 300	Employment and training
2 300	Other education	Group 7	Law, advocacy, and politics
2 400	Research	7 100	Civic and advocacy organizations
Group 3	Health	7 200	Law and legal services
3 100	Hospitals and rehabilitation	7 300	Political organizations
3 200	Nursing homes	Group 8	Philanthropic intermediaries and voluntarism promotion
3 300	Mental health and crisis intervention	Group 9	International
3 400	Other health services	Group 10	Religion
Group 4	Social services	Group 11	Business and professional associations, unions
4 100	Social services	Group 12	[Not elsewhere classified]
4 200	Emergency and relief		
4 300	Income support and maintenance		

Standard Industrial Classification system (ISIC) but elaborates on it to provide more detail than ISIC allows within particular categories (e.g., health and social assistance). This system has worked well to differentiate civil society organizations, though occasional updates were needed as the project expanded into different regions and new categories of organizations were encountered.

Terminology

For the sake of convenience, we will generally use the term "civil society organizations" or "civil society sector" to refer to the institutions that meet this fivefold structural-operational definition. To be sure, this term is often used in a broader sense to encompass individual citizen activity as well.[4] To emphasize our focus on the more collective and organized forms of civil society, we will generally use the term "civil society organization" or "civil society sector" rather than simply "civil society" to depict the range of social phenomena that is the focus of our attention. This term has gained the widest acceptance internationally to refer to the organizations with which we are concerned. Other terms that will occasionally be used interchangeably to refer to the same set of entities will be "nonprofit sector," "nonprofit organizations," "third sector," and "voluntary organizations." Each of these terms carries its own baggage, but the "civil society" term seems the closest to gaining truly universal usage and has the advantage of avoiding the negative connotations associated with the terms "nonprofit" or "nongovernmental."

Data Sources and Methodology

In order to ensure a reasonable degree of comparability in the basic data generated about the organizations identified above, we developed a data assembly approach that specified a common set of target data items, offered guidance on likely sources of such data, and then relied on Local Associates to formulate detailed strategies for generating the needed information in each country.

The principal focus in this basic descriptive portion of the project was on the overall scope and scale of civil society organization activity and the resources required to support it. Because it is a notoriously imprecise measure, we devoted little attention to the number of organizations and focused instead on variables more indicative of the level of effort these organizations mobilize. These included the number of workers, both paid and volunteer, expressed in full-time equivalent terms; the expenditures; the sources of revenue; and the primary activity.[5]

Broadly speaking, four types of data sources were employed to generate estimates of these key variables:

- Official economic statistics (e.g., employment surveys and population surveys), particularly those that included coverage of civil society organizations, giving, or volunteering. Where the civil society organizations were not separately identified in the data source, as was often the case, a variety of estimating techniques were used to determine the civil society organization share of particular industry aggregates. Local Associates typically worked closely with relevant officials in statistical agencies to secure the requisite data. With the 2003 publication of the UN *Handbook on Nonprofit Institutions in the System of National Accounts,* produced by Johns Hopkins Center for Civil Society Studies personnel with the assistance of Helen Tice, formerly of the US Bureau of Economic Affairs, additional data on nonprofit institutions began to become available in the roughly 30 countries that have implemented this *Handbook* and produced the nonprofit institution "satellite accounts" it calls for;
- Data assembled by umbrella groups or intermediary associations representing various types of civil society organizations or industries in which civil society organizations are active;

- Specialized surveys of civil society organizations; and
- Population surveys, particularly those focusing on giving and volunteering.

The extent of reliance on these different types of sources varied greatly from country to country and even from field to field. Where existing data systems could be tapped to locate relevant information about a class of nonprofit organizations in a country, these were heavily mined. Where such data systems were inadequate or a class of organizations not covered by them, special surveys were carried out. Depending on the legal arrangements and registration systems in place, these surveys began with existing core lists of organizations or with lists that had to be built from the ground up. As the project moved its focus from areas with more developed data systems and more formalized civil society sectors to those with less developed data systems and less formal organizations, the extent of reliance on specially designed, bottom-up surveys naturally expanded. Thus, in Africa and Southeast Asia, detailed "snowball sampling" or "hypernetwork sampling" techniques were used to build profiles of the civil society sector from the ground up by going house to house or organization to organization in carefully selected geographic areas, asking respondents about the organizations they belonged to or worked with, and continuing this process until no new organizations were encountered. These results were then blown up to estimate national totals. On the opposite end of the spectrum are the Nonprofit Institution Satellite Accounts assembled by national statistical offices of several countries, including Australia, Belgium, Brazil, Canada, the Czech Republic, Israel, Japan, Mexico, Norway, and Portugal in compliance with the United Nations *Handbook on Nonprofit Institutions in the System of National Accounts.*

Further Insights to the Data and Approach

In interpreting the findings presented here, several features of the analysis should be borne in mind:

- Employment data—both paid and volunteer—are expressed in full-time equivalent (FTE) terms to make them comparable among countries and organizations. Thus, an organization that employs 20 half-time workers would have the same number of "full-time equivalent" workers (i.e., 10) as an organization that employs 10 people full-time. Similarly, an organization that employs 10 full-time paid workers would have the same "workforce" as an organization that engages 50 volunteers who work one day a week, or one-fifth time, each. Part-time workers, paid and volunteer, were converted to full-time equivalent terms by dividing the number of hours they work by the number of hours considered to represent a full-time job in the respective country.

- Unless otherwise noted, average figures reported here are unweighted averages in which the values of all countries are counted equally regardless of the size of the country or of its civil society sector.
- Although data were collected at different time periods (between 1995 and 2008), we have attempted to minimize the consequences of the different base years by focusing on the *relative* size of the civil society sector in a country rather than the *absolute* size since the relative size is not likely to change much over the three- or four-year period we are examining. Thus, for example, we measure the workforce of the civil society sector in a country as the *percentage* of the economically active population that works for civil society organizations in either paid or volunteer positions.[6]
- As noted above, religious as well as secular organizations were included within the project's definition of the civil society sector, and an effort was made in most countries to capture the activity of both *religious worship organizations* (e.g., churches, mosques, synagogues, choirs, and religious study groups) and *religiously affiliated service organizations* (e.g., schools, hospitals, and homeless shelters). Generally, where a distinction between these two was possible, the affiliated service organizations were assigned to the relevant service field in which they chiefly operate (e.g., health, education, and social services). The organizations primarily engaged in religious worship, by contrast, were assigned to the special category of "religious organizations" (ICNPO Category 10). Since comparable data on religious worship organizations could not be gathered in all countries, the cross-country comparisons here generally exclude the religious worship organizations (but not religiously affiliated service organizations). However, where this exclusion affects the results significantly, we also note what difference the inclusion of religious worship organizations would make in the countries for which data are available.
- The revenues of civil society organizations come from a variety of sources. For the sake of convenience, we have grouped these into three categories: *fees,* which includes private payments for services, membership dues, and investment income; *philanthropy,* which includes individual giving, foundation giving, and corporate giving; and *government* or *public sector support,* which includes grants, contracts, and voucher or third-party payments from all levels of government, including government-financed social security systems that operate as quasi-nongovernmental organizations.

Notes

1. Quoted in Ragin 1987, 1.
2. Religious organizations can take at least two different forms: (1) places of religious worship and (2) service organizations, such as schools and hospitals with a

religious affiliation. Both of these are included within the project's definition of a civil society organization, though, as noted below, where it was possible to differentiate the two, the religiously affiliated service organizations were grouped together with other service organizations in the relevant field and the religious worship organizations identified separately. Not all countries were able to collect information on the religious worship organizations, however.

3. A revised edition of the United Nations *Handbook on Nonprofit Institutions in the System of National Accounts* scheduled for release in 2017 recommends generating comparable data on a subset of cooperatives and mutual societies found to operate under a significant limitation on their distribution of profit. For a discussion of the "social economy" concept, see Defourny and Develtere 1999.

4. For an illustration of the confusion attending the "civil society" concept, see Fowler 2002. Although claiming to use a different concept than the one adopted here, Fowler defines civil society in terms quite consistent with the definition adopted in this project: "an arena of voluntary formal and informal collective citizen engagement distinct from families, state, and profit-seeking institutions." The emphasis on "collective" engagement in this definition is similar to our focus on organizations.

5. See the Further Insights section for a discussion of the full-time equivalent conversion. Other components of the project examined additional facets of the civil society sector in the target countries, such as the legal framework, the history, religious and cultural traditions, and the policy context.

6. Readers of our previous reports will note that the basis of comparison used here differs slightly from that used previously. In particular, we compare nonprofit employment here to the economically active population in the countries covered rather than to the nonagricultural workforce as in previous reports. This change was made necessary because of the huge size of the agricultural workforce, the large informal economy, and the resulting relatively small size of the formally recorded "workforce" in many of the countries now covered by the project. In India, for example, no more than 10 percent of the economically active population—meaning the population of working age that is able to work—is recorded in government documents as part of the formal "labor force." This change in the base of the percentages means that the relative size of the nonprofit sector reported here appears lower than in previous reports for some of the countries covered. This is so because the economically active population is generally larger than the nonagricultural labor force. The economically active population is essentially the population of working age that is not institutionalized or otherwise unavailable for productive work, whether they are formally employed, self-employed, producing for their own consumption, or looking for work. See International Labour Organization 1988.

Dimensions of the Civil Society (CS) Sector by Country

Country	CS workforce as % of EAP	Volunteers as % of CS workforce	Share of CS workforce in expressive activities (%)	Share of CS workforce in service activities (%)
Argentina	5.9	45.7	42.4	54.4
Australia	8.8	33.5	25.4	57.3
Austria	7.8	72.2	50.3	48.7
Belgium	13.1	25.8	14.2	85.2
Brazil	3.3	18.5	48.6	51.3
Canada	12.3	26.5	28.1	68.0
Chile	5.0	48.8	41.6	55.8
Colombia	2.3	24.0	24.7	72.8
Czech Republic	1.7	16.0	30.8	68.5
Denmark	8.8	43.9	42.9	50.5
Finland	5.7	53.8	58.1	40.9
France	9.0	34.2	37.1	62.0
Germany	6.8	45.0	37.1	54.8
Hungary	2.0	18.8	36.9	60.2
India	1.5	56.0	12.2	82.8
Ireland	10.9	21.2	18.4	80.3
Israel	11.8	12.4	13.6	81.7
Italy	4.3	42.6	38.7	58.8
Japan	8.0	19.3	14.8	79.3
Kenya	2.1	39.1	16.5	59.0
Korea, Republic of	4.2	40.4	42.6	57.4
Mexico	3.1	33.0	34.9	59.0
Netherlands	15.9	36.3	30.1	64.4
New Zealand	9.6	66.7	45.1	46.2
Norway	7.3	62.2	60.0	37.9
Pakistan	1.0	44.6	23.1	76.9
Peru	2.1	38.2	4.3	94.9
Philippines	1.9	62.0	41.8	56.9
Poland	0.9	21.2	46.7	49.0
Portugal	4.5	26.7	37.5	62.5
Romania	0.7	56.5	39.5	55.8
Russian Federation	1.2	36.3	57.1	33.9

Government share of CS revenue (%)	Philanthropy share of CS revenue (%)	Fee share of CS revenue (%)	Gov't social spending as % of GDP	Income level
17.2	18.6	64.2	12.4	Medium-high
33.5	9.5	56.9	17.1	High
50.0	12.8	37.2	26.0	High
68.8	3.3	27.9	27.2	High
5.7	9.7	84.5	14.0	Medium-high
48.5	12.8	38.7	17.8	High
45.2	19.4	35.4	14.0	Medium-high
14.9	14.9	70.2	10.0	Medium-low
64.7	18.0	17.3	26.0	High
40.1	7.0	53.0	27.9	High
36.0	7.1	56.8	32.1	High
62.8	9.5	27.7	28.3	High
64.8	3.4	31.8	29.6	High
52.2	11.8	36.0	22.7	Medium-high
36.1	12.9	51.0	2.6	Low
74.5	10.3	15.2	19.4	High
63.6	18.0	18.4	22.9	High
36.1	3.3	60.7	23.7	High
38.3	0.9	60.8	17.7	High
4.8	14.8	80.4	2.0	Low
35.5	2.1	62.5	5.7	High
11.0	10.6	78.5	6.8	Medium-high
62.6	5.1	32.4	19.7	High
24.6	20.0	55.4	18.9	High
36.0	7.5	56.5	25.2	High
5.9	44.2	49.8	1.9	Low
18.1	12.2	69.8	8.8	Medium-low
4.5	14.7	80.9	1.7	Medium-low
24.1	15.5	60.4	25.9	Medium-high
39.6	11.5	48.9	21.1	High
45.1	26.5	28.4	12.4	Medium-high
15.2	33.3	51.5	12.5	Medium-high

(*continued*)

Country	CS workforce as % of EAP	Volunteers as % of CS workforce	Share of CS workforce in expressive activities (%)	Share of CS workforce in service activities (%)
Slovakia	1.0	27.7	63.8	29.6
South Africa	3.4	49.1	48.1	51.5
Spain	4.3	34.8	25.9	71.1
Sweden	9.6	73.7	67.0	29.9
Switzerland	6.9	37.2	42.9	55.0
Tanzania	1.9	75.2	31.4	51.2
Uganda	2.4	59.3	28.4	67.8
United Kingdom	11.0	53.0	46.0	50.1
United States	9.2	32.4	29.0	66.2
41-country average	**5.7**	**40.4**	**36.6**	**59.1**
41-country median	**4.5**	**38.2**	**37.5**	**57.3**
Skewness	0.62	0.39	−0.04	0.19

DATA SOURCES: Johns Hopkins Comparative Nonprofit Sector Project Data Files, ccss.jhu.edu. Data on government social spending and GDP for 27 high-income countries come from OECD at https://stats.oecd.org/Index.aspx?DataSetCode=SOCX_AGG. Government social spending percentages for remaining countries are author estimates based on GDP data from national statistical sources and data on social welfare spending compiled from information available online from government agencies and research organizations.

* EAP = Economically active population.

Government share of CS revenue (%)	Philanthropy share of CS revenue (%)	Fee share of CS revenue (%)	Gov't social spending as % of GDP	Income level
22.1	23.7	54.2	19.9	Medium-high
41.6	24.9	33.5	3.5	Medium-high
32.1	18.8	49.0	21.5	High
28.7	9.1	62.3	36.4	High
34.5	7.9	57.5	7.7	High
26.9	20.2	52.9	4.3	Low
7.1	38.2	54.7	4.3	Low
45.2	11.3	43.5	22.8	High
30.0	14.1	55.9	15.9	High
35.3	14.4	50.3	16.84	
36.0	12.8	53.0	17.81	
0.17	1.31	−0.14	−0.07	

BIBLIOGRAPHY

Acemoglu, Daron, and James A. Robinson. 2012. *Why Nations Fail: The Origins of Power, Prosperity, and Poverty*. New York: Crown Business.

Agard, Kathryn Ann (ed.). 2011. *Leadership in Nonprofit Organizations: A Reference Handbook*. Los Angeles: Sage Publications.

Amenomori, Takayoshi. 1993. "Defining the Nonprofit Sector: Japan." *Working Papers of the Johns Hopkins Comparative Nonprofit Sector Project*, no. 15, edited by Lester M. Salamon and Helmut K. Anheier. Baltimore: The Johns Hopkins Institute for Policy Studies. Available at: http://ccss.jhu.edu/publications-findings/?did=167.

Andersen, Johannes, Jørgen Goul Andersen, and Lars Torpe. 2000. *Hvad folket magter—demokrati, magt og afmagt*. Copenhagen: Jurist- og Økonomforbundets Forlag.

Anheier, Helmut K., and Lester M. Salamon. 2006. "The Nonprofit Sector in Comparative Perspective." In Walter W. Powell and Richard Steinberg (eds.), *The Nonprofit Sector: A Research Handbook*, 2nd edition, pp. 89–116. New Haven: Yale University Press.

Anufriev, N. P. 1917. Правительственная регламентация образования частных обществ в России: Вопросы административного права. (*Governmental Regulation of the Private Communities Establishment in Russia.*) Issues of the Administrative Law, 1M.

Arthur, Brian W. 1994. *Increasing Returns and Path Dependence in the Economy*. Ann Arbor: University of Michigan Press.

Avakyan, S. 1996. *Политический плюрализм и общественные объединения в РФ: конституционно-правовые основы.* (*Political Pluralism and Public Associations in the Russian Federation: Constitutional-and-Legal Foundations.*) Moscow: The Russian Juridical Publishing House.

Backhaus-Maul, Holger, and Thomas Olk. 1994. "Von Subsidiarität zu 'outcontracting:' Zum Wandel der Beziehungen von Staat und Wohlfahrtsverbänden in der Sozialpolitik." In Wolfgang Streeck (ed.), *Staat und Verbände*, pp. 100–135. Opladen: Westdeutscher Verlag.

Bakvis, Herman. 1981. *Catholic Power in the Netherlands*. Kingston, ON: McGill Queen's University Press.

Banfield, Edward. 1958. *The Moral Basis of a Backward Society*. New York: Free Press.

Bauer, Arnold. 1975. *Chilean Rural Society from the Spanish Conquest to 1930*. New York: Cambridge University Press.

BBC. 2015. "Russia targets 'undesirable' foreign organisations." *BBC World News*, May 15, 2015. www.bbc.com/news/world-europe-32751797.

Belich, James. 2001. *Paradise Reforged: A History of the New Zealanders from the 1880s to the Year 2000*. Auckland, NZ: Allen Lane/The Penguin Press.

Bellah, Robert, Richard Madsen, William M. Sullivan, Ann Swidler, and Steven Tipton. 1985. *Habits of the Heart: Individualism and Commitment in American Life*. New York: Harper and Row.

Beller, Steven. 2007. *A Concise History of Austria*. Cambridge: Cambridge University Press.

Belyaeva, N. Yu. 1994. Беляева Н.Ю. Правовое регулирование и этические нормы в благотворительном секторе// *Помоги ближнему! Благотворительность вчера и сегодня*. Под ред. В. В. Меньшикова. (*"Legal Regulation and Standards of Ethics of the Charity Sector" in V. V. Menshikov [ed.], Help Your Neighbor! Charity Yesterday and Today*.) Moscow: Polygran.

Bender, Johan, Christian R. Jansen, and Erik Korr Johansen. 1977. *Arbejdsløshed i Danmark: fra 1800 til i dag*. Copenhagen: Gyldendal.

Ben-Ner, Avner, and Benedetto Gui (eds.). 1993. *The Independent Sector in the Mixed Economy*. Ann Arbor: The University of Michigan Press.

Ben-Ner, Avner, and Theresa Van Hoomissen. 1993. "Independent Organizations in the Mixed Economy: A Demand and Supply Analysis." In Avner Ben-Ner and Benedetto Gui (eds.), *The Independent Sector in the Mixed Economy*, pp. 27–58. Ann Arbor: The University of Michigan Press.

Berger, Peter, and John Neuhaus. 1977. *To Empower People: The Role of Mediating Structures in Public Policy*. Washington, DC: American Enterprise Institute.

Berger, Stefan, and David Broughton (eds.). 1995. *The Force of Labour*. Oxford: Berg Publishers.

Bethell, Leslie (ed.). 1991. *Mexico Since Independence*. Cambridge: Cambridge University Press.

Blackburn, Simon. 2001. *Ethics: A Very Short Introduction*. Oxford: Oxford University Press.

Borzenkov, A. G. 1998. Борзенков А.Г. Политизированные самодеятельные инициативы молодежи на востоке России (1960-е–начало 1990-х гг.)// Проблемы истории местного управления Сибири XVI–XX веков: Материалы III региональной научной конференции (19–20 ноября 1998 г.). Новосибирск, 1998. С.272. (*Politicized Amateur Initiatives of Youth in the East of Russia [1960s–early 1990s]. Issues of the Local Government History in Siberia in 16th–20th centuries: Material of the 3rd Regional Scientific Conference November 19-20, 1998.*) Novosibirsk.

Bourdieu, Pierre. 1984. *Distinction: A Social Critique of the Judgment of Taste*. Cambridge: Harvard University Press.

Bourjaily, Natalia. 2006. "Some Issues Related to Russia's New NGO Law," *International Journal of Not-for-Profit Law* 8(3): 5–6. Available at: www.icnl .org/research/journal/vol8iss3/special_1.htm.

Bradley, Joseph. 1994. "Public Associations and Civil Society Development in Pre-Revolutionary Russia." *Social Sciences and Modern Age* 5, 77–89.

Brandsen, Taco, and Ulla Pape. 2015. "The Netherlands: The Paradox of Government-Nonprofit Partnerships." *VOLUNTAS: International Journal of Voluntary and Nonprofit Organizations* 26(6): 2267–2282.

Brenner, Robert. 1982. "Agrarian Class Structure and Economic Development in Pre-Industrial Europe." *Past & Present* 97:16–113.

Brook-Shepherd, Gordon. 1996. *The Austrians: A Thousand-Year Odyssey*. New York: Carroll and Graf.

Buchenau, Jürgen. 2007. *Plutarco Elias Calles and the Mexican Revolution*. Lanham, MD: Rowman & Littlefield.

Burger, Ary, Paul Dekker, Tymen van der Ploeg, and Wino van Veen. 1997. "Defining the Nonprofit Sector: The Netherlands." *Working Papers of the Johns Hopkins Comparative Nonprofit Sector Project*, no. 23, edited by Lester M. Salamon and Helmut K. Anheier. Baltimore: The Johns Hopkins Institute for Policy Studies. Available at: http://ccss.jhu.edu/publications-findings/?did=181.

Butcher, Jacqueline, and María Guadalupe Serna (eds.). 2006. *El Tercer Sector en México: Perspectivas de Investigación*. México DF: The Mexican Center for Philanthropy (CEMEFI) e Instituto de Investigaciones.

Cadena Roa, Jorge (ed.). 2004. *Las Organizaciones Civiles Mexicanas Hoy*. México DF: Universidad Nacional Autónoma de México, Centro de Investigaciones Interdisciplinarias en Ciencias y Humanidades.

Chang, Cyril F., and Howard P. Tuckman. 1996. "The Goods Produced by Nonprofit Organizations." *Public Finance Review* 24(1): 25–43.

Chernykh, A. I. 1993. Черных А. И. По пути к гражданскому обществу. Реформы 1960-х годов в России/ Проблемы формирования гражданского общества/ Отв. ред. З. Т. Голенкова. (*"On the Way to the Civil Society: Reforms of the 1960s in Russia" in Z. T. Golenkova [ed.], Problems of the Formation of Civil Society*.) Moscow: ИС РАН.

Cheyne, Christine, Mike O'Brien, and Michael Belgrave. 2005. *Social Policy in Aotearoa/New Zealand: A Critical Introduction*. Auckland, NZ: Oxford University Press.

Clarence-Smith, William G. 1985. *The Third Portuguese Empire 1825–1975: A Study in Economic Imperialism*. Manchester: Manchester University Press.

Coatsworth. John H. 1978. "Obstacles to Economic Growth in Nineteenth-Century Mexico." *The American Historical Review* 83(1): 80–100.

Cohen, Theodore, and Herbert Passin. 1987. *Remaking Japan: The American Occupation as New Deal* (Studies of the East Asian Institute). Glencoe, IL: Free Press.

Coleman, James. 1990. *Foundations of Social Theory*. Cambridge, MA: Harvard University Press.

Collins, Randall. 1986. *Weberian Sociological Theory*. Cambridge: Cambridge University Press.

Cook, Linda J. 2015. "New Winds of Social Policy in the East." *VOLUNTAS: International Journal of Voluntary and Nonprofit Organizations* 26(6): 2330–2350.

Cox, Robert H. 1993. *The Development of the Dutch Welfare State*. Pittsburgh: University of Pittsburgh Press.

Dalziel, Raewyn. 1993. "Political Organisations." In Anne Else (ed.), *Women Together: A History of Women's Organisations in New Zealand*, pp. 55–69. Wellington, NZ: Historical Branch, Department of Internal Affairs/Daphne Brassell Press.

de Tocqueville, Alexis. 1835, 1840. *Democracy in America*. Available at: http://ebooks.adelaide.edu.au/t/tocqueville/alexis/democracy/complete.html.

Defourny, Jacques, and Patrick Develtere. 1999. "The Social Economy: The Worldwide Making of a Third Sector." In Jaques Defourny, Patrick Develtere, and Bénédicte Fonteneau (eds.), *L'economie sociale au Nord et au Sud*, pp. 25–50. Paris: Université de Boeck.

Defourny, Jacques, Patrick Develtere, and Bénédicte Fonteneau (eds.). 1999. *L'economie sociale au Nord et au Sud*. Paris: Université de Boeck.

Drake, Paul W. 1996. *Labor Movements and Dictatorships: The Southern Cone in Comparative Perspective*. Baltimore: The Johns Hopkins University Press.

Durie, Mason. 2005. *Ngā Tai Matatū: Tides of Māori Endurance*. Melbourne, Australia: Oxford University Press.

Eberle, Thomas S., and Kurt Imhof (eds.). 2007. *Sonderfall Schweiz*. Zurich: Seismo.

Edwards, Michael. 2004. *Civil Society*. Cambridge: Polity Press.

———. 2011. *The Oxford Handbook of Civil Society*. Oxford: Oxford University Press.

Else, Anne (ed.). 1993. *Women Together: A History of Women's Organisations in New Zealand*. Wellington, NZ: Historical Branch, Department of Internal Affairs/Daphne Brassell Press.

Erne, Emil. 1988. *Die schweizerischen Sozietäten: Lexikalische Darstellung der Reformgesellschaften des 18. Jahrhunderts in der Schweiz*. Zürich: Chronos.

Esping-Andersen, Gøsta. 1990. *The Three Worlds of Welfare Capitalism*. Princeton: Princeton University Press.

Etzioni, Amitai. 1993. *The Spirit of Community: Rights, Responsibilities, and the Communitarian Agenda*. New York: Crown Publishers.

Evans, Peter B., Dietrich Rueschemeyer, and Theda Skocpol (eds.). 1985. *Bringing the State Back In*. Cambridge: Cambridge University Press.

Evers, Adalbert, and Jean Louis Laville. 2004. "Defining the Third Sector in Europe." In Adalbert Evers and Jean Louis Laville (eds.), *The Third Sector in Europe*, pp. 11–42. Cheltenham, UK: Edward Elgar.

Favela Gavia, Diana. 2004. "La regulación jurídica de las organizaciones civiles en México: en busca de la participación democrática." In Jorge Cadena Roa (ed.),

Las Organizaciones Civiles Mexicanas Hoy. México DF: Universidad Nacional Autónoma de México, Centro de Investigaciones Interdisciplinarias en Ciencias y Humanidades.

Fowler, Alan. 2002. "Civil Society Research Findings from a Global Perspective: A Case for Redressing Bias, Asymmetry, and Bifurcation." *VOLUNTAS: International Journal of Voluntary and Nonprofit Organizations* 13(3): 287–300.

Franco, Raquel C. 2005. "Defining the Nonprofit Sector: Portugal." *Working Papers of the Johns Hopkins Comparative Nonprofit Sector Project*, no. 43. Baltimore: Johns Hopkins Center for Civil Society Studies. Available at: http://ccss.jhu.edu/publications-findings/?did=203.

Franco, Raquel C., S. Wojciech Sokolowski, Eileen M. H. Hairel, and Lester M. Salamon. 2006. *The Portuguese Nonprofit Sector in Comparative Perspective.* Porto and Baltimore: Universidade Catolica Portuguesa and Johns Hopkins University. Available at: http://ccss.jhu.edu/publications-findings/?did=359.

Fukuyama, Francis. 1995. *Trust: The Social Virtues and the Creation of Prosperity.* New York: Free Press.

Galbraith, John Kenneth. 2001. *The Essential Galbraith.* Boston: Mariner Books.

Gamson, William. 1990. *The Strategy of Social Protest,* 2nd edition. Belmont: Wadsworth Publishing Company.

Gella, Aleksander. 1988. *Development of Class Structure in Eastern Europe.* Albany: State University of New York Press.

Gellner, Ernest. 1995. "The Importance of Being Modular." In John R. Hall (ed.), *Civil Society: Theory, History, Comparison,* pp. 32–55. Cambridge: Polity Press.

Gerschenkron, Alexander. 1992. "Economic Backwardness in Historical Perspective." In Mark Granovetter and Richard Swedberg (eds.), *The Sociology of Economic Life,* pp. 111–130. Boulder: Westview Press.

Giddens, Anthony. 1987. *The Nation-State and Violence.* Berkeley: University of California Press.

Golenkova, Z. T. (ed.). 1993. *Проблемы формирования гражданского общества. (Problems of the Formation of Civil Society.)* Moscow: ИС РАН.

Gramsci, Antonio. 1999. *Selections from the Prison Notebooks.* New York: International Publishers.

Granovetter, Mark. 1985. "Economic Action and Social Structure: The Problem of Embeddedness." *American Journal of Sociology* 91(3): 481–510.

Granovetter, Mark, and Richard Swedberg (eds.). 1992. *The Sociology of Economic Life,* 1st edition. Boulder: Westview Press.

Green, David, and Lawrence Cromwell. 1984. *Mutual Aid or Welfare State.* Sydney: G. Allen & Unwin.

Grimshaw, Patricia. 1987. *Women's Suffrage in New Zealand,* 2nd edition. Auckland, NZ: Auckland University Press.

Gromov, A. V., and O. S. Kuzin. 1990. *Громов А.В., Кузин О.С. Неформалы: кто есть кто? (Members of the Unofficial Organizations: Who Are Who?)* Moscow: Mysl.

Haber, Stephen J. 1992. "Assessing the Obstacles to Industrialisation: The Mexican Economy, 1830–1940." *Journal of Latin American Studies* 24(1): 1–32.

Habermann, Ulla. 2001. *En postmoderne helgen?—om motiver til frivillighed.* Lunds Dissertations in Social Work. Lunds University.

Habermann, Ulla, and Bjarne Ibsen. 1997. Den frivillige sektor i Danmark—150 års historisk udvikling. I: *Frivilligt socialt arbejde i fremtidens velfærdssamfund.* Bet. Nr. 1332. Bilagsdel. Copenhagen: Socialministeriet.

Habermas, Jürgen. 1989[1962]. *The Structural Transformation of the Public Sphere: An Inquiry into a Category of Bourgeois Society.* Cambridge, MA: The MIT Press.

Haider, Astrid, Ulrike Schneider, Robert Leisch, and Klaus Stöger. 2008. Neue Datengrundlage für den Non-Profit-Bereich. *Statistische Nachrichten* 63(8): 754–761.

Hall, John R. (ed.). 1995a. *Civil Society: Theory, History, Comparison.* Cambridge, UK: Polity Press.

———. 1995b. "In Search of Civil Society." In John R. Hall (ed.), *Civil Society: Theory, History, Comparison,* pp. 1–31. Cambridge: Polity Press.

Halperin, S. William. 1964. *Germany Tried Democracy: A Political History of the Reich from 1918 to 1933.* New York: The Norton Library.

Hansmann, Henry. 1987. "Economic Theories of Nonprofit Organizations." In Walter W. Powell (ed.), *The Nonprofit Sector: A Research Handbook,* pp. 27–42. New Haven: Yale University Press.

Harvey, David. 2007. *A Brief History of Neoliberalism.* Oxford: Oxford University Press.

Hastings, James (ed.). 1914(1914). *Encyclopedia of Religion and Ethics,* vol. 6. New York: Charles Scribner's Sons.

Hausner, Jerzy, Bob Jessop, and Klaus Nielsen (eds.). 1995. *Strategic Choice and Path Dependency in Post Socialism, Institutional Dynamics in the Transformation Process.* Aldershot, UK: Edward Elgar.

Heclo, Hugh. 1974. *Modern Social Politics in Britain and Sweden.* New Haven, CT: Yale University Press.

Heerma van Voss, Lex. 1995. "The Netherlands." In Stefan Berger and David Broughton (eds.), *The Force of Labour: The Western European Labour Movement and the Working Class in the Twentieth Century,* pp. 39–70. Bern: Berg.

Heinrich, Volkhart F. 2005. "Studying Civil Society Across the World: Exploring the Thorny Issues of Conceptualization and Measurement." *Journal of Civil Society* 1(3): 211–228.

Heitzman, James, and Robert L. Worden. 1996. *India: A Country Study,* 5th edition. Washington, DC: Government Printing Office.

Heitzmann, Karin, and Ruth Simsa. 2004. "From Corporatist Security to Civil Society Creativity: The Nonprofit Sector in Austria." In Annette Zimmer and Eckhard Priller (eds.), *Future of Civil Society: Making Central European Nonprofit Organisations Work,* pp. 713–731. Wiesbaden: VS Verlag für Sozialwissenschaften.

Helmig, Bernard, Christoph Bärlocher, and Georg von Schnurbein. 2009. "Defining the Nonprofit Sector: Switzerland." *Working Papers of the Johns Hopkins*

Comparative Nonprofit Sector Project, no. 46. Baltimore: The Johns Hopkins Center for Civil Society Studies. Available at: http://ccss.jhu.edu/publications -findings/?did=224.

Helmig, Bernard, Markus Gmür, Christoph Bärlocher, Georg von Schnurbein, Bernard Degen, Michael Nollert, Monica Budowski, Wojciech Sokolowski, and Lester M. Salamon. 2011. "The Swiss Civil Society Sector in a Comparative Perspective." *VMI Research Series,* volume 6. Fribourg: Institute for Research on Management of Associations, Foundations and Cooperatives (VMI), University of Fribourg. Available at: http://ccss.jhu.edu/publications-findings/?did=309.

Henriksen, Ingrid. 1999. "Avoiding Lock-In: Cooperative Creameries in Denmark, 1882–1903." *European Review of Economic History* (3)1: 57–78

———. 2003. "Freehold Tenure in Late Eighteenth-Century Denmark." *Advances in Agricultural Economic History* 2: 21–40.

———. 2006. "An Economic History of Denmark." In *EH.Net Encyclopedia,* edited by Robert Whaples. Available at: http://eh.net/encyclopedia/an-economic -history-of-denmark.

Henriksen, Lars Skov, and Peter Bundesen. 2004. "The Moving Frontier in Denmark: Voluntary-State Relationships Since 1850." *Journal of Social Policy* 33(4): 605–625.

Henriksen, Lars Skov, and Bjarn Ibsen (eds.). 2001. *Frivillighedens udfordringer— nordisk forskning om frivilligt arbejde og frivillige organisationer.* Odense: Odense Universitetsforlag.

Hoppe, Göran, and John Langton. 1994. *Peasantry to Capitalism: Western Östergöt- land in the Nineteenth Century.* Cambridge: Cambridge University Press.

Howe, Richard Herbert. 1978. "Max Weber's Elective Affinities: Sociology within the Bounds of Pure Reason." *American Journal of Sociology* 84(2): 366–385.

Howell, Jude, and Jenny Pearce. 2001. *Civil Society and Development: A Critical Exploration.* Denver: Lynne Rienner.

Hyde, J. K. 1973. *Society and Politics in Medieval Italy: The Evolution of the Civil Life, 1000–1350.* New York: Macmillan.

Ibsen, Bjarne, and Ulla Haberman. 2005. "Defining the Nonprofit Sector: Den- mark." *Working Papers of the Johns Hopkins Comparative Nonprofit Sector Project,* no. 44. Baltimore: The Johns Hopkins Center for Civil Society Studies. Available at: http://ccss.jhu.edu/publications-findings/?did=50.

ICA, INP. 2007. Jekonomicheskie Posledstvija Novogo Zakonodatel'stva o Nekommercheskih Organizacijah (*Economic Consequences of the New Legislation on Nonprofit Organizations*). Moscow: Institute for Civic Analysis, Institute of the National Project "Social Contract."

Instituto Nacional de Estadística y Geografía. 2011. "Sistema de Cuentas Naciona- les de México. Cuenta satélite de las instituciones sin fines de lucro de México 2008." Aguascalientes: Instituto Nacional de Estadística y Geografía. Available at: http://ccss.jhu.edu/publications-findings/?did=178.

International Labour Organization. 1988. *Current International Recommendations on Labour Statistics.* Geneva: International Labour Organization.

Irarrázaval, Ignacio, Eileen M. H. Hariel, S. Wojciech Sokolowski, and Lester M. Salamon. 2006. *Comparative Nonprofit Sector Project: Chile.* Santiago: Focus. Available at: http://ccss.jhu.edu/publications-findings/?did=38.

James, Estelle. 1987. "The Independent Sector in Comparative Perspective." In Walter W. Powell (ed.), *The Independent Sector: A Research Handbook,* pp. 27–42. New Haven: Yale University Press.

———. 1993. "Why Do Different Countries Choose a Different Public-Private Mix of Educational Services?" *Journal of Human Resources* 7(1): 571–592.

Jørgensen, Anja, Peter Bundesen, and Lars Skov Henriksen. 2001. "Frivillig Organisering Og Offentligt Ansvar." *Nordisk Sosialt Arbeid* 21(4): 1–5.

Katzenstein, Peter. 1985. "Small Nations in an Open International Economy: The Converging Balance of State and Society in Switzerland and Austria." In Peter B. Evans, Dietrich Rueschemeyer, and Theda Skocpol (eds.), *Bringing the State Back In.* Cambridge: Cambridge University Press, pp. 227–251.

Khlystova, E. I. (ed.) 1998. Теория социальной работы. (*The Theory of Social Work.*) Moscow: Yurist.

Klausen, Kurt K. 1995. "Et historisk rids over den tredje sektors udvikling i Danmark." In Kurt K. Klausen and Per Selle (eds.), *Frivillig organisering i Norden.* pp. 35–50. Oslo: Tano. Available at: www.gbv.de/dms/ub-kiel /189572957.pdf.

Klausen, Kurt K., and Per Selle (eds.). 1995a. *Frivillig organisering i Norden.* Oslo: Tano. Available at: www.gbv.de/dms/ub-kiel/189572957.pdf.

———. 1995b. "The Third Sector in Scandinavia." *VOLUNTAS: International Journal of Voluntary and Nonprofit Organizations* 7(2): 99–122.

Kornbluh, Peter. 2004. *The Pinochet File: A Declassified Dossier on Atrocity and Accountability. A National Security Archive Book.* New York: New Press.

Kornhauser, William. 1959. *The Politics of Mass Society.* Glencoe, IL: Free Press.

Korpi, Walter, and Joakim Palme. 2003. "New Politics and Class Politics in the Context of Austerity and Globalization: Welfare Regress in 18 Countries, 1975–1998." *American Political Science Review* 97(3): 425–446.

Kramer, Ralph. 1981. *Voluntary Agencies in the Welfare State.* Berkeley, CA: University of California Press.

Krashinsky, Michael. 1986. "Transaction Costs and a Theory of Non-Profit Organisations." In Susan Rose-Ackerman (ed.), *The Economics of Non-Profit Institutions.* Oxford: Oxford University Press.

Kriesi, Hanspeter. 1995. *Le système politique Suisse.* Paris: Economica.

Kruger, Daniel W. 1969. *The Making of a Nation: A History of the Union of South Africa, 1910–1961.* Johannesburg: Macmillan.

Krugman, Paul. 1991. "History and Industry Location: The Case of the Manufacturing Belt." *The American Economic Review* 81(2): 80–83.

Kymlicka, Will. 2002. *Contemporary Political Philosophy: An Introduction.* New York: Oxford University Press.

Larner, John. 1980. *Italy in the Age of Dante and Petrarch: 1216–1380.* New York: Longman.

Lijphart, Arendt. 1999. *Patterns of Democracy: Government Forms and Performance in Thirty-Six Countries.* New Haven: Yale University Press.

Linz, Juan J., and Alfred Stepan. 1996. *Problems of Democratic Transition and Consolidation: Southern Europe, South America, and Post-Communist Europe.* Baltimore: Johns Hopkins University Press.

Lipset, Seymour Martin. 1980. "Some Social Requisites of Democracy: Economic Development and Political Legitimacy." In Seymour Martin Lipset, *Political Man: The Social Bases of Politics.* Baltimore: Johns Hopkins University Press.

Ljubownikow, Sergej, Jo Crotty, and Peter W. Rodgers. 2013. "The State and Civil Society in Post-Soviet Russia: The Development of a Russian-style Civil Society." *Progress in Development Studies* 13(2): 153–166.

Loaeza, Soledad. 1998. *Clases Medias y Política en México.* México DF: El Colegio de México.

Lorentzen, Håkon. 1993. *Frivillighetens integrasjon: Staten og de frivillige velferdsprodusentene.* Institut for samfunnsforskning Rapport 93:10. Oslo University.

Loveman, Brian. 2001. *The Legacy of Hispanic Capitalism,* 3rd edition. New York: Oxford University Press.

Maxwell, Michael P. 2006. "NGOs In Russia: Is the Recent Russian NGO Legislation the End of Civil Society in Russia?" *Tulane Journal of International and Comparative Law* 15(1): 235–264.

McKinlay, Brian. 1979. *A Documentary History of the Australian Labour Movement, 1850–1975.* Richmond, Australia: Drummond.

Menshikov, V. V. (ed.). 1994. *Помоги ближнему! Благотворительность вчера и сегодня. (Help Your Neighbor! Charity Yesterday and Today.)* Moscow: Polygran.

Mersianova, Irina V., and Lev I. Yakobson. 2010. *Philanthropy in Russia: Public Attitudes and Participation.* Moscow: Publishing House of the State University. Available at: www.hse.ru/data/2011/04/11/1210548893/Philanthropy%20 in%20Russia.pdf.

Meyer, Jean. 1991. "Mexico in the 1920s." In Leslie Bethell (ed.), *Mexico Since Independence.* Cambridge: Cambridge University Press.

Miller, Raymond. 2005. *Party Politics in New Zealand.* Auckland, NZ: Oxford University Press.

Mohmand, Shandana Khan, and Haris Gazdar. 2007. "Social Structures in Rural Pakistan." *Thematic paper prepared under TA4319, Determinants and Drivers of Poverty Reduction and ADBs Contribution in Rural Pakistan.* Islamabad: Asian Development Bank. Available at: www.researchgate.net/publication /237295405_Social_Structures_in_Rural_Pakistan.

Monroy, Mario. 1993. *¿Socios? ¿Asociados? ¿En sociedad? Asimetrías entre Canadá, Estados Unidos, y México.* México, DF: CEERMALC-CIPRO.

Moore, Barrington. 1966. *Social Origins of Dictatorship and Democracy: Lord and Peasant in the Making of the Modern World.* Boston: Beacon Press.

Neumayr, Michaela, Ulrike Schneider, Michael Meyer, and Astrid Haider. 2007. "The Nonprofit Sector in Austria: An Economic, Legal and Political Appraisal."

Working Paper of the Institute for Social Policy, No. 01/2007. Vienna: WU Vienna University of Economics and Business.

Neville, Mette. 1998. *Andelsboligforeningsloven med kommentarer*, 2nd edition. Copenhagen: GadJura.

Nisbet, Robert. 1962. *Power and Community*, 2nd edition. New York: Oxford University Press.

Nkrumah, Kwame. 1973. *Revolutionary Path*. New York: International Publishers.

Nollert, Michael. 2007. "Sonderfall im rheinischen Kapitalismus oder Sonderweg im liberalen Wohlfahrtskapitalismus? Zur Spezifitiit des Sozialstaats Schweiz." In T. Eberle & K. Imhof (eds.), *Sonderfall Schweiz*, pp. 153–171. Zurich: Seismo.

Nowland-Foreman, Garth. 1997. "Can Voluntary Organisations Survive the Bear Hug of Government Funding under a Contracting Regime? A View from Aotearoa/New Zealand." *Third Sector Review* 3: 5–39.

Olson, Mancur. 1965. *The Logic of Collective Action: Public Goods and the Theory of Groups*. Cambridge: Harvard University Press.

Olssen, Erik. 1988. *The Red Feds: Revolutionary Industrial Unionism and the New Zealand Federation of Labour 1908–1913*. Auckland, NZ: Oxford University Press.

Olvera, Alberto J. 2004. "Representaciones e ideologías de los organismos civiles en México: crítica de la selectividad y rescate del sentido de la idea de sociedad civil." In Jorge Cadena Roa (coord.), *Las Organizaciones Civiles Mexicanas Hoy*. México DF: Universidad Nacional Autónoma de México, Centro de Investigaciones Interdisciplinarias en Ciencias y Humanidades.

Omer-Cooper, J. D. 1988. *History of Southern Africa*. Cape Town: David Philip.

Payne, Stanley G. (n.d.). "Portugal under the Nineteenth-Century Constitutional Monarchy." In *A History of Spain and Portugal*, vol. 2. The Library of Iberian Resources Online, chapter 22. Available at: http://libro.uca.edu/payne2/payne22.htm.

Pennerstorfer, Astrid, Ulrike Schneider, and Christoph Badelt. 2013. "Der Nonprofit-Sektor in Österreich." In Ruth Simsa, Michael Meyer, and Christoph Badelt (eds.), *Handbuch der Nonprofit Organisationen. Strukturen und Management*, pp. 55–75. Stuttgart: Schäffer-Poeschel.

Pestoff, Victor A. 1995. "Citizens as Co-producers of Social Services in Europe. From the Welfare State to the Welfare Mix." Stockholm: *Stockholm University School of Business Research Report* 1995(1).

Petersen, Jørn Henrik. 2004. "Den Danske Velfærdsstats Oprindelse." In Niels Ploug, Ingrid Henriksen, and Niels Kærgård (eds.), *Den Danske Velfærdsstats Historie*, pp. 42–66. Copenhagen: SFI. Available at: www.sfi.dk/Default.aspx?ID=4681&Action=1&NewsId=218&PID=9267.

Phillips, Jock. 2012. *Te Ara: The Encyclopedia of New Zealand*. Available at: www.TeAra.govt.nz/en/class/page-3.

Ploug, Niels, Ingrid Henriksen, and Niels Kærgård (eds.). 2004. *Den Danske Velfærdsstats Historie*. Copenhagen: SFI. Available at: http://www.sfi.dk/Default .aspx?ID=4681&Action=1&NewsId=218&PID=9267.

Pope Leo XIII. 1891. *Rerum Novarum*. Vatican City: Libreria Editrice Vaticana. Available at: http://w2.vatican.va/content/leo-xiii/en/encyclicals/documents/hf_l -xiii_enc_15051891_rerum-novarum.html.

Powell, Walter W. (ed.). 1987. *The Nonprofit Sector: A Research Handbook*. New Haven: Yale University Press.

Powell, Walter W., and Richard Steinberg (eds.). 2006. *The Nonprofit Sector: A Research Handbook*, 2nd edition. New Haven: Yale University Press.

Preston, Paul. 1987. *The Triumph of Democracy in Spain*. London: Routledge.

Putnam, Robert. 1993. *Making Democracy Work: Civic Traditions in Modern Italy*. Princeton: Princeton University Press.

Ragin, Charles. 1987. *The Comparative Method*. Berkeley, CA: University of California Press.

Ragin, Charles C., and Howard S. Becker. 1992. *What Is the Case? Exploring the Foundations of Social Inquiry*. New York: Cambridge University Press.

Rahman, Fazlur. 1987. "Islam." In Mircea Eliade (ed.), *The Encyclopedia of Religion*, pp. 303–322. New York: Macmillan.

Reygadas, Rafael. 1998. "Abriendo Veredas, iniciativas públicas y sociales de las redes de las organizaciones civiles." México: Convergencia de Organismos Civiles por la Democracia.

Rice, Geoffrey W. (ed.). 1992. *The Oxford History of New Zealand*, 2nd edition. Auckland, NZ: Oxford University Press.

Richardson, Len. 1992. "Parties and Political Change." In Geoffrey W. Rice (ed.), *The Oxford History of New Zealand*, 2nd edition, pp. 201–229. Auckland, NZ: Oxford University Press.

Romero, Luis Alberto. 2002. *A History of Argentina in the Twentieth Century*. College Station, PA: Penn State University Press.

Rose-Ackerman, Susan (ed.). 1986. *The Economics of Non- Profit Institutions*. Oxford: Oxford University Press.

———. 1996. "Altruism, Nonprofits and Economic Theory." *Journal of Economic Literature* 34: 701–728.

Rosen, George. 1967. *Democracy and Economic Change in India*. Berkeley, CA: University of California Press.

Roth, Bert. 1973. *Trade Unions in New Zealand Past and Present*. Wellington, NZ: Reed Education.

Rueschemeyer, Dietrich, Evelyn Hueber Stephens, and John D. Stephens. 1992. *Capitalist Development and Democracy*. Chicago: University of Chicago Press.

Sachße, C. 1994. "Subsidiarität: Zur Karriere eines sozialpolitischen Ordnungsbegriffes." *Zeitschrift für Sozialreform* 40(1): 717–731.

Sailer, Lee Douglas. 1978. "Structural Equivalence: Meaning and Definition, Computation and Application." *Social Networks* 1: 73–90.

Salamon, Lester M. 1972. "Protest, Politics, and Modernization in the American South: Mississippi as a 'Developing Society.' " Harvard University Doctoral Thesis. Cambridge, MA: Harvard University.

———. 1995. *Partners in Public Service: Government-Nonprofit Relations in the Modern Welfare State*. Baltimore: The Johns Hopkins University Press.

———. 2010. "Putting Civil Society on the Economic Map of the World." *Annals of Public and Cooperative Economics* 81(2): 1167–1210.

———. 2012a. *America's Nonprofit Sector: A Primer*, 3rd edition. New York: The Foundation Center.

———(ed.). 2012b. *The State of Nonprofit America*, 2nd edition. Washington, DC: Brookings Institution Press.

Salamon, Lester M., and Helmut K. Anheier (eds.). 1997a. *Defining the Nonprofit Sector: A Cross-National Analysis*. Manchester: Manchester University Press.

———. 1997b. "In Search of the Nonprofit Sector: The Question of Definitions." In Lester M. Salamon and Helmut K. Anheier (eds.), *Defining the Nonprofit Sector: A Cross-National Analysis*. Manchester: Manchester University Press.

———. 1998. "Social Origins of Civil Society: Explaining the Nonprofit Sector Cross-Nationally." *Voluntas: International Journal of Voluntary and Nonprofit Organizations* 9(3): 213–248.

Salamon, Lester M., Helmut K. Anheier, Regina List, Stefan Toepler, S Wojciech Sokolowski, and Associates. 1999. *Global Civil Society: Dimensions of the Nonprofit Sector*. Baltimore: The Johns Hopkins Center for Civil Society Studies. Available at: http://ccss.jhu.edu/publications-findings/?did=58.

Salamon, Lester M., Vladimir B. Benevolenski, and Lev I. Jakobson. 2015. "Penetrating the Dual Realities of Government-Nonprofit Relations in Russia." *VOLUNTAS: International Journal of Voluntary and Nonprofit Organizations* 26(6): 2178–2214.

Salamon, Lester M., and Megan A. Haddock. 2015. "SDGs and NPIs: Private Nonprofit Institutions—The Foot Soldiers for the UN Sustainable Development Goals." *CCSS Working Papers*, no. 25. Baltimore: Johns Hopkins Center for Civil Society Studies. Available at: http://ccss.jhu.edu/publications-findings/?did =451.

Salamon, Lester M., and S. Wojciech Sokolowski. 2014. "The Third Sector in Europe: Towards a Consensus Conceptualization." *TSI Working Paper*, no. 2. Seventh Framework Programme, European Union. Brussels: Third Sector Impact. Available at: http://thirdsectorimpact.eu/documentation/tsi-working -paper-no-2-third-sector-europe-towards-consensus-conceptualization/.

Salamon, Lester M., S. Wojciech Sokolowski, and Associates. 2004. *Global Civil Society: Dimensions of the Nonprofit Sector*, vol. 2. Bloomfield: Kumarian Press.

Salamon, Lester M., S. Wojciech Sokolowski, and Megan A. Haddock. 2011. "Measuring the Economic Value of Volunteer Work Globally: Concepts, Estimates, and a Roadmap to the Future." *Annals of Public and Cooperative Economics* 82(3): 217–252.

Salamon, Lester M., S. Wojciech Sokolowski, Megan Haddock, and Helen Stone Tice. 2012. *Portugal's Nonprofit Sector in Comparative Context*. Baltimore: Johns Hopkins Center for Civil Society Studies. Available at: http://ccss.jhu.edu/publications-findings/?did=374.

Salamon, Lester M., Jorge Villalobos, S. Wojciech Sokolowski, Lorena Cortes, Megan Haddock, and Cynthia Martines. 2012. "The Mexican Nonprofit Sector in Comparative Context." Baltimore: Johns Hopkins University Center for Civil Society Studies and Mexico City: Mexican Center for Philanthropy. Available at: http://ccss.jhu.edu/publications-findings/?did=383.

Sandel, Michael J. 1996. *Democracy's Discontent: American in Search of a Public Philosophy*. Cambridge: Belknap Press of Harvard University Press.

Sanders, Jackie, Mike O'Brien, Margaret Tennant, S. Wojciech Sokolowski, and Lester M. Salamon. 2008. *The New Zealand Nonprofit Sector in Comparative Perspective*. Wellington: Office for the Community and Voluntary Sector, Government of New Zealand. Available at: http://ccss.jhu.edu/publications-findings/?did=378.

Sardica, José Miguel. 2011. "The Memory of the Portuguese First Republic throughout the Twentieth Century." *E-Journal of Portuguese History* 9(1). Available at: www.brown.edu/Departments/Portuguese_Brazilian_Studies/ejph/html/issue17/pdf/v9n1a04.pdf.

Schneider, Ulrike, and Joachim Hagleitner. 2005. "Österreichische NPO im Spiegel der Arbeitsstättenzählung 2001." *Research Paper of the Institute for Social Policy*. Vienna: WU Vienna University of Economics and Business.

Schneider, Ulrike, and Astrid Haider. 2009. "Nonprofit Organisationen in Österreich 2006." *Research Paper of the Institute for Social Policy*. Vienna: WU Vienna University of Economics and Business.

Seibel, Wolfgang. 1990. "Government/Third Sector Relationships in a Comparative Perspective: The Cases of France and West Germany." *VOLUNTAS: International Journal of Voluntary and Nonprofit Organizations* 1(1): 42–60.

Seligman, Adam B. 1992. *The Idea of Civil Society*. New York: Free Press.

Shchiglik, A. I. (ed.). 1988. Органы общественной самодеятельности как форма социалистической демократии: Опыт СССР и ГДР. (*Local Community Bodies as the Form of the Socialist Democracy: Experience of the USSR and GDR.*) Moscow: Science.

Simsa, Ruth, Michael Meyer, and Christoph Badelt (eds.). 2013. *Handbuch der Nonprofit Organisationen. Strukturen und Management*. Stuttgart: Schäffer-Poeschel.

Simsa, Ruth, Christian Schober, and Doris Schober. 2006. *Das Wiener Vereinswesen im 20. Jahrhundert: Geschichte, Entwicklung und Hintergründe*. Vienna: Project Report.

Singh, Mohinder (ed.). 1996. *Social Policy and Administration in India*. New Delhi: MD Publications.

Skocpol, Theda. 1992. "State Formation and Social Policy in the United States." *American Behavioral Scientist* 35(4/5): 559–584.

———. 1995. *Social Policy in the United States: Future Possibilities in Historical Perspective.* Princeton, NJ: Princeton University Press.

Smith, Adam. 1759. *The Theory of Moral Sentiments.* Available at: http://en .wikisource.org/wiki/The_Theory_of_Moral_Sentiments.

Sokolowski, S. Wojciech. 2000. "The Discreet Charm of the Nonprofit Form: Service Professionals and Nonprofit Organizations." *VOLUNTAS: International Journal of Voluntary and Nonprofit Organizations* 11(2): 141–159.

———. 2011. "Philanthropic Leadership in Totalitarian and Communist Societies." In Kathryn Ann Agard (ed.), *Leadership in Nonprofit Organizations: A Reference Handbook,* pp.138–145. Los Angeles: Sage Publications.

Solsten, Eric (ed.). 1993. *Portugal: A Country Study.* Washington, DC: Government Printing Office.

Spooner, W. A. 1914. "The Golden Rule." In James Hastings (ed.), *Encyclopedia of Religion and Ethics,* vol. 6. New York: Charles Scribner's Sons.

Statistics Collection. 1986. Некоторые вопросы организационной работы местных Советов народных депутатов в 1985 году: Стат. сб. (*Some Issues of the Organizational Work of the Local Councils of People's Deputies in 1985.)* Москва: Отдел по вопросам работы советов Президиума Верховного Совета СССР. (Moscow: The Department for Issues Relating to the Work of the Councils of the Presidium of the Supreme Soviet of the USSR.)

Statistics New Zealand. 2007. *Non-Profit Institutions Satellite Account: 2004.* Wellington, NZ: Statistics New Zealand, Tatauranga Aotearoa. Available at: http://ccss.jhu.edu/publications-findings/?did=311.

Stepan, Alfred. 1985. "State Power and the Strength of Civil Society in the Southern Cone of Latin America." In Peter B. Evans, Dietrich Rueschemeyer, and Theda Skocpol (eds.), *Bringing the State Back In,* pp. 317–343. Cambridge: Cambridge University Press.

Stephens, Evelyn Hueber, and John D. Stephens. 1992. *Capitalist Development and Democracy.* Chicago: University of Chicago Press.

Streeck, Wolfgang (ed.). 1994. *Staat und Verbände.* Opladen: Westdeutscher Verlag.

Svedberg, Lars, and Eva Jeppsson Grassman. 2001. "Frivilliga insatser i svensk Välfärd—med utblickar mot de nordiska grannländerna." In Lars Skov Henriksen and Bjarn Ibsen (eds.), *Frivillighedens udfordringer—nordisk forskning om frivilligt arbejde og frivillige organisationer.* Odense: Odense Universitetsforlag.

Swilling, Mark, Bev Russell, S. Wojciech Sokolowski, and Lester M. Salamon. 2004. "South Africa." In Lester M. Salamon, S. Wojciech Sokolowski, and Associates, *Global Civil Society: Dimensions of the Nonprofit Sector,* vol. 2, pp. 110–125. Bloomfield: Kumarian Press.

Tapia Álvarez, Mónica, and Gisela Robles Aguilar. 2006. *Retos institucionales del marco legal y financiamiento a las organizaciones de la sociedad civil.* Mexico: Alternativas y Capacidades. Available at: www.alternativasycapacidades.org /sites/default/files/RetosInstitucionales.pdf.

Tennant, Margaret. 2007. *The Fabric of Welfare: Voluntary Organisations, Government and Welfare 1840–2005.* Wellington, NZ: Bridget Williams Books.

Timberger, Ellen Kay. 1978. *Revolution from Above: Military Bureaucrats and Development in Japan, Turkey, Egypt and Peru.* New Brunswick: Transaction Publishers.

Titmuss, Richard M. 1974. *Social Policy: An Introduction.* London: Allen and Unwin.

Trotsky, Leon. 1906. *Results and Prospects.* Available at: www.marxists.org/archive /trotsky/1931/tpr/rp-index.htm.

Tumanova, A. C. 2008. Общественные организации и русская публика в начале XX века. (*Public Associations and Russian Public in the beginning of the 20th century.*) Moscow: New Chronograph.

Tusell, Javier. 2011. *Spain: From Dictatorship to Democracy.* New York: John Wiley & Sons.

United Nations. 2003. *Handbook on Non-Profit Institutions in the System of National Accounts.* New York: United Nations.

United States Senate. 1975. *Covert Action in Chile, 1963–1973, Staff Report Of The Select Committee To Study Governmental Operations With Respect To Intelligence Activities.* Washington DC: Government Printing Office. Available at: http://fas.org/irp/ops/policy/church-chile.htm.

Valenzuela, Arturo. 1978. *The Breakdown of Democratic Regimes: Chile.* Baltimore: Johns Hopkins University Press.

Veldheer, Vic, and Ary Burger. 1999. "History of the Nonprofit Sector in the Netherlands." *Working Papers of the Johns Hopkins Comparative Nonprofit Sector Project*, no. 35, edited by Lester M. Salamon and Helmut K. Anheier. Baltimore: The Johns Hopkins Institute for Policy Studies. Available at: http://ccss.jhu.edu/publications-findings/?did=182.

Villadsen, Kaspar. 2004. "Filantropiens genkomst—Medborgerskab, fællesskab og frihed under ombrydning." *Dansk Sociolog* 15(1): 46–63. Available at: http://ej .lib.cbs.dk/index.php/dansksociologi/article/view/228/240.

Wachter, Andrea. 1983. *Antisemitismus im österreichischen Vereinswesen für Leibesübungen 1918-38 am Beispiel der Geschichte ausgewählter Vereine.* PhD Dissertation. Vienna: University of Vienna.

Weber, Max. 1958. *The Protestant Ethic and the Spirit of Capitalism.* New York: Charles Scribner's Sons.

———. 1978. *Economy and Society.* Berkeley: University of California Press.

Weisbrod, Burton. 1977. *The Voluntary Independent Sector.* Lexington: Lexington Books.

Wilson, Monica, and Leonard M. Thompson. 1969. *Oxford History of South Africa.* Oxford: Oxford University Press.

Wollebæk, Dag, and Per Selle. 2000. "Participation in Voluntary Associations and the Formation of Social Capital." Paper presented at the ARNOVA conference, New Orleans, November 2000.

World Values Survey. 1991. Available at: www.religioustolerance.org/rel_ratefor.htm.

Wright, Thomas C. 1982. *Landowners and Reform in Chile.* Urbana: University of Illinois Press.

————. 2007. *State Terrorism in Latin America: Chile, Argentina and International Human Rights*. Lanham, MD: Rowman and Littlefield Publishers.

Wuthnow, Robert. 1991. *Acts of Compassion: Caring for Others and Helping Ourselves*. Princeton: Princeton University Press.

Yakobson, Lev I. 2007. Якобсон Л. И. Российский третий сектор: от импорта к импортозамещению: Некоммерческий сектор—экономика, право и управление. Материалы международной научной конференции. (*The Russian Third Sector: From Import to Import Substitution: Nonprofit Sector-Economics, Law and Government. Materials of the International Scientific Conference.*) Moscow: National Research University Higher School of Economics.

Yamauchi, Naoto. 2004. "Is the Government Failure Theory Still Relevant? A Panel Analysis Using US State Level Data." *Annals of Public and Cooperative Economics* 75(2): 227–263.

Zhukova, I., V. Kononov, Yu Kotov, et al. 1988. Самодеятельные инициативы: Неформальный взгляд. ("Amateur Initiatives: Informal View.") *The Communist* 9: 63–67.

Zimmer, Annette, and Eckhard Priller (eds.). 2004. *Future of Civil Society: Making Central European Nonprofit Organisations Work*, pp. 713–731. Wiesbaden: VS Verlag für Sozialwissenschaften.

Zivildienstverwaltung. 2006. *Zivildienst in Österreich*. Available at: www .zivildienstverwaltung.at.

Zukin, Sharon, and Paul DiMaggio (eds.). 1990a. *Structures of Capital: The Social Organization of the Economy*. Cambridge: Cambridge University Press.

————. 1990b. "Introduction." In Sharon Zukin and Paul DiMaggio (eds.), *Structures of Capital: The Social Organization of the Economy*, pp. 1–36. Cambridge: Cambridge University Press.

ABOUT THE AUTHORS

Lester M. Salamon

Dr. Lester M. Salamon is a professor at the Johns Hopkins University; director of the Johns Hopkins Center for Civil Society Studies, Institute for Health and Social Policy at the Johns Hopkins Bloomberg School of Public Health; research professor at the Johns Hopkins School of Advanced International Studies–Bologna Center; and senior research professor at the National Research University Higher School of Economics, Moscow. He previously served as director of the Center for Governance and Management Research at the Urban Institute in Washington, DC, and as deputy associate director of the US Office of Management and Budget in the Executive Office of the President. Dr. Salamon pioneered the empirical study of the nonprofit sector in the United States and has extended this work to other parts of the world. He is the author or co-author of over 50 articles and author or editor of more than 20 books, including *The Resilient Sector Revisited: The New Challenge to Nonprofit America* (Brookings Institution Press, 2015); *America's Nonprofit Sector: A Primer,* 3rd edition (Foundation Center, 2012); *The State of Nonprofit America,* volume 2 (Brookings Institution Press, 2012); *Rethinking Corporate Social Engagement: Lessons from Latin America* (Kumarian Press, 2010); *The Tools of Government: A Guide to the New Governance* (Oxford University Press, 2002); *Global Civil Society: Dimensions of the Nonprofit Sector,* volume 2 (Kumarian Press, 2004); *New Frontiers of Philanthropy: A Guide to the New Tools and Actors Reshaping Global Philanthropy and Social Investing* (Oxford University Press, 2014); and *Partners in Public Service: Government-Nonprofit Relations in the Modern Welfare State* (Johns Hopkins University Press, 1995). He serves on the editorial boards of *Annals of Public and Cooperative Economics, Administration and Society, Transaction, The Journal of Chinese Governance, Voluntas,* and *Nonprofit and Voluntary Sector Quarterly.*

S. Wojciech Sokolowski

Dr. S. Wojciech Sokolowski is senior research associate for the Johns Hopkins Center for Civil Society Studies, Institute for Health and Social Policy at the

Johns Hopkins Bloomberg School of Public Health. Dr. Sokolowski received his PhD in sociology from Rutgers University. He has taught at the Defense Language Institute, Hartnell College, Rutgers University, and Morgan State University. Dr. Sokolowski is the author of *Civil Society and the Professions in Eastern Europe: Social Change and Organization in Poland* (Plenum/Kluwer, 2001) and a coauthor of *Measuring Volunteering: A Practical Toolkit* (Independent Sector/United Nations Volunteers, 2001); *Global Civil Society,* volumes 1 and 2 (Kumarian Press, 2004); *Handbook on Nonprofit Institutions in the System of National Accounts* (United Nations, 2003), and the International Labour Organization *Manual on the Measurement of Volunteer Work* (ILO, 2011). He has advised national statistical agencies in the United States and abroad on the development of data systems reporting on nonprofit institutions. His publications have appeared in *VOLUNTAS: International Journal of Voluntary and Non-Profit Organizations, Annals of Public and Cooperative Economics, Nonprofit Management & Leadership, Northwestern Journal of International Human Rights, Journal of Civil Society, the International Journal of Contemporary Sociology, the International Journal of Cultural Policy*, and several edited volumes.

Megan A. Haddock

Megan A. Haddock is international research projects manager for the Center for Civil Society Studies, Institute for Health and Social Policy at the Johns Hopkins University. She is a lead author of the ILO *Manual on the Measurement of Volunteer Work* (2011) and has published articles related to documenting the contribution of volunteering to development, particularly with regard to the UN's Sustainable Development Goals, in the journal *Voluntaris* and for the International Forum for Volunteering in Development. She has coauthored several Center publications, book chapters, a paper that appeared in the *Annals of Public and Cooperative Economics*, ISTR conference papers, and articles for newspapers and magazines. Ms. Haddock received her master's in public policy from the Johns Hopkins Institute of Policy Studies and her BA from Carleton College.

CONTRIBUTORS

CHRISTOPH BÄRLOCHER, University of Fribourg (Switzerland), Institute for Management on Associations, Foundations, and Cooperatives

THOMAS P. BOJE, Roskilde University, Department of Society and Globalization

LORENA CORTÉS VÁZQUEZ, The Mexican Center for Philanthropy (CEMEFI)

BERNARD DEGEN, University of Basel (Switzerland), Department of History

RAQUEL CAMPOS FRANCO, Católica Porto Business School, Universidade Católica Portuguesa

TORBEN FRIDBERG, SFI: The Danish National Centre For Social Research

MARKUS GMÜR, University of Fribourg (Switzerland), Institute for Research on Management of Associations, Foundations, and Co-Operatives (VMI)

ULLA HABERMANN, University of Southern Denmark (SDU) (retired)

BERND HELMIG, University of Mannheim Business School (Germany)

BJARNE IBSEN, University of Southern Denmark, Odense, Centre for Sports, Health, and Civil Society

IGNACIO IRARRAZAVAL, Centro de Políticas Públicas, Pontificia Universidad Católica de Chile

OLGA KONONYKHINA, Hertie School of Governance (Germany)

MARK LYONS (deceased), formerly Professor of Social Economy, University of Technology (Australia)

CYNTHIA MARTÍNEZ, The Mexican Center for Philanthropy (CEMEFI)

IRINA MERSIANOVA, National Research University Higher School of Economics (Russia), Center for Studies of Civil Society and the Non-profit Sector

Michael Meyer, WU Vienna University of Economics and Business, Institute for Nonprofit-Management

Michaela Neumayr, WU Vienna University of Economics and Business, Institute for Nonprofit Management

Michael Nollert, University of Fribourg (Switzerland), Department of Social Sciences, Division of Sociology, Social Policy, and Social Work

Astrid Pennerstorfer, WU Vienna University, Department of Sociology

Ulrike Schneider, Vienna University of Technology, Institute of Statistics and Mathematical Methods in Economics

Jorge Villalobos, The Mexican Center for Philanthropy (CEMEFI)

Georg Von Schnurbein, University of Basel (Switzerland), Center for Philanthropy Studies

CORE STAFF, LOCAL ASSOCIATES, ADVISORS, AND SPONSORS, 1991–2016

Core Staff

Director: Lester M. Salamon; *Research Staff:* Helmut Anheier, Kathryn Chinnock, Andrew Green, Megan Haddock, Eileen Hairel, Les Hems, Regina Rippetoe List, Stefan Toepler, Wojciech Sokolowski; *Communications and Administrative Staff:* Brittany Anuszkiewicz, Mimi Bilzor, Chelsea Newhouse, Jacquelyn Perry, Wendell Phipps, Marcy Shackelford, Robin Wehrlin

Local Associates

Argentina: Mario Roitter, Centro de Estudios de Estado y Sociedad (CEDES)
Australia: Mark Lyons, University of Technology, Sydney, and Centre for Social Impact (Deceased)
Austria: Ulrike Schneider, Vienna University of Technology, Institute of Statistics and Mathematical Methods in Economics
Belgium: Sybille Mertens, Centre D'Économie Sociale, Universite de Liège, *and* Jacques Defourny, Centre D'Économie Sociale, Universite de Liège
Brazil: Leilah Landim, Instituto de Estudos da Religiâo, *and* Neide Beres, UN Volunteers and Instituto Brasileiro de Geografia e Estatística
Canada: Michael Hall, Imagine Canada
Chile: Ignacio Irarrazaval, Centro de Políticas Públicas, Pontificia Universidad Católica de Chile
Colombia: Rodrigo Villar, Independent Researcher
Czech Republic: Martin Potuçek, Charles University, Institute of Sociological Studies, *and* Pavol Fric, Charles University, Institute of Sociological Studies
Denmark: Ole Gregersen, Social Forsknings Instituttet, *and* Thomas P. Boje, Roskilde University, Department of Society and Globalization
Egypt: Amani Kandil, Arab Network for NGOs
Finland: Susan Sundback, Åbo Akademi University, Institute of Public Administration
France: Edith Archambault, Centre d'économie de la Sorbonne, MATISSE

Germany: Eckhard Priller, Wissenschaftszentrum Berlin, AG Sozialberichterstattung; *and* Annette Zimmer, Institut für Politikwissenschaft, Westfalische Wilhelms-Universität Münster

Hungary: István Sebestény, Civitalis Association, *and* Renáta Nagy, Central Statistical Office

India: Rajesh Tandon, Society for Participatory Research in Asia, *and* S. S. Srivastava, Society for Participatory Research in Asia

Ireland: Freda Donoghue, National College of Ireland

Israel: Benjamin Gidron, Ben Gurion University, Israeli Center for Third-Sector Research; *and* Hagai Katz, Ben Gurion University, Israeli Center for Third-Sector Research

Italy: Gian Paolo Barbetto, Istituto de Ricerca Sociale

Japan: Naoto Yamauchi, Osaka School of International Public Policy

Kenya: Karuti Kanyinga, University of Nairobi, Institute for Development Studies; *and* Winnie Mitullah, University of Nairobi, Institute for Development Studies

Korea, Republic of: Tae-kyu Park, Yonsei University

Lebanon: Hashem El Husseini, Lebanese University

Mexico: Gustavo Verduzco, El Colegio de Mexico, AC

Morocco: Salama Saidi, Association Rawabit

The Netherlands: Paul Dekker, Social and Cultural Planning Office, *and* Bob Kuhry, Social and Cultural Planning Office

New Zealand: Diana Suggate, Ministry of Social Development

Norway: Hakon Lorentzen, Institutt for Samfunnsforkning; Karl Henrik Sivesind, Institutt for Samfunnsforkning; *and* Per Selle, Norwegian Research Centre in Organization and Management

Pakistan: Hafiz Pasha, Social Policy Development Centre, *and* Muhammad Asif Iqbal, Social Policy Development Centre

Peru: Felipe Portocarrero, Centro de Investigación de la Universidad del Pacífico, *and* Cynthia Sanborn, Centro de Investigación de la Universidad del Pacífico

The Philippines: Ledivina Cariño, University of the Philippines (Deceased)

Poland: Slawomir Nalecz, Nonprofit Organizations Research Unit, Polish Academy of Sciences

Portugal: Raquel Campos Franco, Católica Porto Business School, Universidade Católica Portuguesa

Romania: Carmen Epure, Civil Society Development Foundation

Russia: Oleg Kazakov, LINKS—Moscow, *and* Irina Mersianova, National Research University Higher School of Economics

Slovakia: Helena Woleková, SPACE Foundation

South Africa: Mark Swilling, Graduate School of Public and Development Management, University of Witwatersrand

Spain: Jose Ignacio Ruiz Olabuenaga, Centro de Investigación de Expectativas Sociales (CINDES)

Sweden: Filip Wijkstrom, Stockholm School of Economics

Switzerland: Bernd Helmig, University of Mannheim Business School, Public and Nonprofit Management; *and* Georg von Schnurbein, University of Basel, Center for Philanthropy Studies

Tanzania: Laurean Ndumbaro, University of Dar es Salaam, *and* Amos Mhina, University of Dar es Salaam

Thailand: Amara Pongsapich, Chulalongkorn University

Turkey: Mustafa Özer, Department of Economics, Anadolu University

Uganda: John-Jean Barya, Centre for Basic Research

United Kingdom: Jeremy Kendall, Department of Social Policy and Administration, London School of Economics and Political Science; Martin Knapp, Department of Social Policy and Administration, London School of Economics and Political Science; *and* Les Hems, Guidestar UK

United States: Lester M. Salamon, Johns Hopkins Center for Civil Society Studies, Johns Hopkins University; *and* S. Wojciech Sokolowski, Johns Hopkins Center for Civil Society Studies, Johns Hopkins University

Advisory Committees

International Advisory Committee

Nicole Alix, UNIOPSS; *Farida Allaghi,* AGFUND; *Manuel Arango,* Mexican Center on Philanthropy (CEMEFI); *David Bonbright,* Aga Khan Foundation; *Mauricio Cabrera Galvis,* Fundación FES; *John Clark,* The London School of Economics; *Pavol Demes,* The German Marshall Fund; *Barry Gaberman,* The Ford Foundation; *Cornelia Higginson,* American Express Company; *Stanley Katz,* Princeton University; *Kumi Naidoo,* CIVICUS; *Miklos Marschall,* Transparency International; *John Richardson,* European Foundation Centre; *Gerry Salole,* European Foundation Centre; *S. Bruce Schearer,* The Synergos Institute; Luc Tayart de Borms, King Baudoin Foundation

Local Advisory Committees

Argentina: Heber Camelo, UN Economic Commission for Latin America (CEPAL); *Marita Carballo,* GALLUP-Argentina; *Juana Ceballos,* Cáritas; *Ricardo Ferraro,* Fundación YPF; *Ernesto Gore,* Universidad de San Andrés; *María Herrera Vegas,* Fundación Bunge y Born; *Rafael Kohanoff,* Gobierno de la Ciudad Autónoma de Buenos Aires; *María Rosa Martíni,* Foro del Sector Social; *Dolores Olmos de Taravella,* Fundación Juan Minetti; *Beatriz Orlowski de Amadeo,*

CENOC, Secretaría de Desarrollo Social; *Catalina Smulovitz,* Universidad Torcuato Di Tella; *Andrés Thompson,* W. K. Kellogg Foundation.

Australia: Margaret Bell, Australian Council of Volunteering; *Steven Bowman,* Australian Society of Association Executives Limited; *Jeff Byrne,* Industry Commission; *Elizabeth Cham,* Australian Association of Philanthropy; *Gabrielle Gelly,* Australian Conservation Foundation; *Steve Haynes,* Confederation of Australian Sport; *Betty Hounslow,* Australian Council of Social Service; *Philip Hughes,* Christian Research Association; *Richard Madden,* Australian Institute of Health and Welfare; *Russel Roggers,* Australian Bureau of Statistics; *Fergus Thomson,* National Council of Independent Schools' Associations; *David Throsby,* Macquarie University.

Belgium: Each of the following agencies has one representative: Banque Nationale de Belgique (Chair); Fondation Roi Baudoin; Confédération des entreprises non marchandes; Ministère de l'emploi et de l'environnement; Ministère des affaires sociales; Ministère de la Région wallonne; Ministère de la Région Bruxelles-Capitale; Ministère de la Communauté flamande; Ministère de la Communauté française; Comission Communautaire Commune.

Chile: Francisco Ruiz, Banco Central; *José Venegas,* Banco Central; *Ximena Aguilar,* Banco Central; *Iván Castro,* Chiledeportes; *Karin Berlien,* Chiledeportes; *Óscar Agüero,* Consejo Nacional de la Cultura y de las Artes; *Juan Francisco Lecaros,* Corporación Simón de Cirene; *Alessandra Muzio,* Corporación Simón de Cirene; *Mónica Silva,* Escuela de Administración Universidad Católica de Chile; *Teresa Valdés,* Facultad Latinoamericana de Ciencias Sociales; *María Teresa Infante,* Fundación Miguel Kast; *Leonardo Moreno,* Fundación para la Superación de la Pobreza; *Sergio Oyanedel,* Fundación Teletón; *Mónica Espósito,* Hogar de Cristo; *Andrés Rencoret,* Ministerio de Justicia; *Marcela Jiménez,* Ministerio de Planificación y Cooperación; *Fuad Chain,* Ministerio Secretaría General de Gobierno; *Francisco Soto,* Ministerio Secretaría General de Gobierno; *Ana María de la Jara,* ONG Cordillera; *Alicia Amunátegui,* Sociedad Protectora de la Infancia/Feniprom.

Colombia: *Inés de Brill,* CCONG; *Mauricio Cabrera,* FES; *Marco Cruz,* Fundación Antonio Restrepo Barco; *Mauricio Londoño,* National Department of Planning; *Jose Bernardo Toro,* Fundación Social; *Olga Lucia Toro,* Centro Colombiano de Filantropía.

Czech Republic: Fedor Gál (Chair), Business Leader; *Helena Ackermannová,* Donors Forum; *Milan Damohorský,* ISS Charles University; *Ivan Gabal,* Gabal

Consulting; *Petr Háva*, ISS Charles University; *Miroslav Purkrábek*, ISS Charles University; *Jana Ryšlinková*, ICN.

Egypt: Salwa El Amir, National Center for Social Research; *Nazli Maoud*, Faculty of Political and Economic Science; *Abd El Monem Said*, Center for Political and Strategic Studies; *Nabil Samuel*, Coptic Angelic Organization for Social Services.

Finland: Krister Sthåhlberg (Chair), Åbo Akademi University; *Olavi Borg*, University of Tampere; *Maija Innanen*, Finnish Sport Federation; *Leila Kurki*, Finnish Confederation of Salaried Employees; *Kari-Pekka Mäkiluoma*, Federation of Finnish Municipalities; *Rolf Myhrman*, Ministry of Social Affairs and Health; *Martti Siisiäinen*, University of Lapland; *Hannu Uusitalo*, Academy of Finland; *Jouko Vasama*, Association of Voluntary Health, Social and Welfare Organizations.

France: Laurence Delmotte (Chair), Fondation de France; *Jean Bastide*, CNVA; *Chantal Bruneau*, Ministère de la Jeunesse et des Sports; *Marie-Thérèse Cheroutre*; *Olivier Dargnies*, Délégation à la qualité de la vie, Ministère de l'Environment; *Anne David*, FONDA; *Mireille Delbeque*, Délégation Formations et Développement, Ministère de la Culture; *Léon Dujardin*, Secours Populaire Français; *Ghislaine Esquiague*, Délégation interministérielle à la ville; *Hugues Feltesse*, UNIOPSS; *Francis Lacloche*, Caisse des Dépots et Consignations; *Jacqueline Lauriau*, Ministère de la Recherche; *Jacqueline Mengin*, CELAVAR; *Marie Dominique Monferrand*, Réseau Information Gestion; *Guy Neyret*, INSEE; *Claudine Padieu*, Direction de l'Action Sociale, Ministère des Affaires Sociales; *Guy Pailler*, Association des Paralysés de France; *Daniel Rault*, Délégation interministérielle à l'innovation sociale et à l'économie sociale; *Jean Pierre Reisman*, Ministère de la Culture; *Philippe Saint Martin*, Ministère du Travail et des Affaires socials, Direction de l'action sociale; *Denis Tzarevcan*, Fondation d'enterprise du crédit Coopératif.

Germany: Rupert Graf Strachwitz (Chair), Maecenata Institut für Dritter-Sektor-Forschung; *Ulli Arnold*, Universität Stuttgart; *Klaus Balke*, Nationale Kontakt und Informationsstelle zu Anregung und Unterstützung von Selbsthilfegruppen; *Rudolph Bauer*, Universität Bremen; *Hans-Jochen Brauns*, DPWV Landesverband Berlin; *Peter-Claus Burens*, Stiftung Deutsche Sporthilfe; *Marita Haibach*; *Albert Hauser*, Caritasverband der Erzdiözese München und Freising; *Christoph Mecking*, Bundesverband Deutscher Stiftungen; *Bernd Meyer*, Deutscher Städtetag; *Klaus Neuhoff*, Universität Witten/Herdecke; *Eckart Pankoke*, Universität der Gesamthochschule Essen; *Heide Pfarr*, Hans-Böckler-Stiftung; *Peter Philipp*, Daimler Chrysler AG; *Stephanie Rüth*, BfS-Service GmbH; *Gabriele Schulz*, Deutscher

Kulturrat; *Wolfgang Seibel,* Universität Konstanz; *Marlehn Thieme,* Deutsche Bank Stiftung; *Alfred Herrhausen,* Hilfe zur Selbsthilfe; *Gerhard Trosien,* Deutscher Sportbund; *Olaf Werner,* Friedrich-Schiller-Universität Jena; *Wolfgang Zapf,* Wissenschaftszentrum Berlin für Sozialforschung.

Hungary: Marianna Török (Chair), Centre for Nonprofit Information and Education (NIOK); *János Bocz,* Central Statistical Office; *Beatrix Gõz,* Ministry of Finance; *Gábor Gyorffy,* PHARE Program; *Béla Jagasics,* Landorhegy Foundation-Nonprofit Service Centre; *Anikó Kaposvári,* Foundation for the Education on Human Rights and Peace; *Judit Monostori,* Central Statistical Office; *László Sík,* Ministry of Finance.

India: Indu Capoor, CHETNA; *Mathew Cherian,* Charities Aid Foundation; *Murray Culshaw,* Murray Culshaw Advisory Services; *Noshir Dadawala,* Centre for Advancement of Philanthropy; *Swapan Garain,* Tata Institute of Social Sciences; *Mr. Jagdananda,* Centre for Youth and Social Development; *Joe Madiath,* Gram Vikas, Berhampur; *Harsh Mandar,* Action Aid, New Delhi; *Ajay Mehta,* National Foundation of India; *Vijai Sardana,* Aga Khan Foundation; *Mark Sidel,* Ford Foundation; *Pushpa Sundar,* Indian Centre for Philanthropy.

Ireland: Joyce O'Connor (Chair), National College of Ireland; *Roger Acton,* Disability Federation of Ireland; *Mel Cousins,* Barrister-at-Law and Personal Advisor to Minister for Social, Community and Family Affairs; *Raymond Jordan,* Department of Education; *Bernadette Kinsella,* Secretariat of Secondary Schools; *Mick Lucey,* Central Statistics Office; *Paul Marron,* Central Statistics Office; *Ernest Sterne,* Secondary Education Committee; *James Williams,* Economic and Social Research Institute.

Israel: Ya'acov Kop (Chair), Center for Social Policy Research; *J. Aviad,* KRB Foundation; *H. Ayalon,* Amal Network; *Yehoshua David,* Income Tax Commission; *S. N. Eisenstadt,* Hebrew University; *Yoram Gabbai,* Bank HaPoalim; *Y. Galnoor,* Hebrew University; *D. Lehman-Messer,* Ministry of Justice; *A. Mantver,* Joint Distribution Committee–Israel; *Moshe Sikron,* Central Bureau of Statistics.

Kenya: Patrick O. Alila, former Director, Institute for Development Studies, University of Nairobi; *Chairperson of the Board of Trustees,* Chandaria Foundation; *Njeri Karuru,* former Project Coordinator, Women and Law in East Africa; *Jaindi Kisero,* Nation Newspapers; *Martha Koome,* former Chairperson, FIDA; *Gibson Kamau Kuria,* Law Society of Kenya; *Betty C. Maina,* former Executive Director, Institute of Economic Affairs; *David S. O. Nalo,* former Director, Central Bureau of Statistics; *Elkana Odembo,* Philanthropic Foundation; *Martin Oloo,* former

Regional Programme Officer, Aga Khan Foundation; *Oduor Ongwen*, National Council of NGOs; *Alois Opiyo*, Undugu Society of Kenya; *Kassim Owango*, the Kenya National Chamber of Commerce and Industry; *Aina Tade*, former Programme Officer, Ford Foundation.

Korea, Rep. of: Hong-sup Cho, Hangyurae Daily Newspaper; Kyu-whan Cho, Angels' Heaven Social Welfare Corporation; *Woo-Hyun Cho*, Yonsei University Medical College; *Ho-jin Jung*, Daesan Foundation for Rural Culture and Society; *Soobok Jung*, formerly at the Korean NGO Times; *Min-young Kim*, People's Solidarity for Participatory Democracy; *Hyung-Jin Lee*, Arche Publishing House; *Chang-ho Lee*, Joongang Daily Newspaper; *Kang-Hyun Lee*, Volunteer 21; *Kwang-Joo Lee*, Bank of Korea; *Eun-Kyung Park*, YWCA; *Yong-Joon Park*, Global Care; *Pyong-Ryang Wi*, Citizens Coalition for Economic Justice.

Lebanon: Muhammad Barakat, Institutions of Social Welfare; *Role el-Husseini Begdashe*, Lebanese University; *Faheem Dagher*, Pediatrician; *Hasan Hammoud*, Lebanese American University; *Marwan Houry*, Lebanese University; *Naamat Kanaan*, Ministry of Social Affairs.

Mexico: Marie Claire Acosta Urquidi, Comisión Mexicana de Defensa y Promoción de Derechos Humanos; *Sergio Aguayo Quezada*, El Colegio de Mexico; *Rubén Aguilar Valenzuela,* Causa Ciudadana; *Luis F. Agullar Villanueva*, Secretaría de Gobernación; *Manuel Arango Arias*, CEMEFI; *Vicente Arredondo Ramírez*, Fundación Demos; *Manuel Canto Chac*, Universidad Autónoma Metropolitana; *Alfonso Castillo Sánchez*, Unión de Esfuerzos por el Campo; *Norman Collins*, Ford Foundation; *Julio Faesler Carlisle*, Consejo para la Democracia; *Rosa María Fernández Rodriguez*, Consultant; *Sergio García*, Foro de Apoyo Mutuo; *Jesús Luis García Garza*, Universidad Iberoamericana; *Claudio X. González Guajardo,* Oficina de la Presidencia de la República; *Ricardo Govela Autrey,* Philos; *Luis Hernández Navarro*, Coordinadora Nacional de Organizaciones Cafetaleras; *Alonso Lujambio*, Instituto Tecnológico Autónomo de México; *María Angélica Luna Parra*, México Ciudad Humana; *Dionisio Pérez Jácome*, Unidad de Promoción de Inversiones; *Federico Reyes Heroles,* Revista Este País; *Rafael Reygadas Robles-Gil*, Convergencia; *Alejandra Sánchez Gabito*, Consultant; *Jairo Sánchez Méndez*, Banco Interamericano de Desarrollo; *Martha Smith de Rangel,* CEMEFI; *Guillermo Soberón Acevedo,* Fundación Mexicana para la Salud; *Ekart Wild*, Fundación Frederich Ebert; *Alfonso Zárate*, Grupo Consultor Interdiciplinario.

Morocco: M. Bennani, Ministry of Planning; *Ait Haddout*, former Director of the Cooperatives Department; *K. El Madmad*, University of Ain Chock, UNESCO

Chair on Migration and Human Rights; *C. Ben Azzou,* Statistician, former Moroccan Ambassador to Indonesia.

Netherlands: Th. van Oosten (Chair), Juliana Welzijn Fonds; *B. M. Jansen,* Algemeen Bureau Katholiek Onderwijs; *J. H. L. Meerdink,* Prins Bernhard Fonds; *L. Roosendaal,* Centraal Bureau voor de Statistiek; *A. J. P. Schrijvers,* Universiteit Utrecht; *A.J. Spee,* Ministerie van Onderwijs, Cultuur en Wetenschappen; *Th. J. van Loon,* Nederlandse Organisaties Vrijwilligerswerk; *W. Woertman,* Ministerie van Volksgezondheid Welzijn en Sport.

New Zealand: Garth Nowland-Foreman, Unitec New Zealand; *David Robinson,* Social and Civic Policy Institute; *Peter Glensor,* Community Sector Taskforce; *Donna Matahaere-Atariki,* Arai Te Uru Whare Hauora; *Peter McIlraith,* Combined Community Trusts of New Zealand; *Robyn Munford,* Massey University; *Bob Stephens,* Victoria University of Wellington; *Tuwhakairiora Williams,* Independent Researcher; *Diana Suggate,* Ministry of Social Development, Office for the Community and Voluntary Sector; *Chungui Qiao,* Ministry of Social Development, Centre for Social Research and Evaluation.

Norway: Jon Olav Aspås, Ministry of Health and Social Affairs; *Erling Berg,* Ministry of Finance; *Paul Glomsaker,* Ministry of Culture and Church Affairs; *Steinar Kristiansen,* Research Council of Norway; *Dag Nissen,* Ministry of Foreign Affairs; *Åsa Steinsvik,* Ministry of Children and Family Affairs; *Ottil Tharaldsen,* Ministry of Labour and Government Administration; *Liv Westby,* Ministry of the Environment.

Pakistan: Rolando Bahamondes, Canadian High Commission; *Kaiser Bengali,* Social Policy and Development Centre; *R. Kamal,* Pakistan Institute of Development Economics; *Mazhar Ali Khan,* Voluntary Social Welfare Agencies; *Munir M. Merali,* the Aga Khan Foundation; *Khawar Mumtaz,* Pakistan NGO Forum; *Mehtab Akbar Rashidi,* Shahrah-e-Kamal Ataturk; *Ghazi Salahuddin,* Journalist; *Sardar Wasimuddin,* Royal Embassy of Japan.

The Philippines: Lourdes Casas-Quezon, Philippine National Red Cross; *David Chiel,* Ford Foundation; *Sheila Coronel,* Philippine Center for Investigative Journalism; *Victoria Garchitorena,* Ayala Foundation; *Emil Q. Javier,* Consultative Group on International Agricultural Research; *Horacio Morales,* La Liga Citizens' Movement for Renewal and Reform.

Poland: Alina Baran, Central Statistical Office; *Natalia Bolgert,* Bank of Socio-Economical Initiatives and Forum of Non-Governmental Initiatives

Association; *Janusz Gałęziak,* Ministry of Labor and Social Policy; *Helena Góralska,* Member of Parliment, Public Finance Commission; *Miroslawa Grabowska,* Institute of Sociology, University of Warsaw; *Hubert Izdebski,* Faculty of Law, University of Warsaw; *Wojciech Łażewski,* Caritas-Poland; *Piotr Marciniak,* NGOs and Legislation Project; *Krzysztof Ners,* Deputy Minister of Finance; *Joanna Stare,ga-Piasek,* Member of Parliment, Public Finance Commission; *Edmund Wnuk-Lipiński,* Institute of Social Policy, Polish Academy of Science; *Zbigniew Woźniak,* University of Poznań; *Mirosław Wyrzykowski,* Institute for Public Affairs; *Witold Zdaniewicz,* Catholic Church Statistics Institute.

Romania: Sorin Antohi, Central European University; *Aurora Liiceanu,* University of Bucharest; *Dan Manoleli,* Romanian Parliament Expert; *Liviu Matei,* Ministry of National Education; *Mihaela Miroiu,* National School for Political and Administrative Studies; *Dumitru Sandu,* University of Bucharest; *Ancuta Vamesu,* Civil Society Development Foundation; *Mihaela Vlasceanu,* University of Bucharest.

Slovakia: Pavol Demeš (Chair), Slovak Academic Information Agency; *Martin Bútora,* Milan Simecka Foundation; *Olga Cechová,* Institute for Law Approximation; *Katarína Košťálová,* Slovak Academic Information Agency; *Milan Olexa,* Statistical Office of the Slovak Republic.

South Africa: Eve Annecke, Sustainability Institute; *Colleen du Toit,* South African Grantmakers Association; *Nomboniso Gasa,* Centre for Civil Society, University of Natal; *Adam Habib,* Centre for Civil Society, University of Natal; *Firoz Khan,* School of Public Management and Planning, University of Stellenbosch; *Christa Kuljian,* Mott Foundation; *Alan Mabin,* Graduate School of Public and Development Management, University of the Witwatersrand, Johannesburg; *Eugene Saldanha,* Non-Profit Partnership; *Hanlie Van Dyk,* Department of Public Service and Administration, South African Government.

Switzerland: Martina Ziegerer, ZEWO Foundation; *Franz Marty,* Raiffeisen Group; *Ernst Buschor,* Bertelsmann Foundation; *Philippe Küttel,* Swiss Federal Statistic Office; *Marco Blatter,* Swiss Olympic Association; *Herbert Ammann,* Schweizerische Gemeinnützige Gesellschaft; *Beat von Wartburg,* SwissFoundations; *Jürg Krummenacher,* Caritas Switzerland.

Tanzania: H. Halfan; Gertrude Mongella, Advisor to UN Secretary General on Gender Issues; *Estomish Mushi,* Deputy President's Office; *M. Rusimi; Edda Sanga,* Radio Tanzania; *Issa Shivji,* University of Dar es Salaam.

Turkey: Davut Aydin, Anadolu University; *Mehmet Ali Caliskan*, YADA Foundation; *Ugras Ulas Tol*, YADA Foundation; *Ali Simsek*, Anadolu University; *Zafer Erdogan*, Anadolu University; *Aysel Celikel*, Support for Modern Life Association; *Sevim Conka*, Educational Volunteers Foundation for Turkey; *Güven Savul*, Confederation of Turkish Trade Unions; *Muammer Niksarlı*, National Union of Cooperatives of Turkey; *Celal Ulgen*, Union of Turkish Bar Associations; *Ahmet Ozdemir Aktan*, Turkish Medical Association; *Zeki Bostancı*, Turkish Statistical Institute; *Hasan Akdemir*, Turkish Statistical Institute; *Aysegül Ünügür*, Association of Turkish Women.

Uganda: Xavier Mugisha, Institute of Statistics and Applied Economics, Makerere University; *Tumusime Mutebile*, Ministry of Finance; *Olivia Mutibwa*, Makerere University; *Kiyaga Nsubuga*, Ministry of Local Government.

United Kingdom: Ian Bruce (Chair), Royal National Institute for the Blind; *Michael Brophy*, Charities Aid Foundation; *Richard Corden*, Charity Commission; *Paul Fredericks*, Charity Commission; *Les Hems*, The Johns Hopkins University; *Janet Novak*, Voluntary and Community Services, Department of National Heritage; *Cathy Pharaoh*, Charities Aid Foundation; *Roger Ward*, ONS.

Funders

Academy of Finland
Aga Khan Foundation
Aga-Khan Foundation–Portugal
Anadalou University (Turkey)
Arab Gulf Fund (AGFUND)
Atlantic Philanthropies
Associazione Casse di Risparmio Italiane
Associazione Ricreativa e Culturale Italiana
Australian Bureau of Statistics
Australian Research Council
Austrian Science Foundation
Banca di Roma
Banco di Napoli
Bank of Sweden Tercentenary Foundation
Calouste Gulbenkian Foundation (Portugal)
Canadian Fund (Slovakia)
Caritas Ambrosiana
Cassa di Risparmio delle Province Lombarde

Cassa di Risparmio di Puglia
Cassa di Risparmio di Torino
Charles Stewart Mott Foundation (United States)
Charities Aid Foundation (United Kingdom)
Civil Society Development Foundation (Czech Republic)
Civil Society Development Foundation (Romania)
Civil Society Development Foundation (Slovakia)
Colombian Center on Philanthropy
Combined Community Trusts of New Zealand
David and Lucile Packard Foundation
Department of Welfare (South Africa)
Deutsche Bank Foundation (Germany)
FIN (Netherlands)
Fondation de France
Fondazione Giovanni Agnelli
Fondazione San Paulo di Torino
Ford Foundation
FORMEZ
Foundation for an Open Society (Hungary)
Fundación Andes (Chile)
Fundación Antonio Restrepo Barco (Colombia)
Fundación BBVA (Spain)
Fundación FES (Colombia)
Fundación Minera Escondida (Chile)
Gerbert Rüf Stiftung (Switzerland)
Humboldt Foundation/Transcoop (Germany)
Ilídio Pinho Foundation (Portugal)
Imagine Canada
Industry Commission (Australia)
Institute for Human Sciences (Austria)
Instituto de Desarrollo Agropecuario (Chile)
Inter-American Development Bank
Inter-American Foundation
Joseph Rowntree Foundation (United Kingdom)
Juliana Welzijn Fonds (Netherlands)
Kahanoff Foundation (Canada)
King Baudouin Foundation (Belgium)
Körber Foundation (Germany)
Luso-American Foundation (Portugal)
Ministry for Public Administration (Sweden)

Ministry of Church and Education (Norway)
Ministry of Culture and Sports (Norway)
Ministry of Education, Culture and Science (Netherlands)
Ministry of Environment (Norway)
Ministry of Family and Children (Norway)
Ministry of Family/World Bank (Venezuela)
Ministry of Foreign Affairs (Norway)
Ministry of Health and Social Affairs (Sweden)
Ministry of Health, Sports and Welfare (Netherlands)
Ministry of Social Affairs and Health (Finland)
Ministry of Social Development (New Zealand)
National Department of Planning (Colombia)
National Research Fund (Hungary)
Norwegian Research Council
OPEC
Open Society Foundation (Slovakia)
Productivity Commission (Australia)
Research Council of Norway
Rockefeller Brothers Fund
Sasakawa Peace Foundation (Japan)
SENAC (National Commercial Training Service–Brazil)
Servicio de Cooperación Técnica (Chile)
Skoll Foundation
Socialministeriet (Ministry of Social Affairs, Denmark)
SPES–Associazione Promozione e Solidarietà (Italy)
Swedish Council for Research in the Humanities and Social Services
Swedish Red Cross
Telefonica CTC Chile
Tindall Foundation (New Zealand)
United Nations Development Programme (UNDP)
United Nations Volunteers
Université de Fribourg, Verbandsmanagement Institute (Switzerland)
United States Agency for International Development (USAID)
United States Information Service
University of Wıitwatersrand (South Africa)
W. K. Kellogg Foundation (United States)
Yad Hadaniv Foundation (Israel)

Page numbers in *italics* refer to tables and figures.

Chile *(continued)*
   Latin America, 181, 184, 188–89;
   foreign powers' influence on, 195;
   mining industry in, 181; mutual
   associations in, 190; neoliberal reforms
   in, 192, 194; organizations legalized in,
   191; organized labor in, crackdown
   on, 192; political compromise in, 190;
   political instability in, 190, 192, 195;
   power relationships in, 181–82, 193–94;
   reforms in, 191–92; social origins theory
   and, 181, 189–95; welfare partnership
   pattern in, 107, 113–14, 182, 183,
   185–86, 188–91, 193–94; workers'
   organizations in, 189
China, 126
Christian Austrian People's Party, 207, 208
Christian Democratic Party (Chile), 191,
   195
Christian Democrats (Austria), 198
Christian Social Federation of Swiss Trade
   Unions, 140
Christian Social Party (Austria), 204, 205,
   209
church attendance, 53, 54, 72n19
citizen action, individual, 25
citizen self-management, 140
citizenship theory, 49
civic associations, 138
civic republicanism, 49
civic virtue, 49, 50
civil rights movement (US), 101–2
civil society: other names for, 20; as public
   space, 22; social class power relationships and (*see* social class); social
   origins theory and, 78–79, 81–82.
   See also social origins theory
civil society development: foreign powers'
   role in, 96, 195; liberal pattern of, 84,
   86–87, 99–102, 137–38 (*see also* liberal
   pattern); patterns of, 10, 81, 83–89;
   power relationships and, 115, 122, 125;
   social democratic pattern of, 84, 85,
   87–88, 107–10 (*see also* social democratic pattern); statist pattern of, 84, 85,
   88, 110–14 (*see also* statist pattern);
   traditional pattern of, 83–86, 92–99
   (*see also* traditional pattern); welfare
   partnership pattern of, 84, 87, 88, 102–7
   (*see also* welfare partnership pattern)

civil society institutions, democratization
   and, 46
civil society organizations: activities of,
   30–31; data on, 3; dynamism of, 33–34;
   embeddedness and, 6, 7; expressive
   functions of, 31 (*see also* civil society
   sector: expressive activities of); financial
   support for, 3; functions of, 29–31; vs.
   government agencies, 23; growth and
   development of, 6; individualism and,
   72n26; vs. kin-based groups, 23, 24;
   motivations for starting, 69–70; policy
   functions of, 29–30; preference theories
   and, 2–3, 6, 7, 9; restrictions on, 88,
   110, 113–14; revenue sources for, 5,
   32–33, 39, 40 (*see also* civil society
   sector: revenue sources for); roles of,
   1–2; service functions of, 30–31 (*see also*
   civil society sector: service activities of);
   social functions of, 29; staffing of, 31;
   workforce of, 34
civil society sector: as American phenomenon, 5; charitable contributions and, 5;
   components of, 11; composition of,
   23–24; cross-national variations in,
   34–39; data on, 3; defining, 21–26;
   development and, 1, 35; diversity in, 1,
   19–20, 21, 27; economic development
   and, 46–49; economic impact of, 5,
   27–28; expressive activities of, 146–47,
   161, 172, 200, 213–14, 226–27, 240–41,
   254, 255; functions of, 35–39; global, 20;
   growth in, 33; as instrument of suppression, 126; labor movements and, 102–6,
   108–9, 120, 126, 140–42, 163–67,
   176–77, 197, 219; as major industry, 27,
   28; in national economic statistics, 12;
   nonservice activities of, 69–70; organizational dimension of, 21–22; paid vs.
   volunteer workforce in, 38; per-capita
   GDP and, 47; popular beliefs about, 4–5;
   population diversity and, 63; as power
   source, 7; predictability of, 89; preference
   theories and, 48, 51, 55–68; religion and,
   50–51; religious traditions and, 6;
   revenue growth of, 34; revenue sources
   for, 148–49, 162, 172–74, 175, 186, 187,
   201–3, 216–17, 218, 228, 229, 242, 243,
   255–56; rise of, 2; scale of, 34–35; scope
   of, 22–23; secular thought on, 49–50;

James, Estelle, 58
Japan, 88, 111–12, 120
Johns Hopkins Comparative Nonprofit
Sector Project, 3, 4–5, 9, 13n, 20, 21,
26–27
Juarez, Benito, 113

Kenya, 39; traditional pattern in, 98–99
Kenya African National Union, 98
Kenya African Union, 98
Kenyatta, Jomo, 98–99
Kikuyu Central Association, 98
Kingitanga (King movement; N.Z.), 153
kin relations, 24, 51–52, 79, 98–99
Korea (Republic of), statist pattern in, 114
Kornhauser, William, 22

labor: crackdown on, 192; organized,
106, 143, 150–55, 157, 169, 176, 177;
organized religion and, 105, 109; weak
position of, 131–32. *See also* labor
movements; unions
Labour Party (Australia), 157–58, 165–66
Labour Party (N.Z.), 144, 150–52, 154,
155
Larner, John, 54
Latin America: colonial origins of, 189;
CSS activity in, 107; government
support in, for CSOs, 188; philanthropy
in, 188; power relations in, 113.
See also individual nations
Lenin, V. I., 231
Leo XIII, 55, 90n24. See also *Rerum
Novarum*
Liberal Alliance (Chile), 190
Liberal Democratic Party (Chile), 190
Liberal Party (Australia), 166
Liberal Party (Chile), 190
Liberal Party (N.Z.), 150
liberal pattern of civil society development,
84, 86–87, 126; characteristics of,
99–101, 110, 164; conditions leading
to, 99–102. *See also* Australia; New
Zealand; Switzerland; United Kingdom
liberation theology, 246
Libya, 127
Lijhpart, Arendt, 59–60, 69, 179
Lipset, Seymour Martin, 46
Local Government Reform Act (1970;
Denmark), 220

macroeconomic environment, power
relationships and, 68
*Manual on the Measurement of Volunteer
Work* (ILO), 12
Māori population, 153–54
market failure, assumption of, 55–56
market-failure/government-failure theory,
55, 56, 60–65, 68–69, 106, 179
Marriage Guidance (N.Z.), 153
mass membership organizations, 113, 232
Mau Mau uprising, 98
Meiji Restoration, 88, 112
median voters, 56, 57, 64, 69
member-serving organizations, 26
Mexico: Catholic Church in, 244, 245;
civil society development in, 243–49;
civil society sector in, 1, 39, 107,
237–43; class struggle in, 194; political
instability in, 244–45, 248; power
amplifiers in, 237–38, 248; power
relationships in, 237–38, 245, 247–49;
protest movements in, 246–47;
revolution from above in, 243–44;
social movements in, 246–47; social
origins theory and, 242, 243–49;
statist pattern in, 113–14, 237–43,
247; urban movements in, 246
Middle East, civil society development in,
127
Mill's method of difference, 94
modern world, routes to, 8, 75–76
modularity, 72n21
Moi, Arap, 99
Moore, Barrington, Jr., 8, 75, 77, 78, 80,
81, 83, 95, 97
Moral Basis of a Backward Society
(Banfield), 50
moral entrepreneurs, 58, 67–68
Mozambique, 258
Mussolini, Benito, 109
Mutsuhito (Meiji), 112
mutual associations, 25, 139, 140, 258

National Party (N.Z.), 144, 154
National Party of Australia, 166
National Revolutionary Party (PNR;
Mexico), 113, 244, 245
natural order, 51
neoliberalism, 107, 121, 141, 144, 154–55,
158, 166–67, 192, 194, 221–22

Netherlands, the, 213; battle of schools in, 106, 177–78; civil society sector in, 1, 52, 169–76; consensus democracy in, 179–80; government's mediating role in, 177–78; organized labor in, 105, 106, 169, 176, 177; pacification in, 106, 170; philanthropy in, 52, 72n18; pillarization in, 177, 178; power relationships in, 179; religious differences in, 60–61, 105, 169–70, 176; social democratic leanings in, 105; social origins theory and, 169–70, 176–80; social welfare policy in, 106; welfare partnership pattern in, 106, 170, 172–76, 178–79

Neuhaus, John, 22

New Deal, 101

New Zealand, 158; affluence of, 151; civil society development in, 150–55; civil society sector in, 144–49; class structure of, 143; colonization of, 149–50; legal environment in, 150; liberal pattern in, 99, 110, 143, 145, 149, 154, 155; Māori population in, 153–54; neoliberal reforms in, 144, 154; nonprofit-state cooperation in, 152–53, 154; organized labor in, 143, 150–51; power amplifiers in, 155; power relationships in, 155; social democratic pattern in, 153–55; social origins theory and, 155; unexpected dimensions in, 149–54; usehold policy in, 151–52; volunteer workers in, 35; welfare partnership pattern in, 106, 154–55; welfare state in, 152; women's suffrage in, 153

New Zealand Labour Party, 151

Nisbet, Robert, 22

Nkrumah, Kwame, 22, 126

nobility, 79

non-distribution constraint, 57

nongovernmental organizations (NGOs), 26

nonprofit institution section (NPI), 14n6

nonprofit institutions, 23–24, 26, 41–42n2

Nonprofit Institutions Serving Households, 20

nonprofit organizations, 57–59. See also civil society organizations

nonprofit sector, 13n1. See also civil society sector

nonservice activities, 69–70

Norway, 35, 39, 178, 213

NPI Handbook (UN), 12, 14n6, 44n22

NPISH. See Nonprofit Institutions Serving Households

nursing homes, for-profit, 67

Olson, Mancur, 55

organization, importance of, 22

Pakistan: civil society sector in, 1; philanthropy in, 39; traditional pattern of civil society development in, 97

Paremata Māori (Māori Parliament), 153

parliamentary systems, government funding and, 59–60

path dependence, 8, 82, 86, 90n19, 91

Pearce, Jenny, 7

Peru, 35–39, 107

philanthropy: church attendance and, 53, 54; CSOs and, 39; government support and, 34; as revenue source for CSOs, 34, 39; social welfare spending and, 62–63. See also civil society organizations: revenue sources for

Philippines, 39

pillarization, 177, 178

Pinochet, Augusto, 107, 192, 193, 195

Pio, Louis, 219

pluralism, 83

PNR. See National Revolutionary Party

Poland, 123n36, 224

political institutions, significance of, 76–77

political parties: as power amplifiers, 143, 194, 237, 248; role of, in class-centered political outcomes, 76–77; welfare partnership pattern and, 104, 195

Politics of Mass Society (Kornhauser), 22

Popular Unity alliance (Chile), 192

Portugal: bifurcated system, 257; Carnation Revolution in, 119, 251, 260–62; Catholic Church in, 157; civil society development in, 251, 257–62; civil society sector in, 252–57, 259, 260; class changes in, 258; delayed democratization in, 119; hybrid character of, 255–56; Liberal Revolution of 1920, 257; Misericórdias in (see Misericórdias), 257; mutual associations in, 258; mutualist movement in, 259; "New State" regime in, 259; organized labor in, 109; political instability in, 259; power relations in, 118–19, 251, 257; social origins theory and, 257–62; statist pattern in, 251, 254, 256; welfare partnership pattern in, 119, 251, 254, 256

Portuguese Republican Party, 259

power: diffusers of, 143; social science and, 75

power amplifiers, 82, 143, 155, 157, 164, 167, 194, 237–38

power relationships: civil society development and, 115, 122, 125; configurations of, 82–88; embeddedness and, 7; macroeconomic environment and, 68; parties to, 8; patterns of, 93–94; social class relations and, 8, 80–89, 91, 115, 117, 122, 155, 194, 195. See also social origins theory

preference theories, 2–3, 6, 7, 9, 48, 51, 69; democracy and, 59–60; testing of, 59–68; types of, 55–59; welfare partnership pattern and, 103

premodern societies: social classes in, 79–80; persistence of relationships in, 95–96; social forces' strength in, 95

PRI. See Institutional Revolutionary Party

Prisoners' Aid and Rehabilitation (N.Z.), 153

Private Institutions of Social Solidarity (Portugal), 260

proporz, 207, 208

Protestant Ethic and the Spirit of Capitalism, The (Weber), 50–51

Protestantism, capitalism and, 50–51

Public Chamber (Russian Federation), 233

public goods, 55–56

public space, civil society as, 22

Putin, Vladimir, 113, 118

Putnam, Robert, 7, 14–15n14, 49–50, 52, 54–55, 71n14, 86, 95, 121

Quanta Cura (Pius IX), 105

Radical Party (Chile), 190

reciprocity, 2, 49–50

Reform Party (N.Z.), 150

religion: adherence to, 53–54; altruism and, 69; civil society sector and, 50–51, 54; competition and (see Netherlands, the: religious differences in); diversity and, 67–68; ethical norms and, 52; legitimizing premodern power relations, 95; modularity of, 54; as motivator for nonprofit organizations, 58; organized labor and, 105, 109; power relationships and, 54, 55; social origins theory and, 54; social power and, 69

Rerum Novarum (Leo XIII), 90n24, 177, 181, 190, 195–96n2

revolution from above, 76, 110, 112, 231, 243–44, 259

Robinson, James A., 2, 86

Rogernomics, 144

Romania, 35, 39, 114, 115, 123n36, 224

Rose-Ackerman, Susan, 58

Rueschemeyer, Dietrich, 8, 48, 71n2, 77, 80, 83

rural countryside, class relationships in, 75–76

Russia, 88, 123–24n36, 126; Bolshevik revolution in, 113, 229, 231; charitable associations in, 230; civil society development in, 229–35; civil society sector in, 1, 52, 113, 223, 229, 237; CSOs in, 230, 233; government–civil society relations in, 233–34; power relations in, 118, 248–49; proletarian revolution in, 104; Russia, social origins theory and, 229–35; state power in, 118; statist pattern of civil society development in, 112–13, 118, 224, 226, 228, 229, 234

Russian Orthodox Church, 236n5

Salamon, Lester, 54, 60

Salazar, António de Oliveira, 109, 119, 226, 259

salvation, economic success and, 51

Saudi Arabia, 127

Scottish Enlightenment, 49

secular thought, on civic virtue, 49–50

Seibel, Wolfgang, 7

self-governance, 24

self-help groups, 120, 126, 214, 215, 165

sentiment theories, 2, 3, 6, 7, 9, 48–54, 68, 69; limitations on, 51–55; social values and, 81; Switzerland and, 137, 142
Skocpol, Theda, 8, 77, 80
Slovakia, 39, 123n36, 224
Smith, Adam, 49
SNA. *See* System of National Accounts
social actors: collective power of, 79; cultural norms and, 81; power of, 80; relationships among, 10
social capital, 49–50
social class: power relationships and, 8, 80–89, 91, 115, 117, 122, 155, 194, 195; in premodern societies, 79–80; shifts in, 117; social relationships among, 116; state as, 79
Social Democratic League (*Sociaal-Democratische Bond* [SDB]; Netherlands), 105, 176
Social Democratic Party (Austria), 207, 208, 209
Social Democratic Party (Denmark), 219
Social Democratic Party (Germany), 204
Social Democratic Party (N.Z.), 151
social democratic pattern of civil society development, 87–88, 157; characteristics of, 107–8, 110, 199–200, 211, 219; conditions leading to, 107–10; working class and, 109. *See also* Austria; Denmark; Sweden
Social Democratic Workers Party (Sweden), 108
Social Democratic Workers' Party (Netherlands), 176
social economy organizations, 25
social enterprises, 25
social institutions, church-based, 103–4
social movement organizations, 25
social organization, 120
social origins analysis, 8, 12–13. *See also* social origins theory
social origins of civil society theory, 78. *See also* social origins theory
Social Origins of Dictatorship and Democracy (Moore), 75
social origins theory (social origins of civil society theory), 9–10, 13, 52, 75; and Australia, 157, 163–67; and Austria, 197, 200, 208–9; and Chile, 181, 189–95; civil society and, 78–79, 81–83

(*see also* civil society development); and the civil society sector, 8, 9–10, 92; and Denmark, 211, 217–22; factors in, 13; and Germany, 102–5; and Mexico, 242, 243–49; and the Netherlands, 169–70; and New Zealand, 155; outliers and, 115–22; and Portugal, 257–62; predictive power of, 93, 126–27; religion and, 54; shaping of, 81–82; and Switzerland, 131, 137–42
social power: mobilization of, 70; religion and, 69
Social Reform Act (1933; Denmark), 219
social relationships: durability of, 8, 95; fluctuations in, 116
Social Security Act (1938; N.Z.), 152
social services, religious group competition and, 105
social welfare: research on, 77; state's role in, 101–2
Socialist Party (Austria), 197, 198, 204–5, 206
Socialist Party (N.Z.), 151
Socialist Workers Party (Chile), 190
socioeconomic classes, 79–81, 83–86, 90, 111, 126, 210–12
SOCS theory. *See* social origins theory
solidarity, 7, 95
South Africa: apartheid in, 120–21; delayed democratization in, 119–21; philanthropy in, 39; volunteer workers in, 35
Soviet Union: citizen initiative bodies in, 232; civil society in, 227, 231–34; collapse of, 104, 118; mass membership organizations in, 232; revolution from above, 231. *See also* Russia
Spain: charitable giving in, 53; delayed democratization in, 119; organized labor in, 109
sports clubs, 191, 204, 206, 219
Stalin, Joseph, 113, 231–32
state: governing forms of, 76; role of, in class-centered political outcomes, 76–77; role of, in social welfare protections, 101–2; as social class, 79
statist pattern of civil society development, 88, 110–14, 116, 127; characteristics of, 114, 118, 229, 234, 237; conditions leading to, 110–11. *See also* Mexico; Portugal; Russia

structural equivalence, 82–83, 86, 90n20
subsidiarity, 81, 104, 260
supply-side preference theories, 57–59
supply-side theories, 67–70
Sweden, 151, 158, 213; civil society development in, 1, 39; power amplifiers in, 143; social democratic pattern in, 104, 108–10; social democratic welfare model in, 178; state religion in, 109; volunteer workers in, 35
Swiss Federation of Trade Unions, 140
Switzerland, 184, 199; business associations in, 140; citizen self-management in, 140; civic associations in, 138; civil society development in, 131, 139–42; civil society sector in, 132–37; Helvetic Republic period in, 139; industrialization of, 139–42; labor movement in, 140, 142; liberalization of, 139; liberal pattern in, 99, 102, 115, 131–32, 137–42; sentiment model and, 142; social origins theory and, 131, 137–42
sympathy, moral sentiment of, 49
Syria, 127
System of National Accounts, 12, 14n6, 20, 26, 41–42n2

Tanzania, 35
Te Aute College Students' Association (N.Z.), 153
Theory of Moral Sentiments (Smith), 49
Thomas Aquinas. *See* Aquinas, Thomas
Titmuss, Richard, 77
traditional authority, 95
traditional pattern of civil society development, 83–86, 116; characteristics of, 94–95; conditions leading to, 92–99. *See also* India; Kenya
Treaty of Maastricht (1992), 260
trust: as norm, 2; cultural value of, 50; institutional roots of, 50; levels of, 51–52; nonprofits and, 57
trust theory, 65–66, 68
Turkey, 127

Uganda, 35, 39
Union of South Africa, 120

unions, 102, 143. *See also* labor
United Kingdom, 158; charitable giving in, 53; liberal pattern in, 99, 100–101. *See also* British colonial system
United Labour Party (N.Z.), 151
United Nations, 12; Statistical Commission, 26; Statistics Division, 12; Sustainable Development Goals, 2
United States, 158; choice in, for trust-sensitive services, 66–67; decentralized social policies in, 77; involvement of, in Chile, 195; liberal pattern in, 99, 101

Villa, Pancho, 244
voluntary associations, 51, 150
voluntary organizations, 96
volunteers: behavior of, 22; in civil society workforce, 25, 28, 29, 132, 134 (*see also* civil society sector: volunteer participation in); social democratic pattern and, 110

Wealth of Nations, The (Smith), 49
Weber, Max, 50–51, 71n13, 79, 81, 95
Weisbrod, Burton, 55–57, 59
welfare partnership pattern of civil society development, 81, 84, 87, 88, 126; characteristics of, 172, 179; conditions leading to, 102–7; criteria for, 107; liberal pattern and, 102. *See also* Chile; Germany; Netherlands, the
welfare partnerships, 5
welfare regimes: civil society and, 5, 27; classifications of, 77–78; patterns of, 8
working class, 143, 167; liberal pattern and, 100–102; social democratic pattern and, 109–10; statist pattern and, 114; welfare partnership pattern and, 87, 102–5

Yeltsin, Boris, 118
Young Māori Party, 153

Zapata, Emiliano, 244
Zapatista Army for National Liberation (EZLN), 246